THE PASTOR'S BIBLE STUDY®

VOLUME THREE

A NEW INTERPRETER'S® BIBLE STUDY

THE PASTOR'S BIBLE STUDY®

VOLUME THREE

A NEW INTERPRETER'S® BIBLE STUDY

Abingdon Press
Nashville

THE PASTOR'S BIBLE STUDY®
Volume Three
A NEW INTERPRETER'S® BIBLE STUDY

This book is printed on acid-free paper.

Cataloging-in-publication information applied for with the Library of Congress

ISBN-10: 0-687-49330-7
ISBN-13: 978-0-687-49330-2

06 07 08 09 10 11 12 13 14 — 10 9 8 7 6 5 4 3 2 1

MANUFACTURED IN THE UNITED STATES OF AMERICA

Contents

Contributors

David Albert Farmer, General Editor, is an ordained American Baptist minister. He earned his M.Div. (1981) and Ph.D. in Homiletics and doctoral minors in New Testament Theology and Pastoral Care (1984) from Southern Baptist Theological Seminary. He is Visiting Professor of Preaching at Palmer Theological Seminary in Philadelphia and also teaches at Wilmington College in Delaware. He has served seven congregations and is now pastor of Silverside (American Baptist) Church in Wilmington, Delaware. He was editor of *Pulpit Digest* for 18 years and *The African American Pulpit* for three years. He is author of *Unmerited Favor: Teaching Sermons on the Love and Grace of God, Basic Bible Sermons on Hope, And Blessed is She: Sermons by Women,* and *Pilgrim Prayers for Single Fathers.* He has contributed to several additional books including *The Storyteller's Companion to the Bible.*

Robert E. Van Voorst is a professor of New Testament at Western Theological Seminary in Holland, Michigan. He served for twelve years as the pastor of Rochester Reformed Church in Accord, New York, while he earned the Ph.D. in New Testament from Union Theological Seminary in New York City. He then taught for ten years at Lycoming College in Williamsport, Pennsylvania, a United Methodist college. He also served in that time as an interim supply pastor in four PC(USA) churches and was a visiting professor at Westminster College in Oxford, England. He maintains an active schedule of preaching and teaching in churches, and has lectured to the School for Pastors of the Omaha Presbyterian Seminary Foundation, to the Taiwan Theological Seminary, and to the Theology Faculty of Oxford University. Among his ten books are *Anthology of World Scriptures; Reading the New Testament Today;* and *Jesus Outside the New Testament: An Introduction to the Ancient Evidence.*

Wilda C. M. Gafney is Assistant Professor of Old Testament and Homiletics at Lutheran Theological Seminary at Philadelphia. A native of Maryland, Wilda is a third-generation soldier. She recently completed five years of service as a chaplain in the Army Reserves as pastor to a hospital congregation and providing psychiatric pastoral care. She began her career as a research biologist, working for an independent laboratory with U.S. Navy contracts and concentrated on immunology and biological defense. She was baptized in the African Methodist Episcopal Church, belonged to a non-denominational congregation as a teen "because my Mother liked the youth program there," attended a Baptist school during her junior high years, a Catholic high school and rounded things off by attending Earlham, a Quaker college, earning a B.A. in biology in 1987. She received her M.Div. from Howard School of Divinity in 1997 and a pastoral appointment in the AME Zion Church in 2001. She is the first African American woman scholar to serve on the Lutheran Theological Seminary at Philadelphia faculty.

Deborah J. Spink is the product of the Evangelical and Reformed side of the United Church of Christ. Her grandfather, the Rev. Harry N. Spink Sr., was ordained in the Evangelical church, and her father, the Rev. Harry N. Spink Jr., was ordained in the Evangelical and Reformed church (later to become the United Church of Christ). Deborah received the Bachelor of Science in Music Education from the University of West Chester in Pennsylvania in 1979 and a Master of Divinity in 1985 from Eastern Baptist Theological Seminary. She served as pastor of the United Church of Christ in Warminster, Pennsylvania, then completed her Ph.D. in religion at Temple University. Dr. Spink edited her first book, "Who killed Goliath" in 2001 and is presently a Biblical Studies adjunct professor at the Palmer Theological Seminary in Pennsylvania.

Anne Crumpler comes from a long line of preachers, teachers, and writers; she learned Theology, Bible, and English grammar over the dinner table. She also has a Bachelor of Arts in Philosophy from Chatham College and a Master of Religious Education from St. Meinrad School of Theology. Anne has been an assistant editor in the Department of Youth Publications, the United Methodist Publishing House, and is presently a freelance writer and editor. Anne is a contract editor for *The Upper Room Daily Devotional Guide* and for *Devo'Zine*. She has written bible lessons for *Mature Years* and *Daily Bible Studies,* commentary for *The New International Lesson Annual,* articles for *Devo'Zine* and *Alive Now,* devotions for *The Upper Room Disciplines* and *365 Meditations for Families,* sermon helps for *What Difference Would It Make?* (a program of The Upper Room), and study guides for Lent offered on-line by The Upper Room. Anne lives in Nashville, Tennessee, with her husband, David. They have two children, Rachel and Benjamin.

J. Andrew McTyre is pastor for the Park Central Presbyterian Church in Syracuse, New York. He is also a Fellow with the American Association of Pastoral Counselors and holds a Masters of Divinity degree in pastoral counseling from Southern Seminary in Louisville, Kentucky. He also did graduate work at Rüshlikon Theological Seminary and the Jung Institute in Zürich and at Emory University in Atlanta. His experience includes serving as Co-Pastor with his wife, Sarah, at a united UCC and PCUSA church in Oswego, New York. He was the founding therapist of the Oneida Counseling Ministry in Central New York. He has also supervised a residential drug and alcohol program and taught pastoral counseling at the seminary level. He has published in *Pulpit Digest* and *Word and Witness.*

Sarah S. McTyre is an ordained Presbyterian minister and serves as a consultant for Christian Education in Central New York. She holds a B.A. in English literature from Davidson College in Davidson, North Carolina and a Master of Divinity degree with honors work in pastoral care from Columbia Theological Seminary in Decatur, Georgia. She also did graduate work in Pastoral Theology at Emory University in Atlanta. Her experience includes serving as Co-Pastor with her husband, Andrew, at a united UCC and PCUSA church in Oswego, New York. She was the Assistant Dean of Faculty at Columbia Seminary and served pastorates in Alabama and Georgia. She has published in the *Journal of Pastoral Care* and *Pulpit Digest* and has published liturgical resources for the Presbyterian Church (USA).

Ken Carter is senior pastor of Providence United Methodist Church in Charlotte, North Carolina. He is the author of *The Gifted Pastor* and *A Way of Life in the World*, both published by Abingdon Press. Ken has contributed to eleven other books, including *The Abingdon Preaching Annual*, *The Upper Room Dictionary of Christian Spiritual Formation* (Upper Room) and *Hope For The Future: Theological Voices From The Pastorate* (Eerdmans). His writing has also appeared in *Christian Century*, *Alive Now*, and *The Journal of Pastoral Care*. He is Book Review Editor of the *Circuit Rider*. A graduate of Duke Divinity School, The University of Virginia, and Princeton Theological Seminary, Ken has previously served congregations in East Bend, Winston-Salem and Greenboro, North Carolina. He has been a delegate to the General and Jurisdictional Conferences of the United Methodist Church, and is a Director of the General Board of Higher Education and Ministry. He is married to Pam and they have two daughters, Liz and Abby.

Foreword

This edition of *The Pastor's Bible Study* is the third in an exciting and successful series projected for ten or more volumes. Most of you have been with our ever-growing family of readers from the beginning, and we appreciate your loyalty and support! You know that Abingdon Press, because of its commitment to pastors, conducted research to discover that there were virtually no materials being published to help pastors specifically with our midweek Bible study sessions. This strong addition to their *New Interpreter's Bible* collection of biblical study reference works was the direct result of this research, followed by months and months of dreaming and hard work. Three years into this project, you keep telling us that we are onto something good for you and your congregants.

I am, therefore, pleased to introduce you to *The Pastor's Bible Study*, Volume Three. We follow the same format that we have followed in Volumes One and Two. Half of the fifty lessons are based on readings for Lectionary Year C, featuring the Gospel of Luke and The Book of Genesis. The other twenty-five lessons are thematic, including studies on the Psalms, the Kingdom of God, relationships and table fellowship, and spiritual gifts.

Our contributors to this volume represent a diversity of denominations and interests.

- ♦ Dr. Robert Van Voorst, Professor of New Testament at Western Theological Seminary, Holland, Michigan, provides us with an excellent set of lessons for teaching the Gospel of Luke. His approach is fresh and written for the local congregation.

- ♦ Dr. Wilda C. M. Gafney is Assistant Professor of Old Testament and Homiletics at the Lutheran Theological Seminary of Philadelphia. Her treatment of key texts in Genesis, along with her original translations of many Genesis passages, will excite you and your fellow learners and, unless I'm mistaken, will find their way into your sermons some time in the next year.

- ♦ Dr. Deborah J. Spink provides a creative study of the Psalms as hymns. She presents us with an opportunity to discuss rich theological themes and references to every-day human emotions and experiences that are embedded in these ancient poems. The lessons include modern hymns that convey the themes of the Psalms for congregations today. She is Adjunct Professor of Biblical Studies at Palmer Theological Seminary in Pennsylvania.

- Ms. Anne Crumpler, popular freelance writer and Presbyterian layperson, has provided six lessons on the kingdom of God. Her insightful and conversational commentary deals with the importance and pervasiveness of the theme of God's promises and purpose throughout the Bible. At the beginning of the study, she poses the question: "What happened? Why have people forgotten the kingdom of God and the new promised social order?" Through discussion and soul-searching, congregants will have the chance to find their own answers to this provocative question.

- The Reverend J. Andrew McTyre, pastor of Park Central Church in Syracuse, New York and the Reverend Sarah S. McTyre, a Christian Education consultant to churches in the New York area, are partners in marriage as well as in ministry and writing. They have prepared for us a menu of relationships and relationship-building excercises based on feeding stories and table fellowship. They worked through every detail of this study with the congregation Andrew pastors, before completing their chapters. These lessons are fun as well as thought-provoking, nourishing to both body and spirit.

- Finally, well-known United Methodist pastor and writer, Dr. Ken Carter, offers four pivotal lessons on spiritual gifts, a topic to which we return over and over again as we lead our congregations. His exploration of the biblical context for spiritual gifts leads to discussion of how we can discern and accept our own spiritual gifts. He is serving as pastor of the Providence United Methodist Church in Charlotte, North Carolina.

On behalf of the hard-working and behind-the-scenes editors and production professionals at Abingdon Press, I present to you this volume, in the hopes that, once again, you may help the Bible come alive for truth-seekers in a world all too happy to bypass truth in any form. The truth makes us free.

David Albert Farmer
Wilmington, Delaware

Introduction

The Pastor's Bible Study is the latest in the line of New Interpreter's Bible® products that provide the best in scholarship for the service of the church. Designed to help pastors lead Bible studies for their congregations, this series is intended to enhance the study, teaching, and preaching of the Scriptures.

Each volume includes fifty lessons written by recognized biblical scholars, professors of preaching and pastoral care, and outstanding pastors and church educators. The fifty sessions include:

- Fifteen lessons from the New Testament
- Ten lessons from the Old Testament
- Ten lessons on a special topic (e.g., biblical themes, pastoral care)
- Four or more lessons on relational themes and the Christian life (e.g., social justice, ethics, diversity, the Kingdom of God)
- Four or more lessons on issues of faith (e.g., inspirational themes, prayer, healing, spiritual gifts)

Whether your study group meets for thirty minutes or an hour, for four weeks or the entire year, the flexible structure of the *Pastor's Bible Study* will meet your preparation needs. Its versatile design is also useful whether you choose to follow the lectionary, the canonical order of the Bible, a key biblical theme, or life application.

As you prepare to lead your Bible study, look for the useful sidebars that include teaching aids to facilitate discussion. **Sources** will provide you with resources for further study derived from the lessons. **Study Bible** sidebars will indicate points of integration with the *New Interpreter's Study Bible*.* **Teaching Tips** and **Reflections** foster participation, encourage discussion, and prompt interaction with the biblical text.

Supplementing the studies in this volume is a CD-ROM containing valuable data and suggestions for classroom use, such as:

- The full text of The Pastor's Bible Study: Volume Three, completely searchable by key words.
- An outline of each lesson
- PowerPoint slides
- Supplementary material that can be customized for handouts and screen viewing.

It is our hope that the Pastor's Bible Study will help you lead Bible studies in your congregation, in order to advance and increase the study, teaching, and preaching of the Scriptures.

* Note: The *Pastor's Bible Study* frequently cites material
from *The New Interpreter's Study Bible*,
the recommended text for study participants.

THE GOSPEL OF LUKE

A STUDY BY

ROBERT E. VAN VOORST

Robert E. Van Voorst, a professor of New Testament at Western Theological Seminary in Holland, Michigan, has written ten books, including Anthology of World Scriptures; Reading the New Testament Today; *and* Jesus Outside the New Testament: An Introduction to the Ancient Evidence. *He speaks often on the New Testament in churches and pastor's conferences.*

THE GOSPEL OF LUKE

Outline

I. Introduction
   A. The Forest and the Trees
   B. The Main Features of Luke
   C. Traditional Ways of Reading Luke
   D. Newer Ways of Reading Luke
   E. A Personal Word

II. Session 1—Fresh Vision of the Birth of Jesus: Luke 2:1-14
   A. Separating the Birth Narratives
   B. A Story with World-Wide Significance
   C. Emphasis on Christology
   D. Engaging the Textual Problem

III. Session 2—Get Ready for the Kingdom of God!: Luke 3:1-18
   A. John the Baptizer as Model for the Church
   B. The Desert as Place of Preparation
   C. John the Baptizer's Audience
   D. John the Baptizer's Message

IV. Session 3—Testing Jesus' Commitment, And Ours: Luke 4:1-13
   A. Emphasis on the Spirit
   B. Progression of Testing
   C. Social-Scientific Reading

V. Session 4—Luke's Gospel in Miniature: Luke 4:14-30
   A. Setting in Luke
   B. Purpose of Jesus' Ministry
   C. Jesus Goes on his Way

VI. Session 5—A Back to the Future Ethic: Luke 6:17-31
   A. Sources and Context
   B. A Common Misunderstanding
   C. Blessings and Woes on the Disciples
   D. A New Way of Life Modeled by Jesus

VII. Session 6—Women as Examples of Faith: Luke 7:36-8:3
   A. Story in Three Stages
   B. Women Who Follow and Support
   C. Who was Mary Magdalene?

VIII. Session 7—Lessons on Prayer: Luke 11:1-13
   A. Prayer in the Life of Jesus
   B. Perseverance in Prayer
   C. What Kind of Father?

IX. Session 8—Repentance Renewed: Luke 13:1-9
   A. Repent or Perish
   B. No More Barren Fig Trees
   C. Implications for the Church

X. Session 9—No Gift-Wrapped Crosses, Please!: Luke 14:25-33
   A. The Cost of Discipleship
   B. Literary Context
   C. "Book-Ending with Grace"

XI. Session 10—Who is the Real Prodigal Here?: Luke 15:1-3, 11b-32
   A. Literary Setting of the Parable
   B. The Story Begins
   C. Repentance
   D. Welcome Home!
   E. The Elder Brother

XII. Session 11—Thanksgiving at the Margins: Luke 17:11-19
   A. Historical/Cultural Background
   B. Gospel for the Marginalized
   C. An Illustrative Story

XIII. Session 12—Jesus' Option for the Poor, and Ours: Luke 18:18-30
   A. The Rich Ruler
   B. Social Scientific Setting
   C. Jesus' "Preferential Option for the Poor"

XIV. Session 13—Faithful to the End: Luke 21:25-36
   A. Eschatology Today
   B. Literary Context
   C. Coming of the Son of Man
   D. Moral Alertness

XV. Session 14—The Risen Christ Encounters His Disciples: Luke 24:13-35
   A. Journey Motif
   B. God Gives Understanding
   C. The Nature of Jesus' Body

XVI. Session 15—Transformation Complete: Luke 24:36-53
   A. Literary Context
   B. "What Kind of Body Will We Have?"
   C. The Coming of the Spirit
   D. Ascension Narrated

Introduction

The Pastor's Bible Study on Luke

The Forest and the Trees

When we study the Bible, we are accustomed to studying passage by passage, viewing the individual "trees" of God's word. This approach has considerable advantages, including a close examination of the passage. It also is consonant with the results of historical study of the Gospels, which has established that these passages, or "pericopes," arose as independent oral units. The early church used them separately for the most part until the Gospels were written. However, studying individual passages unconnectedly has its disadvantages. It often neglects the literary context of the passage, the overarching themes and message in a particular Gospel. Examining each "tree"—the individual passages—does give one an in-depth look. However, that "tree" often takes on an added meaning when set in its "forest," the context of its Gospel.

In the Gospel of Luke, or any other portion of scripture for that matter, we must keep the "forest" in sight. An understanding of the overall structure of Luke is quintessential for good theological interpretation. For example, the center section of Luke (Luke 9:51-19:27) begins Jesus' journey toward Jerusalem, a journey toward the passion. The placement of a passage within the journey narrative—the placement of a tree in this forest—affects the theological meaning the author intended for it, and therefore, how we should read it. Another important aspect of the "forest" that should not be forgotten is the immediate context of the passage: trees stand next to other trees. Passages are not haphazardly thrown together, but placed next to other pericopes that assist with interpretation. A reader should diligently notice the cues, such as context, patterns of word usage, narrative structure, etc., that the author has provided in order to interpret the passage faithfully. This study of Luke aims to move Bible teachers and students to a deeper consideration of fifteen Lukan "trees" by probing how they are set in the "forest."

The Main Features of Luke

Before we begin our study of the Gospel of Luke, it would be good to summarize its main features, especially those that distinguish it from the other Gospels. The longest of all four canonical Gospels, Luke is also the most literarily polished. It contains more parables than any other Gospel, many of them only in Luke. Indeed, fully half of its contents are not found in Mark or Matthew. Luke is the only Gospel to have a formal follow-up volume by the same author, the Acts of the Apostles. Although Luke presents Jesus as Messiah ("Christ") of Israel, it also presents Jesus as the divine Lord of the world, who will send his message into the whole world. Luke shows a good knowledge of and appreciation for Judaism, but mostly as a part of Christianity's background. Acts shows Christianity as spreading in the Roman Empire toward Rome itself, but with hints of movement in other directions such as Africa. Within its main presentation of Jesus as Messiah of Israel and Lord of the world, Luke portrays Jesus as God's model for values of humility, prayerfulness, spirituality, and self-denying service. The author weaves a well-developed theology into the carefully structured story. The gospel's overall goal is to challenge the Gentile believers to grow deeper into the faith. Most interpreters see Luke as highly positive toward fuller roles for women, but some recent feminist criticism pointedly questions this. Luke has a special concern for the marginalized, making it a favorite resource for other marginalized readers around the world today. Luke's presentation of Jesus appeals to most Christians today, and even to some who are not Christians, probably more than any other Gospel.

Sources

This material draws on the presentation of Luke-Acts in my *Reading the New Testament Today* (Belmont, Calif.: Wadsworth, 2005). Readers of my contribution to the *Pastor's Bible Study* who want more detail should consult this book, especially its Chapter Two, on the different methods of New Testament interpretation; Chapter Five, an introduction to the Gospels; and Chapter Eight, on Luke. Visit its interactive website at www.wadsworth.com/religion; click on "Student Book Companion Sites" in the navigation bar, then on this book. Use the drop-down box to find the resources for these three chapters.

Traditional Ways of Reading Luke

For readers using a private devotional method, Scripture can be read as a part of one's individual devotional practice. This kind of reading examines the text of Luke for insights into God, Jesus, and Christian living, and is often used in group Bible study. Scripture is also meant to be interpreted within the church body. The writings that now make up the New Testament were designed to edify—to inform and transform for greater faithfulness—the church community, not just the individual. Interpreting the Bible within the context of the church today helps to avoid over-personalizing faith, and assists with faithful interpretation. While devotional and ecclesiastical reading are beneficial, I believe that they must be supplemented by methods based on solid scholarship. Although this can be threatening to some Christians, when they are used "by faith and for faith" these methods can bring deeper understanding of God's living word for us today, directing and empowering Christian life. Using scholarly methods and results to interpret Scripture is a part of loving God "with all your mind" (Luke 10:27).

The main scholarly method for interpreting the Bible for almost two hundred years now is the historical method. Historical reading of the New Testament seeks to understand what its writings meant for their original readers. Here we can only give the main lines of the historical interpretation that informs the fifteen studies of Luke that follow.

Who is the author of Luke? Like the Gospels of Matthew and Mark, Luke is anonymous. No name is present in the text itself, and its title is from the second century. Traditions in the late second century unanimously identify this person as Luke, a physician and co-worker with the Apostle Paul. This may be an "educated guess," or it could be based on oral or literary traditions now lost to us. The oldest Greek manuscript of this document, from about 200 CE, uses the title "Gospel according to Luke." The Muratorian Canon in the late second century also identifies Luke as this Gospel's author. This identification is also found in the mid-second-century writings of Irenaeus (*Against*

Study Bible

For more information on the background of Luke's gospel, see the introduction by Joel Green to the Gospel of Luke in *NISB*, 1847–1850. As you study the text of Luke, pay particular attention to Green's superb study notes, which offer a rich perspective on Luke.

Heresies 3.1.1; 3.14.1) and in later writings (e.g., Eusebius, *History of the Church* 3:4.1-7; 3:24.14-15; 5:8.3; 6:25.6). Based on internal evidence, scholars conclude for good reasons that the same person wrote Luke and Acts. Luke and Acts share a common prologue (Luke 1:1-4, renewed in Acts 1:1-2), a literary style, and distinctive theological themes.

But was this person really Luke? The name "Luke" appears three times in the NT, in Col 4:14, Phlm 24, and 2 Tim 4:11, all clearly with reference to the same person, an associate of the Apostle Paul. 2 Tim 4:11 has little to offer about Luke himself beyond highlighting his faithfulness to Paul in comparison with others. Philemon identifies Luke as a "fellow worker," a term that designates one of Paul's traveling companions and colleagues. Col 4:14 refers to Luke as a "beloved physician." Because Col 4:10-11 refers to Aristarchus, Mark, and Justus as the only Jews present among Paul's coworkers, it appears that Luke is a Gentile. Luke-Acts is indeed compatible with a Gentile author who has had a significant knowledge and appreciation of the Jewish origins of the Christian faith. While it is possible that Luke was the author, we cannot say for sure, due to the paucity of the evidence. However, we can describe the author from Luke-Acts itself, with information that is far more useful in understanding Luke-Acts than just a name. The author was highly educated, especially in literature and rhetoric. This education means that the author likely came from the upper classes of society, whether or not he was a physician. Knowledge of Israel's Scriptures may indicate that the author was a "God-fearer" before becoming a Christian, or (less likely) a convert from paganism directly to Christianity who then learned much about Judaism. The author was a Gentile Christian of either the second or third generation, so most probably never met Jesus or had a firsthand witness about him.

A strong majority of scholarly opinion holds that Luke-Acts was written after 70 CE, the year when the Romans destroyed Jerusalem and its temple. In Luke 19:34-44, Jesus gives details, speaking of siege-works, full encircling of the city to prevent any escape, and the complete destruction of people and buildings ("not one stone standing on another"). Later, he says, "But when you see Jerusalem encircled by armies, then be sure that its destruction is near. Then you who are in Judea must flee to the hills; those that are in the city itself must leave it . . . They will fall by the sword; they will be taken captive into all countries; and Jerusalem will be trampled down by foreigners until their time is gone" (21:20-24). Another important piece of the dating puzzle is that Luke used Mark as one of his sources, so it must be have been written some time after Mark, to account for Mark's spread and standing as a Gospel. If 70 CE is the earliest possible date, the latest possible date is not quite so precise, but most scholars would date Luke before 100. Within this broad 70–100 period, the consensus today is that Luke probably comes from the 80s. Its place of origin is less certain, but Ephesus seems to be the place of composition and destination favored by many scholars today. Ephesus was a large, Greek-speaking city in Asia Minor and an early center of Christianity. However, this is just an educated guess, as very little specific information ties Luke-Acts to any particular place. It could be placed in many Greek-speaking Gentile churches in major cities in the western Mediterranean. Luke-Acts says that the Gospel is for the whole world, and this seems to be born out in the breadth of its first audience when first written.

As for the purpose of Luke, in the prologue (Luke 1:1-4), the author states that he/she writes so that Theophilus, and implicitly readers like him, may be more carefully and accurately informed about the story of Jesus and the early church. This leads us to ask, what exactly did Theophilus and the other readers/listeners need to know that they did not know already? To answer this question, we must look at the special themes of this book. Luke portrays Jesus as originally the Messiah of the Jews, and now the Savior of the whole world. Jesus came to save the lost, including persons that societies and religions marginalized. Jesus journeys from Galilee to Jerusalem, and then the church grows into the whole world. All of this is based on Jesus' life and death for others as an example of prayerfulness, humility and service. Jesus did not

Teaching Tip

The traditional prayer for St. Luke's Day reflects traditional notions of authorship. Whether one concludes that Luke the Physician wrote this or not, it makes a fine prayer for the beginning of study: "Almighty God, who called Luke the physician, whose praise is in the Gospel, to be an evangelist and a physician of the soul; may it please Thee that, by the wholesome medicines of the doctrine delivered by him, all the diseases of our souls may be healed; through the merits of Thy Son, Jesus Christ our Lord. Amen."

break Roman law, but suffers as an innocent. Presumably, some of these characteristic emphases of Luke's Gospel were needed in the churches to which this Gospel was written, for their instruction and growth in faith. According to the influential work of Hans Conzelmann, Luke-Acts' purpose was to set forth his scheme of salvation history in which a long "period of the church" comes between the period of Jesus and the end of time. Others have seen an apologetic purpose to defend Christianity against Roman suspicions or a theological purpose, for example, to specify the identity of the new people of God. In conclusion, it is probably best to read the purpose of Luke from its theological content, not to impose a meaning on its content by first settling on its purpose.

Newer Ways of Reading Luke: Narrative, Social-Scientific, and Feminist

Recent scholarship has turned to other methods to supplement historical study, methods that have given a richer and fuller understanding of Luke's Gospel account. The fresh perspective provided by these newer methods has filled in the gaps that historical study left behind. Although each of these methods could be employed alone, they are most often integrated with historical study, as we will do in the fifteen sessions below.

Narrative reading understands Luke, as a whole and its parts, as a story. Luke is a particularly skilled storyteller. His Greek style is highly literate, and this comes across in most English translations. For those who do narrative-historical reading of Luke, the author's ability to combine and adapt sources into one almost seamless whole is no small feat for any writer! His Center Section and passion narrative show skill in writing that far surpasses Mark and Matthew. Luke is also skilled at narrative rhetoric, so he tells his stories to convince and persuade his readers, not just to inform them. He deftly weaves many sub-themes into his main theme about Jesus as the Savior of the world: the importance of the Holy Spirit and prayer, God's love for the marginalized, and an understanding of eschatology that opens a wider time between the resurrection of Jesus and the end of

Study Bible

For two considerations of some new methods of interpreting the Bible, see John R. Donahue, "Guidelines for Reading and Interpretation," and Edgar V. McKnight, "Varieties of Readings and Interpretations of the Biblical Text," *NISB*, 2261–2273.

Resources

For narrative criticism of Luke, see Robert C. Tannehill, *The Narrative Unity of Luke-Acts: A Literary Interpretation, vol. 1, The Gospel of Luke* (Philadelphia: Fortress Press, 1991); David P. Moessner, *Lord of the Banquet: The Literary Significance of the Lukan Travel Narrative* (Harrisburg, PA: Trinity Press International, 1989); and William S. Kurz, Reading Luke-Acts: Dynamics of Biblical Narrative (Louisville: Westminster/John Knox Press, 1993).

Helpful social-scientific studies include *The Social World of Luke-Acts*, edited by Jerome H. Neyrey (Peabody, MA: Hendrickson, 1991); John J. Pilch, *The Cultural World of Jesus: Sunday by Sunday, Cycle C* (Collegeville, Minn.: Liturgical Press, 1997); based on the readings from Luke in the Roman Catholic lectionary); and James Resseguie, *Spiritual Landscape: Images of the Spiritual Life in the Gospel of Luke* (Peabody, Mass.: Hendrickson, 2004).

For feminist interpretation of Luke, see Jane Schaberg, "Luke," in *The Women's Bible Commentary*, edited by Carol A. Newsom and Sharon H. Ringe (Louisville: Westminster/John Knox, 1992); 275–292; Catherine

(continued on page 23)

the world. Moreover, much of his narrative skill does not become apparent until one reads carefully the Acts of the Apostles, in which the author builds parallels to his Gospel that shed light on its meaning. Luke has said in his preface that he aims to write a careful, orderly account, and readers today can conclude that he has largely succeeded in this.

Social-scientific reading makes use of the paradigms of honor-shame, kinship, and limited goods, to name a few. Honor-shame takes into account the importance of maintaining honor in the ancient world. The most important thing in life, in Mediterranean-Jewish culture, is maintaining honor and keeping away shame (rarely thought of as an individual emotion of "feeling ashamed," but rather as social disapproval). Kinship focuses on familial relationships and the normative behavior within these relationships. On a socio-economic level, a limited goods perspective bears in mind the notion in the ancient world that one can only accrue wealth and goods if someone else loses some of his/her wealth or goods. There are not enough goods in the world for everyone. The reader of Luke encounters a key social relationship in the ancient world at the very beginning of this Gospel: the author may be a client of Theophilus, his patron (social and financial supporter) who is being schooled in the Christian faith. The rest of the Gospel bears out this picture. The author is from the top echelons of society, but nevertheless has a strong message—the strongest of the four Gospels—of indifference to possessions and the dangers of "building wealth." Although God is about to reverse the situations of poverty and wealth, the author shows us a Jesus who ministers in a gracious yet challenging way to rich and poor alike. In this way, the Gospel of Luke is in tune with social values in the ancient Mediterranean, but reforms it with its own particularly Christian values.

Feminist reading pays special attention to the roles given to women in the Bible, and works to change gender inequality that has pervaded society. Feminist criticism has gained momentum in practice since the twentieth century, and continues to provide new insights into biblical study. Women play important roles at key points in its story of Jesus. Women are

(continued from page 22)

Clark Kroeger, "Luke," in *The IVP Women's Bible Commentary*, edited by Catherine Clark Kroeger and Mary J. Evans (Downers Grove, Il.: Inter-Varsity Press, 2002), 561-584; and collected essays in *A Feminist Companion to Luke*, edited by Amy-Jill Levine (Sheffield: Sheffield Academic Press, 2002).

Important commentaries on the Gospel of Luke include Luke Timothy Johnson, *The Gospel of Luke* (Sacra Pagina commentary series; Collegeville, MN: Liturgical Press, 1991); I. Howard Marshall, *The Gospel of Luke: A Commentary on the Greek Text* (Grand Rapids: Eerdmans, 1978); Fred Craddock, *Luke* (Interpretation Series; Louisville: John Knox Press, 1990); and Joseph Fitzmyer, *The Gospel According to Luke* (Anchor Bible Series; 2 volumes; Garden City, NY: Doubleday, 1981, 1985).

prominent at Jesus' conception and birth; note how Matthew's cast of characters in Matthew 1-2 is predominantly male, but in Luke 1-2 the cast is predominantly female. They are present with Jesus more noticeably during his ministry (e.g., 8:1-3), and are the only witnesses at Jesus' death and burial (23:49). They are at the empty tomb (23:55-56, 24:1-3), and two heavenly messengers appear to them first after they visit the empty tomb (24:4-10). Affluent, influential women and poor, unempowered women both figure in Luke's account. His narrative carefully builds the picture of women as disciples, believers, repentant sinners, and finally, credible witnesses. Feminist scholarship disagrees, however, on the significance of all this prominence. On the one hand, some conclude with Jane Schaberg that Luke is a "dangerous text" because it deftly seems to liberate women while portraying them as models of subordinate service, excluded from the power center of the movement and from significant responsibilities. Claiming the authority of Jesus, this portrayal is an attempt to legitimate male dominance in the Christianity of the author's time. On the other hand, most feminist interpreters conclude that a close reading of Luke is promising, because it has insights valuable for the building of a fully egalitarian society and of a theology that preserves and respects women's experience. Which view Luke actually takes, on the whole or with specific pericopes, can only be determined by careful reading of its treatment of women in the context of the whole Gospel.

A Personal Word

I wish to thank the Wednesday evening class at Third Reformed Church in Holland, Michigan, with whom I studied Luke's Gospel in 2003. Thanks also go to my student assistant, April Fiet, for her help in the final steps of preparing this study. Finally, I thank my students in the 2005 "New Testament Language and Interpretation" course at Western Seminary, who formally studied these passages with me. This study is gratefully dedicated to them.

Fresh Vision of the Birth of Jesus

For most Christians, Luke 2 brings strong memories of the Christmas season. Just to hear "In those days a decree went out from Caesar Augustus . . ." is enough to bring warm feelings to people's hearts and sometimes a holiday haze to their minds. This makes a fresh vision of Luke 2 more challenging, but all the more necessary. In order to bring out its full meaning for the faith and life of the church, we must "see it again for the first time." One way to do this is to read Luke 2 in the full context of Luke's Gospel, to see how its infancy narrative has deep significance for the whole of Jesus' story, and for the whole life of the church then and today. Later church traditions and popular ways of celebrating Christmas have obscured the Christmas story with all sorts of legendary, romanticized ideas. These have accumulated on Luke 1-2 like successive layers of varnish on the grain of beautiful wood. Getting deep into Luke will strip these away and allow us to see afresh the rich color and patterns of its original story.

Lectionary Loop

Nativity of the Lord (Christmas Eve and Christmas Day), Year C, Luke 2:1-20

Teaching Tip

"Infancy Narratives"

The phrase "infancy narrative" can be misleading. If you use it, explain that it is a term used by scholars to cover much more than Jesus' infancy; it encompasses Jesus' conception, birth, infancy and (in Luke) his visit to the Jerusalem Temple at age twelve.

Separating the Birth Narratives

First, the careful interpreter must separate Matthew's (Matt 1:18–2:23) and Luke's (Luke 1:26–2:21) nativity narratives from the harmonized understanding that most Christians, and most Christian theology, have. The reason why we have two infancy narratives is that there are two ways to see the story! Luke takes great care to place the birth story into its contemporary historical context, as Luke loves to do, whereas Matthew's account draws on Old Testament stories of the patriarchs' faithfulness to God's commands. Reflecting theological concerns for Jesus' Davidic lineage through Joseph, Matthew focuses on the actions of Joseph. Luke, on the other hand, focuses on Mary and her cousin Elizabeth, John the Baptizer's mother. Although these two gospel accounts contain differences in focus, Matthew and Luke agree that the events surrounding Jesus' birth were of divine origin. In both, Jesus' conception is miraculous; angelic heralds announce the birth of Jesus, and present this child sent by God as God's Son. Great things will be accomplished through this child, things that the angel calls "good news of great joy."

A Story with World-Wide Significance

Second, the world stage of Luke 2 suggests that this story has a worldwide significance; it is set in the whole world, not just Bethlehem and surrounding fields. In verse 1, Luke writes that the emperor demanded that the entire world "should be registered." All people went to the towns from which they came in obedience to the emperor's decree. Although Luke takes care to locate this story in the city of David, the angel proclaims in verse 10 that the birth of Jesus is "good news of great joy for all the people." Clearly, the account of Jesus' birth in Luke is good news for the whole world, not just for those in and around Bethlehem. Note also how Luke reiterates this world stage when he begins the ministry of John the Baptizer (3:1-2), which also introduces the ministry of Jesus. A few historical difficulties in these historical settings (for example, timing and scope of the census, Joseph's and Mary's hometown as Bethlehem or Nazareth) should not obscure for us the theological point that Luke makes in them.

Emphasis on Christology

Third, we must take Luke 1–2 out of its Christmas box, and relate it to Luke's central theological theme, that of Christology. Throughout Luke's account, Jesus is depicted as a virtuous man who is often found praying alone and faithfully keeping God's command-

Teaching Tip

Difficulties with Infancy Legends

People today sometimes have doubts about the traditions that surround the birth of Jesus. Aside from some historical difficulties within Luke 1–2 and Matthew 1–2, post-biblical legends that grow on these four chapters increase the doubts. Every age since Christian antiquity has seen legends and folklore attach themselves to the infancy narratives like barnacles to a ship. Some of these are innocuous enough, but others get in the way of understanding the infancy narratives with the mind and the heart. The opening scene of Shakespeare's *Hamlet*, for example, features this conversation about late-medieval legends about the Christmas season. Marcellus says in all credulity,

Some say that ever 'gainst that season comes
Wherein our Saviour's birth is celebrated,
The bird of dawning singeth all night long;
And then, they say, no spirit dare stir abroad,
The nights are wholesome; then no planets strike,
No fairy takes, nor witch hath power to charm,
So hallowed and so gracious is that time.

To which Horatio, with a more Renaissance attitude not so certain about all this, replies, "So have I heard and do in part believe it."

Today our legends and traditions are less supernatural. Instead, they have

(continued on page 27)

ments. When Jesus was baptized, he was praying (3:21); Jesus often withdrew to pray alone (9:18); it was Jesus' custom to worship each Sabbath day in the synagogue (4:16). He lived a life of such obvious virtue that at the foot of the cross a hard-bitten centurion proclaimed Jesus' innocence (23:47). Luke's emphasis on the virtue of Jesus is based on Jesus' identity as the Son of God. Angelic messengers announce the coming births of both John and Jesus, but from the beginning the reader is told that John is the second, the preparer for one to come who is greater than he. At Jesus' birth the angel could say, "to you is born this day... a Savior, who is the Messiah, the Lord" (2:11).

Jesus' concern for the poor and needy is readily apparent in Luke. This is especially so in the so-called Sermon on the Plain (6:17-49; see Session 5 below). In a series of pronouncements, Jesus blesses those on the margins of society and pronounces woes on the socially powerful. The Lukan infancy narrative prepares the way for this concern for the poor. The savior came into the world through a poor woman, rested in less-than-ideal accommodations (a feed trough, because there was no room in the Holiday Inn), and lived in a working-class family. Those who were first told about Jesus were shepherds, members of a lowly line of work that one should be careful not to romanticize, despite the positive use the Hebrew Bible makes of the shepherd motif. The suffering members of the early church surely took comfort in a savior who was born into such conditions. The marginalized in today's church will likely find it comforting that Jesus was born, lived and died on the fringes of his society.

The Lukan infancy narrative also points to how Jesus will move women from the margins of life more toward the center. Luke's account differs strikingly from the Matthean account in that the author describes the events from Mary's perspective. As noted above, Matthew describes an angel appearing to Joseph in a dream and announcing that Mary's child is "from the Holy Spirit" (Matt 2:20). Luke's account, however, has Mary actually visited by an angel (Luke 1:26-35). Matthew focuses on the righteous response of Joseph to the angel's words, but Luke highlights Mary's

(continued from page 26)

become sentimentalized and romanticized. A part of getting back to the biblical account of Jesus' birth—as difficult as that is in itself!—is dealing in a pastorally sensitive way with these accretions to the popular imagination.

Reflection

Widening Our Focus

In what ways do the differences between the Matthean and Lucan accounts of Jesus' birth enrich our understanding of who Jesus is? How do the similarities confirm central concepts?

Luke claims that the birth of Jesus has worldwide implications. Does the Gospel message of Jesus continue to have worldwide implications today, in our world of competing ideologies and diverse religions?

Voices from/to the Margins

Given Luke's privilege of the poor, how might the church go about proclaiming "good news of great joy" to those who are similarly marginalized? Why might Luke have found it necessary to feature Mary in his gospel account, while Matthew chose to give Joseph's perspective?

A Difficult Message

Luke's message of Jesus as Savior, Lord and Son of God was problematic in the Roman Empire. How is this message problematic even in our society today? How does the reading:

(continued on page 28)

humility and willingness to be a servant. The inclusion of Mary in 2:6-7 clearly illuminates the role of women in God's salvation plan.

Fourth, we must carefully restore the political dimensions of Luke 1–2. Politics and Christmas don't mix for us, but they certainly did for Luke! The story of Jesus' birth is set against the background of Roman domination. Its "Roman peace" (Pax Romana) had its human advantages, often over-stated in today's church. However, it came at the price of religious freedom, especially for religions that claimed the lordship of anyone other than the emperor. Subjects of the empire, whatever their religion, were expected to acknowledge the lordship of the emperor. As a 9 BCE inscription from Priene (now in modern-day Turkey) suggests, Augustus was the object of this kind of reverence: "Providence . . . created the most perfect good for our lives . . . giving us Augustus and filling him with virtue for the benefit of humankind, sending us and those after us a savior who put an end to war and established all things in order. . . . The birthday of the god [Augustus] marked for the world the beginning of good news through his coming." In the Roman Empire, the emperor was increasingly considered "lord" and "god" as a part of imperial ideology that soon would lead to outright emperor-worship. This cosmic imperial ideology became the rationale for all sorts of economic and social repression. The Pax Romana became the "Pox Romana." However, Luke claims that Jesus is Lord, a title that had otherwise been reserved for Caesar. The language here shows that the birth of Christ brings "good news" of a new "Empire" to power, the Kingdom/Reign of God. Jesus is not just the Christ, Israel's long-awaited Messiah, but he—not Augustus or any other human ruler—is "Savior" and "Lord" of the whole world.

Engaging the Textual Problem

Fifth, engaging a textual problem at the end of the narrative brings us to a new understanding of Luke 2. The interpretation, "Peace on earth, goodwill to men" (2:14 in the King James Version) is powerfully

(continued from page 27)
"...and on earth peace among those whom he [God] favors!" (2:14) change your interpretation of this text? Does it clear anything up for you? Are there any new problems that arise with this reading?

engrained in us. We often read it in our holiday haze to mean that God is pleased with the whole human family—maybe we aren't so bad after all! However, a new vision comes when we adopt the better reading: "...and on earth peace among those whom he [God] favors!" Not only does this more accurate reading include women as recipients of God's peace, but this reading also places the emphasis on God. God is the one responsible for giving peace; all of humankind does not receive this peace with the advent of the Lord. Those whom God has found favorable, in God's great mercy, will receive this peace. As we read the Gospel of Luke together, we encounter Jesus and in him become open to receive God's peace.

Sources

Some of the best scholarship on Luke 1–2 and Matthew 1–2 is by my professor at Union Seminary (N.Y.), the late Raymond E. Brown. For a short explanation of his ideas, suitable for laity, see his *An Adult Christ at Christmas* (Collegeville, Minn.: Liturgical Press, 1988). For a full statement, see his magisterial exegetical treatment, *The Birth of the Messiah*, rev. ed. (New York: Doubleday, 1999). There are enough exegetical and theological riches in this book to keep fresh a whole decade of Advent and Christmas study, teaching and preaching!

Other resources include Mark Coleridge, *The Birth of the Lukan Narrative: Narrative as Christology in Luke 1-2* (Sheffield: JSOT Press, 1993), for the often-neglected narrative dimensions of Luke's infancy narrative; and Heidi J. Hornik and Mikeal C. Parsons, *Illuminating Luke* (Harrisburg: Trinity Press International, 2003), for treatment of the Lukan infancy narrative in art.

Get Ready for the Kingdom of God!

John the Baptizer's ministry was one of preparation. Recent scholarship on John has rightly focused more on John's meaning for Judaism, but there is little doubt that John is also significant for the birth of Christianity. Luke makes this point by quoting Isaiah to explain his ministry: "The voice of one crying out in the wilderness: 'Prepare the way of the Lord, make his paths straight'" (Luke 3:4). John proclaimed a message of sharing with others, especially with those in need, and doing one's job justly, a call that drew on the Jewish prophetic tradition. His claims were so powerfully presented that the people began to wonder if he might be the promised Messiah. Indeed, groups claiming some messianic status for John persisted through the first and second centuries, and even today the only group of Gnostics surviving in the modern world, the Mandeans of Iraq, see themselves as continuing John's ministry of baptism. Luke makes it abundantly clear that John is not the Messiah, but the one called to prepare the way for him. In response to the wondering people, John the Baptizer clearly stated, "I baptize you with water; but one who is more powerful than I is coming…" (3:16).

John the Baptizer as Model for the Church

John's ministry, as unique as it was, serves as a model for the prophetic ministry of the church today. God did not give John an easy message to proclaim. Like Jeremiah long before him and Jesus immediately after him, John was called to preach radical repentance to the people of God, and like them, he had to pay the price for faithful ministry. Many of his hearers were

Lectionary Loop

Second Sunday of Advent, Year C, Luke 3:1-6
Third Sunday of Advent, Year C, Luke 3:7-18

Teaching Tip

"John the Baptizer"

Recent scholarship prefers the term "John the Baptizer," a more accurate translation of the Greek, over "John the Baptist." *The Baptist* is more of a title, while "the Baptizer" emphasizes John's action.

resistant to his calls for social justice, for sharing their wealth, and for being washed with the "baptism for repentance." Yet, John the Baptizer faithfully proclaimed the message given to him by God. He understood his place as a servant of God and the importance of being obedient. The church can learn much from John's example. His message of personal and social repentance and reform given to the church in today's world is countercultural, and often offensive. But the church needs to be faithful to God's prophetic word today, just as John the Baptizer was faithful. Like John, the church is called to be a witness to the kingdom of God and open the door for it, whether or not people choose to walk through that door.

The Desert as Place of Preparation

The desert/wilderness sounds to us, as it did to many in the ancient Mediterranean, a hostile, even life-threatening place. For Israel, it had a different meaning. By setting John's story in the desert, Luke would have certainly brought to the reader's mind important events in the life of God's people that also took place in the desert/wilderness. Many of these events were preparatory: the Israelites wandered in the desert as they prepared to enter the land, and Jesus was tempted in the desert prior to his public ministry. Preparation in the desert served to refine God's people, and this refining was often accompanied by an expectation of things to come. John the Baptizer proclaimed a countercultural message in the desert to prepare the way of the Lord, and he preached this message with the expectation that God was about to do something amazing.

John the Baptizer's Audience

In Luke, John the Baptizer addresses his message to several groups of people. To those coming for baptism, John warns that a biological relationship to Abraham does not necessarily protect from "the wrath to come." Trees that bear bad fruit will be chopped down. He instructs those who come to him to "bear fruits worthy of repentance." In verse 11, John the Baptizer describes these "fruits" as compassionate action: sharing an extra coat with someone who is without, and

Source

See Robert Van Voorst, *Reading the New Testament Today*, 170-171, for more on the desert in Mark.

giving food to those who have none. John also addresses a group of tax collectors. Tax collectors were notorious for extracting extra money from people in order to line their personal pocketbooks. Yet, John calls them only to take the "amount prescribed." Similarly, he instructs the soldiers to be content with the wages they are paid, and not to oppress others for money.

Any North American discussion of baptism in the New Testament will usually lead to discussion of church controversies over baptism today. Many mainline Protestant denominations have growing internal conflicts over "infant" versus "believer's" baptism, and some Baptist denominations in North America find themselves backing into this issue as the age of children undergoing "believer's baptism" gets younger and younger. This controversy often leads Christians to search the Scriptures for any possible answers to this issue. Current biblical scholarship almost unanimously concludes that the baptism John offered is not analogous to Christian baptism. Our passage in Luke calls it "baptism for repentance," not for change of religious identity. John himself calls Jesus' baptism radically different from his own. While baptism is a part of this text, Luke does not intend it to be the central focus. Instead, the baptism of repentance is important because it is a step towards the forgiveness of sins, which will become more fully present in Jesus' life, death, and resurrection.

John the Baptizer's Message

This brings the prophetic heritage of Israel into the life of Jesus and the beginnings of the church. The prophetic tradition of Israel held that a king would reestablish David's throne and bring Israel back to the worship of the one true God. Yet no human king could measure up to the characteristics of the expected Davidic king. God would need to intervene. The early church believed that God did intervene in the life, death, and resurrection of Jesus Christ. John heralded the coming of this Messiah, an indication that God had kept his promises to his people. John the Baptizer proclaimed a message that served as a bridge between

Reflections

Cultural Accommodation or Cultural Revolution?

1. In preparing the way of the Lord, John the Baptizer called for radical repentance in the tradition of the Old Testament prophets. As we "prepare the way of the Lord," will we need to call for a similar radical repentance in the church?
2. Is it possible to proclaim the unpopular message of the Gospel in a way that reaches our culture without adapting the message to the culture? If so, how might this be done?
3. What, to you, is the difference between "Christian perfectionism" and secular perfectionism? How can we have less of the latter and more of the former?

Preparation in the Desert

Reflect on a time in your life where you felt as though God were preparing you in the desert. Did this time feel spiritually dry and desolate, or exciting and full of anticipation?

Baptism of Repentance

1. What is meant by "baptism of repentance?" How might our own baptism call us to continuing repentance?
2. Often times, repentance should start within the context of the people of God before the church speaks prophetically to those outside the church. In what ways are we living out a message of repentance? In what ways might the church first need to "take the log out" of its own eye before removing the speck from someone else's eye (Matt. 7:1-5)?
3. What does it mean that Luke calls repentance prior to the Lord's coming "good news?"

God's promises to Israel and the fulfillment of those promises in the person of Jesus Christ.

Another aspect of John's message is holistic repentance and reform. John addresses individuals, social relationships, and political issues. The coming kingdom embraces all these, so they must "get their act together" as it dawns. This is not just repentance for repentance's sake. Rather, it is repentance for relationship: to greet and live with God, coming in the person of God's Son, Jesus. Moreover, repentance begins at home, among God's people. As long as the church is "of the world," as well as in it, we have our own faults to deal with. The church in the world will never be perfect, and forcing such perfection can lead to evils, as the Parable of the Weeds reminds us. Nevertheless, the people of God are called to continuous repentance, a change of mind (the Greek NT term *metanoia*) and a turning of life (the Hebrew Bible term *shub*). Before the church speaks a prophetic word to the world, it must sometimes remove the log from its own eye in order to remove the speck from the eyes of others. John the Baptizer's radical lifestyle indicates that he was carrying out this change for himself, and so the people who heard him were led by his example and his words to repent.

Luke calls this message "the Good News" (3:18), the same term he uses for Jesus' message about the Kingdom of God and the church's message about Jesus as Savior and Lord. The reader of Luke has already encountered this term in 1:19 at the announcement of the conception and birth of John the Baptizer, and in 2:10, the "good news of great joy for all the people" about the birth of Jesus. Now, remarkably enough, the call to repentance in preparation for Jesus is "good news," and John is proclaiming it. It is good news, in the ancient world and today, that people can change, and God is with them to empower and direct this change! This means that the *prophetic* ministry of the church, just like that of Jesus, is conducted in an overall *pastoral* context. Prophecy filled with grace motivates primarily by promise, not by threat.

Finally, we note the eschatological setting of the lectionary. The first Sunday in Advent in every year of

Resources

Many Christian churches, both Protestant and Roman Catholic, have a "call to perfection." For a balanced view of how Christians can resist our culture's version of "perfectionism" while pursuing the Gospel's call to become complete in Christ, see the recent book by Richard Winter, *Perfecting Ourselves to Death: The Pursuit of Excellence and the Perils of Perfectionism* (Downer's Grove, IL: InterVarsity, 2005). See also Guy D. Nave, *The Role and Function of Repentance in Luke-Acts* (Leiden: Brill, 2002).

Solomon Schimmel, *Wounds Not Healed by Time: The Power of Repentance and Forgiveness* (New York: Oxford University Press, 2002).

Frank G. Honeycutt, *Preaching for Adult Conversion and Commitment: Invitation to a Life Transformed* (Nashville: Abingdon, 2003).

the lectionary's three-year cycle is explicitly eschatological, and often deals with the Last Judgment. Year C's gospel readings for the Second and Third Sundays in Advent from Luke 3 continue this eschatological theme. Advent points to both "comings" of Jesus: his birth and his expected return. Preparation for both requires not just feelings of love and good will, but moral reorientation that begins to prepare us in the here and now to live in the Kingdom of God. The words of John the Baptizer continue to ring out their urgent and serious message: Get ready for the Kingdom of God!

Testing Jesus' Commitment to God—and Ours

Many Christians today see the temptation of Jesus as a contest of wills between Jesus and the devil. Supernatural good and supernatural evil collide, and Jesus inevitably wins. When we see it in its first-century context from Luke, it takes on a different meaning. Good and evil do contest with each other, and Jesus does win out over temptation. However, the struggle is real, because it points to the issue of kinship: what sort of Son will Jesus be to his Father?

Emphasis on the Spirit

As the temptation of Jesus begins, Luke characteristically emphasizes the presence and power of the Holy Spirit on Jesus (vv. 1-2). Luke has already emphasized the Spirit: the Holy Sprit was upon John the Baptizer before his birth (1:15); the Spirit overshadowed Mary and she was with child (1:35); the Spirit descended "in bodily form like a dove" while Jesus was praying after his baptism (3:22). In preparation for the temptation narrative, Luke renews its emphasis on the work of the Spirit. It mentions the Spirit twice: Jesus is "full of the Spirit," and was "led by the Spirit." Luke's emphasis on the role of the Spirit in the temptation is noticeably greater than either Matthew or Mark. The accounts in both Matthew (Matt 4:1-11) and Mark (Mark 1:12-13) have Jesus led by the Spirit into the wilderness, but do not comment that Jesus was full of the Spirit. This Lukan addition is important to note, as it has implications for how the reader should understand the narrative that follows. Contrary to what many people think, the Greek for "led by the Spirit" applies to the whole

Lectionary Loop

First Sunday in Lent, Year C

Sources

Bruce Malina and Richard Rohrbaugh, *Social-Science Commentary on the Synoptic Gospels* (Philadelphia: Fortress, 1992), 240-241.

Susan R. Garrett, *The Demise of the Devil: Magic and the Demonic in Luke's Writings* (Minneapolis: Fortress, 1989).

forty days of both fasting and temptation, not just Jesus' transit from the Jordan River to the wilderness as in Mark and Matthew. The testings given in vv. 3-12 come as a culmination at the end of these forty days of testing; they are the devil's final attempt to sway Jesus from his Father's will. Note that at the beginning of the next section after the temptation narrative, Luke says that Jesus is "filled with the power of the Spirit" as he returns to Galilee and begins his ministry.

Progression of Testing

Luke gives us three final temptations; in the ancient Mediterranean, three was the smallest number suggestive of fullness. There seems to be a progression in the tests, not just from "easy" to "hard," but also from "obvious" to "devious." First, the devil tests Jesus' strength over physical needs. Jesus is "famished," but does not allow his physical needs to take over. Instead, Jesus recognizes the importance of honoring his Father above himself. Jesus' response – "One does not live by bread alone" – calls to mind the rest of Deuteronomy 8:3: "…but by every word that comes from the mouth of the LORD." Jesus responds to the devil by reframing the issue; God is the provider, not humankind. In the second testing, the devil changes tactics: he implicitly recognizes Jesus as God's son in the way he frames the test, but tempts Jesus to switch allegiance—and sonship along with it—to the devil. The devil tries to take the worship for himself that only belongs to God. As God's Son, Jesus recognizes that only God should receive worship and references Deuteronomy 6:13: "The LORD your God you shall fear, him you shall serve, and by his name alone you shall swear." Third, the devil tries to beat Jesus at his own game. Recognizing Jesus' respect for the Word, the devil quotes Scripture (Psalm 91:11-12) in an attempt to sway Jesus. Jesus, however, recognizes the devil's quote as a misuse. As a loyal son, Jesus will not test his Father. Adam and Eve failed in their testing (Genesis 1-2), as did Israel in the wilderness (Deuteronomy 6-8), but Jesus leads the way to triumph over temptation for his people.

Reflection

"The Devil Can Cite Scripture"

Consider the famous Shakespearean saying "the devil can cite scripture" in its fuller context. This passage laments the difficulty of telling the real character of a person from the outward appearance in words and looks. In Act 1, scene 3 of "The Merchant of Venice," Antonio says,

Mark you this, Bassanio,
The devil can cite Scripture for his purpose.
An evil soul producing holy witness
Is like a villain with a smiling cheek,
A goodly apple rotten at the heart.
Oh, what a goodly outside falsehood hath!

Reflection

"The Devil Wears Prada"

Consider a contemporary secular view of "gaining the whole world but losing your soul," the cautionary tale by Laura Weisberger, *The Devil Wears Prada* (NY: Random House, 2004). This novel, which is scheduled to be released in 2006 as a film featuring Meryl Streep, centers around Andrea

(Continued on page 39)

Social-Scientific Reading

In their commentary on the Synoptic Gospels using the social scientific perspective, Bruce Malina and Richard Rohrbaugh give an illuminating explanation of the testing/temptation of Jesus. The testing is not just an event that sets the course of Jesus' ministry; it is a testing of his kinship with God. Malina and Rohrbaugh recognize that the testing occurs on a "cosmic level" where true motives are exposed and the truth is revealed. The devil is clearly testing Jesus' loyalty to his Father, and makes this obvious by the way he begins the first test: "If you are the Son of God..." By framing the challenge in this way, the devil seems to imply that if Jesus does not turn the stones into bread, he is not actually the Son of God. Jesus, in an attitude of respect for his Father, answers the devil with the words of his Father, and not his own words. For Jesus to use his own words would be for him to suggest that the authority and honor he has comes from his own doing. Instead, Jesus reminds the devil that all the authority and honor Jesus' possesses come from the Father. Jesus' loyalty to his Father shows that he is not attempting to take honor from the Father for himself. Paul picks up on this theme in Philippians 2 when he writes that Jesus "did not regard equality with God as something to be exploited" (Phil 2:6). As a loyal Son, Jesus did not intend to fulfill his own purposes, but the purposes of God. He remains loyal, and, in doing so, brings honor to the Father. He models for his people what being a true daughter or son looks like.

(Continued from page 38)

Sachs, a small-town woman just out of college who lands the job "a million girls would die for." Hired as the assistant to Miranda Priestly (played by Streep), the fabulously successful editor of *Runway* magazine, Andrea soon discovers that she is working for "the boss from hell," and struggles with the growing temptations of her job.

Reflection

1. The lectionary typically places the temptation narratives at the beginning of Lent.
2. How does this affect how the church reads and applies them?
3. What might be the meaning of Luke's temptation narrative for other periods of the church year, especially seasons of preparation like Lent and a season of the Spirit like Pentecost?

Reflections

Intentional Ambiguity

1. The devil asserts in this passage that he is the "ruler of this world." Jesus does not affirm or deny this assertion, but goes straight to the heart of the temptation. In what sense is this statement true, and in what sense false? How might it contribute to the ambiguity leading up to the actual temptation in verse seven?
2. Luke clearly wants his readers to see the presence of the Spirit in

(Continued on page 40)

(Continued from page 39)
Jesus during these temptations, but mentions the Spirit explicitly only at the beginning. How do you see what happens in vv. 2-13 as a manifestation of the Spirit in Jesus?

Reflections

Temptation/Satan

1. When we are tempted to do wrong, there is usually some inner psychological resistance and struggle preceding our response to temptation (contrary to the quip by Oscar Wilde, "I can resist anything but temptation"). In this passage, the reader is not privy to a struggle inside Jesus; Luke does not give it to us. If it is true here, as the author of the Epistle to the Hebrews says, that Jesus "in every respect has been tested/tempted as we are, yet without sin" (Heb 4:15), what might this testing inside Jesus have looked like?
2. Many people today, including many Christians, do not accept the reality of the devil/Satan. How might this issue influence how we understand this narrative?
3. What types of temptation did Jesus face in this episode, and how these might translate into today's experience for his followers? For example, how might we interpret for today the temptation to turn stones into bread? Some scholars have found the tasks proposed by the devil to be symbols of classic, archetypal temptations: to power, to be like God, etc.

Luke's Gospel in Miniature

After a long prelude, the public ministry of Jesus finally begins, and it begins in a dramatically decisive way. Jesus' rejection at his hometown of Nazareth is one of the most powerful passages in Luke. It explains who Jesus is and what his ministry will be. It even foreshadows what will happen to Jesus at the end of the story, his death and resurrection. Luke 4:16-30 is in effect Luke's "gospel in miniature."

The literary context of Jesus' rejection at Nazareth shows Jesus ministering with power and being greeted with strongly positive praise. In a Lukan summary in 4:14-16 that introduces Jesus' Galilean ministry, Jesus' fame quickly spreads throughout Galilee. He was "praised by everyone" as he taught widely in their synagogues. In the passage that follows his rejection in Nazareth, 4:31-37, Jesus teaches and heals in the synagogue in Capernaum and is greeted with amazement, and his renown reaches even farther. In sum, the dark story of Jesus' rejection in Nazareth is framed with his fame. As in the painting style of Rembrandt, light and darkness come into sharp contrast, to bring the meaning of the whole into view.

Setting in Luke

One other feature of this passage's setting in Luke is important to observe. Mark, Luke's source for this story, and Matthew both situate this story toward the middle of Jesus' Galilean ministry (Mark 6:1-6, Matt 13:53-58). Luke puts it at the beginning of this ministry, albeit with a hint that Jesus has already engaged in ministry in Capernaum. Moreover, Luke fills it out with details of Jesus' teaching, and he adds the attempt

Lectionary Loop

Third Sunday after the Epiphany, Year C, Luke 4:14-21
Fourth Sunday after the Epiphany, Year C, Luke 4:21-30

on Jesus' life. He foreshadows the opposition Jesus will face, his death on a cross, and Jesus' victorious resurrection. This comprehensive passage serves to guide the reader's understanding from this point on: Jesus is the powerful, Spirit-led Savior who is in control of his own life and death.

Purpose of Jesus' Ministry

Jesus' sermon begins, in good synagogue fashion, with the reading of a scripture passage. Jesus finds the passage to read; whether it is fixed by a lectionary or is a free choice by Jesus, we are not told. It begins with a theme dear to Luke, and already very familiar to readers of Luke to this point: "The Spirit of the Lord is upon me." This Spirit began Jesus' human life within Mary his mother (1:35); it prepared Simeon's encounter with him in the temple (2:25-26); it came upon Jesus at his baptism (3:16, 21-22); it preserved him during his temptation in the wilderness (4:1-2); and at the beginning of his Galilean ministry it filled him with power for his ministry (4:11). The Spirit of the Lord directs and empowers Jesus to fulfill several aspects of Isaiah's vision of full salvation. First, Jesus brings good news for the poor. Second, the captives will be freed. Third, the blind will regain their sight. Finally, the oppressed will go free. The Greek word for "go free" is the same word used earlier in Luke to indicate forgiveness of sins. The kingdom of God is breaking into the world in the person of Jesus and those whom the world has humbled will be exalted. This picture from Isaiah is all-encompassing, a telling picture of the Jubilee-orientation of salvation.

Luke then summarizes ("he began to say to them") Jesus' sermon by its theme, "Today this scripture has been fulfilled in your hearing." Luke does not give us the details, but we may surmise that Jesus showed how his ministry is fulfilling what God promised through Isaiah: good news is preached to the poor who gladly receive it, the captives to personal and social sin are set free, the physically and spiritually blind have their vision restored, and the oppressed are being set free. The "year of the Lord"—God's kingdom reign—is dawning in Jesus. All this is met provisionally with approval; the fame of Jesus that surrounds this passage seems at first to rule the day here.

But some say: "Is this not Joseph's son?" Perhaps they meant it as a compliment—"That was a good sermon, Jesus!"—and as a compliment to Jesus' family. Or they could have meant it as a rebuke: "Who does he think he is? Is he not one of us?" Readers of Luke will understand the irony: Jesus is *not* Joseph's son; he is the Son of God. This fundamental misunderstanding of who Jesus is will inevitably lead to a misunderstanding of what he is to do in his ministry, and to his death. If intended as a compliment, Jesus rejects this attempt to win for Joseph's family, and by extension the whole village (many of whom would have been kin of Jesus), the honor that belongs to him alone by virtue of his anointing with the Spirit. If intended as a rebuke, which is more likely in my opinion, he responds with ever-more-pointed attacks on his audience.

Jesus puts two sayings in the mouths of the people: "Doctor, cure yourself!" and "Do here also in your hometown the things that we have heard you did at Capernaum." The first saying serves to foreshadow Jesus' death, and brings to mind the taunting of the soldiers at the foot of the cross: "If you are the King of the Jews, save yourself!" In this lectionary passage, Jesus does save himself from the mob, but there will come a time when Jesus will not save himself. The second saying is a curious one. Luke has not included any material about Jesus' ministry in Capernaum, but this saying makes it clear that Jesus did not begin his ministry in Nazareth. In a chronology more in line with Mark's and Matthew's, Luke alludes to the work of Jesus in Capernaum prior to this event in Nazareth. Second, in verse 24 Jesus quotes a proverb that foreshadows what is to come here in Nazareth. Keeping in line with a long list of God's prophets, Jesus acknowledges that he will not be accepted in his own hometown. Finally, Jesus speaks about Elijah and Elisha, two prophets with whom the crowd were most familiar. Jesus uses these familiar stories to illustrate God's saving purposes among the Gentiles, despite an abundant number of Jews through whom God could have chosen to work. Their reaction

Study Bible

Read carefully the notes for this passage in the *NISB*, pp. 1860–1861. These notes develop both the narrative and theological aspects of this account.

Reflections

Theological Puzzles

1. Heinz Schürmann makes the thought-provoking comment that Jesus' action in escaping from death in 4:30 is a use of the divine protection promised in Psalm 91 that Jesus refused to employ when he was tempted by the devil (4:9-11). What do you think of this assertion? (See *Das Lukasevangelium* [*The Gospel of Luke*]; Herders Theological Commentary on the New Testament, volume 3; Freiburg: Herder, 1969, 240).
2. In his notes to Luke 4:31-32 in the *New Interpreter's Study Bible*, p. 1861, Joel Green states that only in this rejection at Nazareth passage does Luke give us any detail on the content of Jesus' synagogue teaching, so that we probably are to understand the sermon as representative of Jesus' entire preaching in synagogues. Discuss this statement. Could the theological ideas of this sermon also be representative of Jesus' entire ministry, whether in the synagogue or not?

is sudden and powerfully violent. They rise up and as a mob and haul him out of the synagogue. They "cast him out of their city," words that foreshadow the locale of Jesus' crucifixion outside of Jerusalem (Luke 23:26). They take him to the cliff just outside their town, from which they intend to kill him by throwing him headlong onto the rocks below (a sort of reverse stoning). Could there be a more dramatic way to show that Jesus does not belong to their village any longer?

Jesus Goes on His Way

Jesus, simply and without any further ado, "passed through the middle of them" and "went on his way." Is this a "miraculous" escape? Luke's wording does not portray it as such. He probably intends the reader to understand that in God's plan, Jesus foils the lynching at the last moment. He is not "driven along" any longer, and the surging crowd parts like the Red Sea as Jesus calmly walks right through it to the other side. Then Jesus "goes on his way" (literally, "proceeded"). The Greek verb *poreuomai* does not simply mean "he left," but it points here to the journeying that Jesus is about to undertake. This verb is used as Jesus goes on his way not just to minister widely in Galilee, but more significantly he goes on his way to Jerusalem and his death and resurrection there (9:51).

The end of this story foreshadows the death of Jesus and hints at his resurrection. The crowd was enraged by Jesus' words about them, and this certainly would not be the last time that Jesus' words would offend. Indeed, the crowd was so infuriated by him that they wanted to throw him off of the cliff. The "Jesus controversy" was only going to grow over time, eventually leading to the crucifixion. Yet, Luke adds an unmistakable hint of resurrection. Jesus was not going to stay down, but he would rise again. Just as Jesus walked through the middle of the murderous crowd in Nazareth, so too would Jesus prevail over his death and go on his way to his Father.

Resources

See Michael Prior, *Jesus the Liberator: Nazareth Liberation Theology (Luke 4:16-30)* (Sheffield: Sheffield Academic Press, 1995); James A. Sanders, "What Happened at Nazreth?" in *God Has a Story Too: Sermons in Context* (Philadelphia: For-tress, 1979). On the Jubilee language in this pericope, see N. T. Wright, *Jesus and the Victory of God* (Minneapolis: Fortress, 1996), 294–295.

Teaching Tip

If Jesus' ministry is to proclaim good news to the poor and captive, what is your church doing to realize this aspect of Jesus' call to discipleship? What more could your church be doing for the poor and dispossessed of the world?

A Back-to-the-Future Ethic

Most Christians today know the teaching of Jesus in Luke 6:17-49 not in its Lukan form called the "Sermon on the Plain," but in its more well known Matthean form in the "Sermon on the Mount" (Matt 5–7). When we read the Sermon on the Plain, we often unwittingly read it through the Sermon on the Mount. This was true in the ancient church as well, because many scribes who copied the Sermon on the Plain inserted wording from the Sermon on the Mount, thinking to make the Luke 6 more "accurate." So, for professional interpreters and lay interpreters alike, putting Matthew aside as much as possible and seeing Luke 6:17-49 in its own right is a refreshing experience, one that throws new light on Jesus' teaching and the task of following him today.

Lectionary Loop

Third Sunday after Epiphany, Year C, Luke 6:17-26
All Saint's Day, Year C, Luke 6:21-31

Sources and Context

The literary frame for this passage gives a hint about its contents. Immediately before this passage, in 6:17-19, Jesus teaches and heals people in a large crowd, and "all in the crowd were trying to touch him" to access his healing power. Immediately after this passage, in 7:1-10, Jesus heals a believing centurion's servant. All these people put their faith in Jesus into action; they recognize Jesus' power to heal and actively reach out to him. In the Sermon on the Plain itself, Jesus stresses the importance of acting on one's belief in the coming Kingdom. It is not enough to hope for God's coming, but believers must prepare the way for it by living as if it were already here. The power of the future Reign of God reaches back to direct and empower faithful living today (the term that some New

Testament scholars use for this is "proleptic"). This is true for 6:17-31, and it is put even more strongly in the conclusion of the Sermon on the Plain in 6:43-49.

What kind of way of life is this? It is a "back to the future" ethic, one that reaches into the future to see the way of the Kingdom/Reign of God, the rule of God now fully occurring in heaven and coming at the end of time to earth. In Jesus, this Kingdom has come near, and people can live in it by believing in Jesus and following him. When Jesus' disciples follow his teachings, they prepare themselves for the way of life of God's New Age. They live in a partial but significant way "in heaven" although they are on the earth; or, to use more apocalyptic Pauline terms, God in Christ has delivered them from the "present evil age" to live already in the "age to come." Those who listen to Jesus' words are called to live in a radical new way, in imitation of what is to come. Jesus commends those who are mistreated and persecuted for following him, and condemns those who live luxuriously, all in anticipation of the Last Judgment and the establishment of the Reign of God on earth.

A Common Misunderstanding

A common misunderstanding of this teaching in the Sermon on the Plain is that it is not meant to be practiced by most Christians in the here and now. In the medieval world, only monks and nuns were expected to follow these "counsels of perfection." In his thought-provoking book that deals with Jesus' teaching in the sermons in Luke and Matthew, Pinchas Lapide, an Orthodox Jew and expert New Testament scholar, identified eight common misunderstandings of about these teachings of Jesus. Lapide writes that people think the teachings are:

1. Divinely required perfection (and therefore possible)
2. A strategy to frustrate people and send them to the grace of God
3. An "interim ethic" before the coming of the Kingdom of God

Resource

Pinchas Lapide, *The Sermon on the Mount: Utopia or Program for Action?* (Maryknoll, N.Y.: Orbis, 1986). Despite the main title, this book deals fully with the material in Luke 6.

Reflections

A New Way of Life

1. Some biblical scholars who read this against a Jewish background do not like the terms suggest that the Sermon on the Plain is not a system of "ethics" and "morals" as applied to it by others, preferring the Jewish term but is a "halachah" (a Hebrew word used by the rabbis, meaning "walk" or "way of life"). What do you think of this position? How is a "walk" or "way of life" the same or different from a code of ethics?
2. Discuss which of Lapide's "eight misunderstandings" of the teaching of Jesus do you think is most is most prevalent in your church today?
3. Consider this provocative statement by Lapide: these Sermons teach "a Christian way of life that at bottom amounts to a Jewish way of life, and, like it, unfortunately, finds far too few imitators in either community of faith."

4. Impossible utopianism, unsuitable for a world of cold realism
5. Time-bound teachings only for Jesus' own disciples during his ministry
6. "Romantic radicalism" with a few simple but impossibly splendid ideas
7. A resource for self-centered individual religion
8. A historicizing teaching meant for first-century socio-political pragmatism.

Against these misunderstandings, Lapide argued that this teaching urges us to a "realistic utopia": its utopianism comes from Jesus' messianic vision of the future, its realism from the conviction that there is nothing more real and important for this world than the ethics of God's kingdom. Jesus meant his followers to follow these teachings.

Blessings and Woes on the Disciples

The blessings in vv. 21-23 are the good news for the poor Jesus announced in his Nazareth sermon (Luke 4). Jesus speaks these blessings to his disciples. The reader should be careful not to "spiritualize" Jesus' words, as Matthew tends to do. Those whom Jesus blesses are probably physically poor, hungry, grieving, and rejected. Certainly these attributes contain a spiritual dimension, as their history in Israel attests (e.g., the "poor" of Pss 10 and 72), and Jesus may well have intended this dimension in addition to the physical meaning. However, the tendency to neglect the physical nature of these blessings is strong among us, and it overlooks the all-encompassing nature of God's plan of salvation. Jesus ministered to body and soul, and to individuals and society, as a witness to the fullness of salvation in the Kingdom of God.

The woes are also addressed to the disciples! The "you" addressed by Jesus in the blessings is also used here in the "woes" (vv. 20-22, 24-26). These "woes" serve as a prophetic warning, similar to those in OT prophetic literature. The church does not get to skip out on judgment. Instead, the church stands under judgment, just as the world does. Note that the prose sections of vv. 22-23 and v. 26 match each other.

Teaching Tip

Blessing and Woe

The biblical use of the word "woe" is might be unfamiliar to people today. Discuss how it as the opposite of "blessed," entailing divine rejection at the end of time. How do we experience "woe" and "blessing" in our lives? How might "woe" and "blessing" be understood in the context of divine judgment in the end times?

Teaching Tip

This session urges that Christians prepare for the coming of the Kingdom/Reign of God by living as if it was already here. How might one go about living out this faith today, when we cannot physically hear, see, and reach out and touch Jesus?

Reflections

Blessings and Woes

1. As mentioned earlier, Christians often limit the blessings to those who are primarily spiritually poor, hungry etc. How might this understanding limit the fuller meaning intended by Jesus?
2. Does one's interpretation of this passage have implications for the way one lives and how one treats others?
3. How does your church meet the physical needs of the poor and hungry?

"Their ancestors" hated, reviled, and persecuted the prophets of God and spoke well of the false prophets. Jesus warns his disciples not to seek the approval of people like these. Those who walk in the way of God's future world cannot expect approval by those enmeshed in the present world, especially those who are in charge of it.

A New Way of Life Modeled by Jesus

Verses 27-31 are a call to a new way of living. The way of life prescribed by Jesus is contiguous with the holy living John the Baptizer urged, but goes beyond it. "Love your enemies" does not refer primarily to emotions. More than this, love means action. Specifically, Jesus is calling the disciples to "do good to those who hate you." "Turn the other cheek" is now a stock expression, but it literally means "Don't withdraw from relationship, but give them the opportunity to do evil to you again." (In line with general Semitic modesty, this refers only to the cheeks on one's face!) Jesus urges the disciples to live in a way that is dramatically different from those around them, and he does not promise that the road will be easy. Verse 23 serves as a reminder that their lifestyle is not in vain; the new age is indeed coming, and with it God's eternal blessing on their present obedience.

The passage ends with the "Golden Rule." Luke's Golden Rule is not as programmatic as it is in Matthew, where it is the "summary of the law and the prophets." Nevertheless, it forms a fitting conclusion to our passage. Cynics today redefine the Golden Rule as, "Those who have the gold, rule." Only slightly closer to Jesus' meaning is the self-serving misunderstanding, "Do to others as they do to you"; although this looks to us to be very wide of the meaning of the Golden Rule, Jesus takes pains to identify and reject it in 6:32-36. Also in this field of misunderstandings is the so-called "Silver Rule" found in the Jewish Rabbis and Confucius' *Analects*: "Do not do to others what you do not want done to you." In contrast to this rule expressed in the negative, which is fine as far as it goes, Jesus' statement is more comprehensive, positive, and practical. If 6:36 is meant to be a parallel to the Golden Rule in 6:31, this implies that the Golden Rule is the way of mercy that is a response to, and enabled by, God's mercy. Although it has deep theological grounding in God's mercy, it has powerful cultural implications. As an example of the Golden Rule in action, President John F. Kennedy's 1963 anti-segregation speech at the time of the first black enrollment at the University of Alabama is instructive. Kennedy asked whites to imagine themselves as black - and being told that they couldn't vote, go to good public schools, eat at most public restaurants, or sit in the front of the bus. Would whites be content to be treated that way? Of course not, he said, but this is how they treated others. Kennedy said, "The heart of the question is whether we are going to treat our fellow Americans as we want to be treated."

Jesus lived a life that exemplified the Sermon on the Plain. He humbled himself, allowing himself to be poor, hungry and derided by those around him. He blessed those who crucified him, praying for their forgiveness. When all was said and done by Jesus on this earth, God exalted him to the highest place. Jesus did not ask the disciples to live a life that he himself was unwilling to lead. Instead, Jesus made himself an example to follow. His ministry showed the way to live in the presence of the future. His exaltation after his "exodus" to God permitted the coming of the Holy Spirit to complete the transformation of his followers so that we too, as we reach back to the teaching of Jesus, can live in the presence of God's future.

Reflections

Cultural Use of the "Golden Rule"

Do an electronic search on the World-wide Web for the phrase "Golden Rule" or "do unto others," and give an analysis of the results in light of this session. How do people use the Golden Rule today, and how does this relate to how Jesus wants us to use it?

Resources

For full scholarly treatment, see Hans Dieter Betz, *The Sermon on the Mount: A Commentary on the Sermon on the Mount, Including the Sermon on the Plain* (Hermeneia Series; Minneapolis: Augsburg Fortress, 1995).

For more popular studies, see L. John Topel, *Children of a Compassionate God: Luke 6:20-49* (Collegeville, Minn.: Liturgical Press (2001); Megan McKenna, *Blessings and Woes: the Beatitudes and the Sermon on the Plain in the Gospel of Luke* (Maryknoll, NY: Orbis, 1999).

Women as Examples of Faith

Luke portrays women as disciples, believers, repentant sinners, and finally, credible witnesses. Luke often pairs a story about a faithful male character with a story about a faithful female character and thus seems to attempt to balance models of faith between the genders. In this lesson we will examine aspects of women's faith and ministry in the Gospel of Luke.

For many readers of Luke, male and female, the story of the sinful woman's encounter with Jesus (7:36-50) is one of Luke's most powerful passages. It compellingly dramatizes many of the important themes of Luke: God's love for those on the margins of life; the danger of complacency; release from sin; and the importance of deep, adventurous faith. All this comes in a wonderfully crafted narrative that is almost as elusive as it is definitive. To this story the lectionary appends the pericope that follows it in Luke (8:1-3), about the women who followed Jesus and provided for him. Luke no doubt means the second pericope to be read with the first. Together, they show that women's faith and discipleship can serve as a model for all believers.

Story in Three Stages

We can trace three stages in this story. In stage one, Jesus has just been called a "friend of sinners" (7:34). Certainly those who gave Jesus this title meant it as a condemnation, but now the divine truth of it is about to be enacted. Jesus is invited to a formal meal in a Pharisee's house—it is not said if he is the guest of honor, but an invitation to dine in the ancient world is always a mark of special respect. As Jesus is reclining

Lectionary Loop

Proper 6 (11) (Second Sunday after Pentecost), Year C

and eating in the house, a woman "of that city" enters, and Luke adds immediately that she is a known sinner. Luke does not tell us what her sins might be; traditionally it is identified as sexual, but this can be only a supposition on which the text is silent. Being known as a "sinner" had social consequences. Sinners were religiously marginalized, "outsiders" shunned by those who observed God's law. In Jewish literature of the time, it is most often applied to Gentiles. Even though she is reviled by society as a sinner, the way she touches Jesus' feet with her tears, her hair, and her mouth is an act of strong devotion toward Jesus that only a few followers of Jesus demonstrate in Luke.

In stage two, the plot of this short story turns with the objection, "If this man were a prophet, he would have known who and what kind of woman this is who is touching him—that she is a sinner." There is no need to posit supernatural knowledge on Jesus' part. If the Pharisee voices his objection, Jesus probably hears it; if the comment went unvoiced, the look of disdain would have been "written all over his face." The woman is an outsider, but Jesus doesn't treat her that way. Rather, he accepts her touches and displays of devotion. By allowing this sinful woman to associate with him, Jesus brought disgrace to the Pharisee's house. Simon was obviously vexed by this, and his dismay was likely obvious to Jesus. Jesus responds by telling a parable. Two men owed the same moneylender more money than either could pay back (one owed 500, and the other owed 50). Both men needed their debts to be canceled, for the amount was greater than either had. The moneylender canceled both debts, and most likely both debtors were grateful. After telling the parable, Jesus asks Simon a question: "Which one [of the debtors] loved him more?" The Pharisee answers tentatively, like a man who senses that he is being "set up," but can't quite tell how. "I suppose the one who had the bigger debt canceled," he responds. Simon the Pharisee chooses correctly, yet Jesus still needs to explain why.

Women Who Follow and Support

In stage three, the final part of this passage, the drama reaches its climax. Jesus "turns to the woman"

Teaching Tip

Two Washings

Compare the woman's actions in anointing Jesus with the story of Jesus' washing the disciples' feet in John 13:1-20. How does your understanding of this story change if the woman is taking the role of a loving servant, a role Jesus himself took? How is Simon Peter's reaction to being washed (first refusing, then asking that his head and hands be washed, too) an indication of the type of devotion such attention to the body entails?

Resources

For studies of the roles of women in biblical times, see *Women and Christian Origins*, edited by Ross Shepard Kraemer and Mary Rose D'Angelo (Oxford: Oxford University Press, 1999) and *Jewish Women in Greco-Roman Palestine*, by Tal Ilan (Peabody, Mass.: Hendrickson, 1996).

For feminist interpretations of Luke, see Jane Schaberg, "Luke," in *The Women's Bible Commentary*, edited by Carol A. Newsom and Sharon H. Ringe (Louisville: Westminster/John Knox, 1992), 275-292; Catherine Clark Kroeger, "Luke," in *The IVP Women's Bible Commentary* (Downers Grove, IL: InterVarsity, 2002), 561-584; Turid Karlsen Seim, *The Double Message: Patterns of Gender in Luke and Acts* (Edinburgh: T&T Clark, 1994); Barbara Reid, *Choosing the Better Part? Women in the Gospel of Luke* (Collegeville, Minn.: Liturgical Press, 1996); and *A Feminist Companion to Luke*, edited by Amy-Jill Levine (Sheffield: Sheffield Academic Press, 2002).

and thus includes her in the conversation. As Jesus speaks about the woman's "great love," it becomes obvious that Simon is the one with "little love." The woman provided water, kisses, and anointing for Jesus, all things that Simon should have done for Jesus and the other guests, but didn't. Jesus' statement is emphatic: "Therefore, I tell you, her sins, which were many, have been forgiven; hence she has shown great love. But the one to whom little is forgiven, loves little" (v. 47). Jesus makes obvious the point, speaking now directly to the woman: "Your sins are forgiven." The Greek verb *apheontai* (from *aphiemi*) is in the perfect tense, meaning "have been forgiven," which implies the continuing result of past action. The benefits of her forgiveness are ongoing.

Jesus has already made his point, and proven it, so he does not respond directly to their murmuring. Instead, he gives the woman a final assurance, one used elsewhere in Luke (compare to Luke 8:48, 17:19, 18:42), "Your faith has saved you," coupled with a concluding "Go in peace." In her actions, she has shown her faith in Jesus; she has been restored to God, and is on the margins no more. God's shalom is now hers.

Luke then mentions that the disciples are with Jesus. This almost goes without saying, but it is necessary as a transition to the main statement of this section, about the women who accompany Jesus. Luke singles out three: Mary Magdalene, Joanna, the wife of Herod's household manager Chuza, and Susanna. These three had been "cured of evil spirits and [bodily] infirmities." Many other women accompany Jesus on a regular basis. These women "provided for them [some manuscripts: "him," i.e., Jesus] out of their resources."

The Greek word for "providing" (*diakoneo*, from which we get our English word "deacon") carries with it a multitude of meanings. In general, the word denotes any kind of service, but can also mean "to minister to" or "to supply life's necessities." Luke likely had many of these meanings in mind. The women's ministry challenges our assumptions about women's lack of freedom to travel and serve in the first century CE.

Sources

Carolyn Osiek, "Mary [Magdalene]," in Carol Meyers, ed., *Women in Scripture* (Grand Rapids, Mich.: Eerdmans, 2001), p. 122. See also Jane Schaberg, "How Mary Magdalene Became a Whore," *Bible Review 8* (1992), p. 37. For more comprehensive studies of Mary Magdalene, see Susan Haskins, *Mary Magdalen: Myth and Metaphor* (New York: Harcourt Brace, 1993); Carla Ricci, *Mary Magdalene and Many Others: Women Who Followed Jesus* (Minneapolis: Fortress Press, 1994); Esther De Boer, *Mary Magdalene: Beyond the Myth* (Harrisburg, Pa.: Trinity Press International, 1997); or Ingrid Maisch, *Mary Magdalene, The Image of a Woman Through the Centuries* (Collegeville, Minn.: Liturgical Press, 1998).

Did the women serve Jesus only, or for the disciples, as well? Several manuscripts read "who provided for him out of their resources," while many other manuscripts contain the pronoun "them." "Them" is more widely attested than "him," and the context of the passage, in which the Twelve are mentioned, suggests that the women provided for Jesus and the twelve. This lectionary text states that the women ministered to Jesus and the twelve. The women gave what they had at their disposal, a Lukan theme of radical sharing that comes up again in the description of the early Jerusalem church in Acts (compare with Acts 2:44). Jesus urged such commonality in Luke, and these women model it.

Who was Mary Magdalene?

Finally, we should consider a popular issue today in interpreting the passages in this session, the figure of Mary Magdalene. Here I draw on Carolyn Osiek's essay "Mary [Magdalene]," which describes and powerfully critiques the misunderstanding of Mary Magdalene since ancient times and takes to task the portrayal of Mary in Dan Brown's blockbuster book *The DaVinci Code*, as the wife of Jesus. Mary was indeed a close follower of Jesus, as the gospels attest. She was present at his death and burial. She met him after his resurrection; all four gospel accounts testify to her presence at these events. Church tradition from the second century on held that Mary Magdalene was the anointing woman described in this lectionary passage (7:36-50), and assumed that the sinful anointing woman was a prostitute. This assumption about the nature of her "sin" has stirred recent speculation as to the nature of her relationship with Jesus.

However, there is no scriptural evidence to suggest that the woman in 7:36-50 is Mary Magdalene. Luke mentions Mary by name in 8:2, and he easily could have mentioned her name in 7:36-50 if such a reference were appropriate. Indeed, if it were the same person, we would rightly expect Luke to mention her name in 7:36-50. Moreover, the Gospel writers never implied a sexual relationship between Jesus and Mary.

If this is the case, where did these ideas about Mary Magdalene and her relationship to Jesus originate? In

Teaching Tip

Women and the Twelve

Luke 8:1-3 brings up, implicitly but acutely, the question: If women were such faithful followers of Jesus, why was there no woman among the twelve? Twelve is a symbol of the twelve tribes of Israel, all of them named after a male. The inclusion of "twelve" disciples reflects Jesus' mission to call all of Israel to respond to God in faith. Many churches argue that "Since Jesus didn't appoint any female apostles in the twelve, we shouldn't have female ministers today." However, Jesus did not appoint any Gentiles to be among the twelve, either, so by this argument no *Gentiles* could be ministers today, either!

Reflection

Discuss the symbolism of the "twelve." Should this symbol be interpreted as inclusive, because it encompasses all of Israel, or exclusive, because it seems to exclude Gentiles and women?

What are your thoughts on the contributions of women to Jesus' ministry and to the church today? Is Luke suggesting that women are both servants and models of leadership, just as men are? How does your church involve women in leadership and servant roles?

spite of a total lack of evidence in the canonical Scriptures, the Western church, from the second century on, identified Mary as the woman who "was a sinner" in Luke 7:36-50, perhaps because the story occurs immediately before Luke 8:2-3, where she is first named. Mary Magdalene is described as one from whom Jesus cast out seven demons, which does not fit the description of the anointing woman of 7:36-50. The male imagination in late antiquity tended to view women as either saints or sinners, and only one sin could require such dramatic repentance: Mary must have been a reformed prostitute. In the modern period, paintings of Mary Magdalene often make her young and alluring, with sensually flowing hair and just enough clothing out of place to be provocative.

Mary Magdalene deserves to be restored to her Gospel image as prominent disciple and spokeswoman of the gospel. She had the economic means and social freedom to spend her income and time the way she chose. To have acquired her reputation for closeness to Jesus, there must have been a certain depth in their relationship, a tradition borne out in non-canonical writings such as the Gospel of Mary. Her unquestioned presence at both the cross and at the tomb on Easter morning indicates her prominence as a disciple. At the darkest and most uncertain moments, when others had withdrawn—even Jesus' mother, according to the Synoptic Gospels—Mary Magdalene faithfully remained in Jesus' presence.

Reflections

An Interesting Omission

Mark, in his telling of this story, has the remarkable concluding sentence, "Truly, I tell you, wherever the good news is proclaimed in the whole world, what she has done will be told in remembrance of her" (Mark 14:9). Assuming, as the vast majority of NT scholars do, that Luke uses Mark as a source, why might Luke have omitted this?

Tears of Sorrow or Joy?

1. The woman in this story is obviously weeping, but it is less clear what exactly caused her to weep. Was the woman crying tears of sorrow, as she repented? Or, was she crying tears of joy at her forgiveness?
2. When have you felt as if you were overwhelmed with gratefulness for having been forgiven much?

The Result?

In the *NISB* Joel Green asks this good question on p. 1867: Will the community of that city, and in particular the men around that table, respond to this forgiven woman by welcoming her in the community?

Lessons on Prayer

Prayer is an essential element of the Christian life. The prayer life of Jesus' disciples is grounded in his own prayer life, as 11:1 makes plain: "He was praying in a certain place, and after he had finished, one of his disciples said to him, 'Lord, teach us to pray, as John taught his disciples.'" Jesus' faithful reliance on God during his ministry and passion, from his temptation forward, came from his life of prayer.

Prayer in the Life of Jesus

The prayer that Jesus taught develops the attitude of faith in God; it follows the example of Jesus' prayer life; it brings us into the presence of the Kingdom of God. The Lord's Prayer has both common and extraordinary uses: every day in private; every Sunday in church; with Christians in difficult or dangerous situations, such as accidents or military battle; and on the lips of the faithful as they are dying.

David Crump's book *Jesus the Intercessor* contributes greatly to the understanding of Jesus' prayer life, both as recorded in Luke-Acts and after the resurrection. The early Church believed that the risen and ascended Jesus interceded on the church's behalf at the "right hand of God." This belief was grounded in early Jewish belief that God had appointed certain men to serve as intercessors. Crump states that Jesus served in an intercessory capacity during his life, not just after his death and resurrection. Jesus prayed for others as any Jewish person would have, yet his prayers were even more efficacious because of his status in God's kingdom.

Luke records a shorter form of the Lord's Prayer than does Matthew (Matt 6:9-13). This short form is probably

Lectionary Loop

Proper 12 (17), Year C

Source

David Crump, *Jesus the Intercessor: Prayer and Christology in Luke-Acts*. Grand Rapids, Mich.: Baker, 1999.

closer to the original/authentic form of the Lord's Prayer, although there is no way to be sure. The Lord's Prayer in Matthew lays down a *pattern* of prayer: "Pray, then in this way..." (Matt 6:9) However, in Luke, Jesus seems to be instructing his disciples to pray using the exact words that follow. This difference contains some irony—the church has followed Luke's desire for using exact words, but the exact words we use are from Matthew! While it is good to use the exact words, we can pay attention to the model of prayer that the Lord's prayer offers to enhance our own prayer.

First, the Lord's prayer begins by praising God. "Father, hallowed be your name" does not simply mean that the word "God" be treated in a holy way. Instead, this phrase means: "You are holy, and we offer praise to you." The proper place to begin prayer is with the recognition of who God is, particularly God's fatherhood, and with gratitude for the things God has done for us as our Father.

Second, the Lord's Prayer offers petitions that focus on God's kingdom: "(May) your kingdom come." As we pray for the full coming of God's rule, we live more faithfully in the part of his rule that is already present with us in the here and now. Prayer that is kingdom-focused realizes that the reign of God has not fully come. This realization enables members of the church to live more faithfully in an unfaithful world.

Third, Jesus' prayer models dependence on God every day. "Our daily bread" can refer to the everyday, literal bread that one needs for survival. Reliance on God is the key. However, "daily bread" can also refer to the "eschatological bread" to come at the messianic banquet. God will continue to provide in the days to come, especially with the second advent of Christ. The Greek word for "bread" (artos) can refer literally to a loaf of bread, but also carries the meaning of food and nourishment in general, or metaphorically refers to one's support or livelihood. Jesus encourages the disciples to remember continually who provides for them, and to pray for continued care.

Fourth, the Lord's prayer models how we need to pray for God's forgiveness, and reminds us that we must forgive others. We must not to get this backwards: God forgives us first and always, and on this

Reflection

The Gospel of John does not record a version of the Lord's Prayer, but John does portray Jesus as "the bread of life," the one who provides not only food but "true bread from heaven" (John 6:22-35). Discuss the implications of "daily bread" as "bread of life."

basis we forgive others. Righteousness is not works-based: it is not the case that God will forgive us only if we forgive others first. (If that is that case, we are all doomed!) As mentioned earlier in session 7, those who have been forgiven much by God, love and forgive others more fully (cf. Luke 7:37).

Finally, Jesus' prayer shows us how to gird ourselves for the spiritual struggle with evil. In prayer, one must be aware that since the kingdom has not fully come, evil is still a force with which to be reckoned. In Luke, the prayer ends with a petition to be kept from "the time of trial," yet Matthew adds "rescue us from the evil one." The last word in Matthew can mean either "evil" or "evil one." A detailed study of this prayer, and its daily use, should keep both meanings in view.

Perseverance in Prayer

As we examine the inner meaning of the Lord's Prayer, its connection to perseverance in prayer becomes clear. As a religious Jew, Jesus would have prayed every day. The prayer contains internal hints which suggest daily, regular use (i.e. "daily bread"). Faith calls for steady, steadfast perseverance in all of life, and prayer's ability to connect us to God encourages this perseverance.

Jesus knew from Scripture and his own experience that answers do not always come immediately. So, he exhorts us to, "ask, seek, knock" (Luke 11:9). The continuous aspects of the Greek verbs (*aiteite*, "ask;" *zēteite*, "seek;" and *krouete*, "knock") are important; the actions are continuous, not simple, one-time actions. A paraphrase could render this passage: "Keep on asking, keep on seeking, keep on knocking." However, even when we grant this, there is a tension. How long do we have to keep asking, in sometimes desperate situations? As Jesus often does to explain an important point, he uses a parable (Luke 11:5-8): Someone has stopped at a man's house, and the man has no bread to offer his guest. In desperation, the man goes to his friend's house at midnight to ask for a loan of three loaves of bread. The friend responds that it is not a good time to be asking this thing. Yet, the man was persistent in his asking. If friendship was not enough to get the friend to loan him three loaves of bread, his perseverance in asking eventually succeeds. In Luke 11:11-13,

Reflections

Implications for Worship

1. A current trend among some American Protestant Christians is the expression in prayer, "Father–God." What are the strengths and weaknesses of this expression?
2. Prayer in the church today tends to be focused on the needs of individuals. How might the recitation of the Lord's Prayer serve as a reminder of the communal nature of the church?
3. Teaching about the Lord's Prayer requires pastoral sensitivity toward those who have experienced abuse, even while being mindful of the importance of the "father-language" for God in the Bible. What are some ways in which church services can incorporate both masculine and feminine imagery for God (for example, mother imagery in addition to father imagery)?
4. Forgiveness tends to be thought of as a personal and private matter. Yet, the pronouns in the Lord's Prayer are all plural ("our debts"). Reflect on issues for which the church may need to ask corporate forgiveness.

Jesus explains the parable by using a "lesser to greater" method: If you who are evil (we all live in the present evil age and participate in its evil) know how to give good gifts to your children, how much more will a God who is good give perfectly good gifts to his children. In Luke, the good gift from God is that of the Holy Spirit, and it is given to those who ask God for it.

What Kind of Father?

We cannot leave our treatment of Luke 11:1-13 without dealing with a difficult question in the ancient world of Jesus and our world today: What kind of Father is God, anyway? In the ancient world a father had wide-ranging power. This power could be used for coercive purposes, and often was. The expression *pater familias*, "father of the family," adequately encompasses the role of the father in the ancient world as heads of their respective households.

In today's world, many human fathers are physically and emotionally abusive. Tragically, the rate of parental abusiveness (including neglect) has been growing in the United States over the last two generations. Those who suffer under abusive parents often have a great deal of trouble, as children and later as adults, thinking of God as their "Father," even if it is the "Father in heaven." For many people, "God" is not a happy word, but a word that conjures up images of a domineering father and the pain associated with such a father figure. This passage serves as a reminder that our relationship with God as Father is based on Jesus' relationship with God as his Father. In the previous chapter of Luke, Jesus praises his Father, a Father who is only known by the Son. Knowledge of the Father comes through the Son (Luke 10:21-22) Also, as we get to know a new Father, we learn that he is different from our earthly Fathers, who like all human beings can range from imperfection to seemingly absolute evil. The human concept of fatherhood has been touched by the effects of the fall and sin; fatherhood is only perfect in God. We, as Christians, would do well to remember that we are to judge our behavior by God's standard, and not to judge God's character by our flawed enactment of God's standard.

Teaching Tip

Praying the Lukan Lord's Prayer

Have the class pray the Lord's Prayer using the wording of Luke. Then discuss the different thoughts and feelings individuals in the class have toward this form of the Our Father.

Teaching Tip

Praying in Community

Point out the plural pronouns within the prayer, and show how they allude to the communal nature of this prayer. Even when the prayer is said individually, it serves as a reminder that one is always a part of the church.

Resources

N. T. Wright, *The Lord and His Prayer* (Grand Rapids: Eerdmans, 1997); Kenneth Stevenson, *The Lord's Prayer: a Text in Tradition* (Minneapolis: Fortress Press, 2004); Michael Crosby, *The Prayer that Jesus Taught* (Maryknoll, NY: Orbis, 2002); Herman C. Waetjen, *Praying the Lord's Prayer: An Ageless Prayer for Today* (Harrisburg, Pa.: Trinity Press International, 1999); Roberta C. Bondi, *A Place to Pray: Reflections on the Lord's Prayer* (Nashville: Abingdon Press, 1998); William H. Willimon, *Lord, Teach Us: The Lord's Prayer and the Christian Life* (Nashville: Abingdon Press, 1996).

Repentance Renewed

Jesus' journey to Jerusalem continues in Luke. The Gospel writer takes much of the material in this section from Mark's description of Jesus' Galilean ministry, and adds several unique pericopes not found anywhere else in the canonical Gospels. This is the case with the two pericopes in this session. They call the readers to continual repentance with the kind of urgency usually found in biblical calls to repentance.

Any teaching or preaching of this passage must reckon with its context. 13:1-9 comes at the end of a teaching section that began at 12:1. The theme of this long discourse section is "vigilance in the face of crisis" (Joel Green, *NISB*, 1877–78). Like many of the longer teaching passages ("sermons") in the Synoptic Gospels, this one ends with a call to action. The action Jesus demands here is repentance, a changed heart and mind that results in a changed, fruitful life. In the light of its context, 13:1-9 is not an isolated call to "repent or perish," which it could too easily be made out to be. Rather, it calls us to use the present opportunity to amend our lives and become more productive for the Kingdom of God.

Repent or Perish

Jesus' message to the particular group that asked about an atrocity is one of repentance. Jesus responds to specific questions about the meaning of an atrocity that people were talking about: The blood of Galileans had been mixed with their sacrifices, presumably by Pilate. Aware of the Deuteronomic law's tendency to equate suffering with guilt or at least the suspicion of guilt, Jesus reminds his listeners that the Galileans

Lectionary Loop

Third Sunday in Lent, Year C

Study Bible

See comments on the context of this passage in the *NISB*, 1877-1878.

who were killed were no worse sinners than the group standing before him. In an action that no doubt surprises them, Jesus issues a direct ultimatum: "But unless you repent, you will all perish as they did" (Luke 13:3). Jesus continues to drive home his message of repentance by recalling the tragedy of the tower of Siloam falling and killing eighteen people. Again, he reminds the inquiring group that those who were killed were much like those standing before him. He intensifies the ultimatum by calling once more for repentance. All of us are familiar with horrifying tragedies in our own times, and all of us no doubt question why some people perish in these horrible events and why others are spared. Whether those who read Luke's account later on were familiar with these tragedies or not, they are self-explanatory in the narrative, and Jesus' message of repentance is still as poignant to us as it was for his first audience.

Even today, the continual repentance commanded in Luke is of great importance for the church. Jesus warns against presuming that bad things happen only to bad people. All people are in need of repentance, and no one should presume herself or himself to be above it. Jesus' message is one of continuous repentance, but also of hope. Death is not inevitable, but can be avoided through sincere repentance. The use of the word "unless" in Jesus' admonition, "Unless you repent," is pivotal. This small word provides hope in an otherwise bleak pronouncement. Repentance will lead to a restored relationship with God that trusts God in the midst of tragedies in this world. It trusts that God is our loving Father even when tragedy strikes, that God in Jesus suffers with us, and that God is somehow guiding history to its end in the Kingdom of God.

In this passage, Jesus renews the message of John the Baptizer, which calls for inner repentance that leads to changed social behavior (Luke 3:3). Like John, Jesus warns that failure to change one's heart and ways will lead to destruction, and this destruction is imminent (Luke 3:9). Repentance is critical now more than ever because in Jesus God's reign is coming ever closer.

Teaching Tip

"On Friday noon, July the twentieth, 1714, the finest bridge in all Peru broke and precipitated five travelers into the gulf below." With these words begins the 1927 novel by Thornton Wilder, *The Bridge of San Luis Rey* (New York: Harper Perennial Modern Classics), a Pulitzer Prize-winning exploration of reason and irrationality in tragic accidents. This short (133 page) masterpiece will stir questions that this Lukan passage addresses.

Reflection

Repentance/Confession

1. A traditional prayer of confession and repentance that dates from the Middle Ages has the line, "Grant us time to amend our lives." Do you think that this is still a helpful thing to say in prayer today?
2. Reflect on the way in which Jesus' call for repentance mirrors the call issued by John the Baptizer (compare to Luke 3).
3. Give your reflections on this sentence: "The longer one lives as a devoted Christian, the harder it is to repent."

No More Barren Fig Trees

Jesus then tells the crowd a parable (13:6-9) to further explain his point. A man had a fig tree planted in his vineyard, and he came hoping to find fruit on the tree. But, for the third year in a row (which makes the chances of ever finding fruit on it slim), the tree was without yield. The man angrily explains the situation to his gardener, and then commands the gardener to cut down the tree. The gardener asks for one more year. In that time, the gardener promises to dig around the tree and add manure to it. He hopes that this action will cause the tree to produce fruit. After the allotted time, if the tree is still barren, the gardener will cut it down. Through the parable, Jesus explains the urgent situation. The harvester has come, and has found the people unrepentant and unready. Although the people have had ample time to repent and "bear fruit," no good has come from them. But, rather than simply cut the people off, the gardener (Jesus) has asked for one more chance. Jesus is alerting the people to the urgency of the situation. The time has drawn near and they were not ready. Repentance is necessary, and there is no room for hesitation.

Implications for the Church

This passage exemplifies the rest of Luke's eschatology (his understanding of the end times) in Luke-Acts. Believers are living in a period of time before the eschaton (the end of the world), the "middle of time" that is the period of the church, but this period of "middle" time has a limit. One should not presume that there is plenty of time left prior to repenting, nor should one presume to know how quickly the end will come. The end will not come capriciously. Jesus calls people to repent now and live in a way that will proclaim the kingdom until it comes in full, a sort of moral readiness. This emphasis on the end is often neglected in our churches, and may falsely give the impression that Christians need not prepare for the eschaton any time soon. However, Jesus' words are quite clear: "But unless you repent, you will all perish as they did."

Jesus' call for repentance is not an easy one for the church to hear. We usually associate repentance with those outside wanting to come in, but Jesus warns against arrogance that presumes that all those on the inside of his movement are morally or spiritually better than those outside it. All people are indebted to God and need a life of continual change. There is an immediacy and urgency in Jesus' words that is often neglected by the church. Almost two thousand years after the death and resurrection of Jesus, the imminence of Christ's second advent has all but faded away in the minds of many Christians, especially "mainstream" Protestants and Roman Catholics. Yet, Jesus' call for repentance should ring just as true today as it did when it was first spoken. Repentance is necessary for salvation, and the amount of time left between now and Christ's return is becoming constantly narrower.

Just as John the Baptizer came proclaiming the need for repentance, Jesus renewed this call to those around him and to those who would come later. The kingdom of heaven has drawn near in the person of Jesus, and is steadily drawing closer. The harvester will come to check and see if the people have borne fruit, at which time those who do not bear fruit will be cut down. Jesus provides the warning, and his people would do well to heed it.

Reflection

Eschatological Implications

1. What are some ways the church can reclaim the immediacy of Jesus' message?
2. Jesus' warning to the group of people counters the notion that the end will come capriciously. How does this notion fit together with Jesus' claim that the end will come "like a thief?"
3. How are our notions of eschatology tied to how we think about and practice repentance? How might Luke's ideas of eschatology help us today?

No Gift-Wrapped Crosses, Please!

When a new wing containing faculty offices was built at the seminary where I teach, I went in search of some artwork for the walls of my new room. At a local art gallery I found an appropriate piece for a New Testament professor's office, a two-foot tall cross made of large antique nails. It was both beautiful and ugly, as the cross of Jesus was, and like all good art it has the power to raise thought and emotions in the beholder. As I stood at the counter waiting for a salesperson to appear, I became almost absorbed by the cross I held in my hands. Suddenly I heard a chirpy voice from somewhere behind me call out, "Sir, would you like your cross gift-wrapped?" This startled me. It wasn't just because this voice came seemingly out of nowhere, but rather the very idea that a cross should be gift-wrapped struck me at that moment as peculiar. When the sales clerk came into range I said, "No thanks, it's not a gift. Plain wrapping will be fine."

Gift-wrapping crosses may be appropriate for sales people, but to students of the New Testament, it is strange indeed. As a symbol of the Christian faith, the cross is a symbol of death and life. It speaks most directly about Jesus' self-sacrificial death for us, but it also calls us to offer ourselves as a living sacrifice to God. In the words of Luke 14:25-33, followers of Jesus must pick up the cross as they follow him, and count the cost of this discipleship. The cross gives us God's very self, but costs Jesus and us everything. The cross of Christ is a gift, but it does not come gift-wrapped!

Lectionary Loop
Proper 18, Year C

The Cost of Discipleship

This pericope is often known by its theme of "counting the cost of discipleship." The phrase "cost of discipleship" reminds many people of the book by that title written by Dietrich Bonhoeffer. Bonhoeffer's book was published in 1937, as National Socialism consolidated its power in Germany and war and holocaust threatened. It became immediately influential for its understanding of following Jesus, especially in the context of a totalitarian system like National Socialism. In his book, Bonhoeffer expounds upon the notion of sacrificial faith, and contemplates grace through the lens of the Sermon on the Mount. He rails against "cheap grace" that has no transformative value for believers. One of the most memorable lines in the work—"When Christ calls a man, he bids him come and die"—summarizes eloquently and prophetically Bonhoeffer's understanding of true discipleship. Ultimately, the believer is striving for union and participation with the risen Christ. *The Cost of Discipleship* would have had a lasting impact quite on its own, but Bonhoeffer's death at the hands of the Nazis gave it the imprimatur of his death. (The German title is simply *Nachfolge*, "Discipleship"; when the English version was first published in 1948, it was under the title "The Cost of Discipleship," and Bonhoeffer's death may have had something to do with that change.)

In Luke 14:25-33, the emphasis is not simply on the cost of discipleship, but on *counting the cost of discipleship*. Jesus uses two "hard sayings" to get the crowd's attention and urge them to this consideration. First, Jesus tells the large crowds that they must "hate" their families, and even their own lives in order to be his disciples. Such a saying would be significantly more difficult to hear for people in the ancient Mediterranean than for twenty-first century people in the Western world. While the use of the word "hating" is definitely hyperbolical, this saying probably had such a strong effect in the culture that it certainly seemed as though Jesus really meant disciples needed to *hate* their families. In the Mediterranean world, families were the basis for everything an individual

Reflection

Price Tag on Discipleship

1. What does "giving up all you have" mean for us today? Do you think Jesus means this literally? If we were to follow this command literally, what would happen?
2. Dietrich Bonhoeffer's death is widely hailed as a martyrdom. Without taking anything away from the astonishing accomplishments of his life, and without passing easy judgment on what was certainly a very complicated moral situation for Bonhoeffer and others, we can raise here the question that some have asked about his death: is it correct to call him a "martyr" when one of the main reasons he died was because he participated in an act of deadly violence against Adolf Hitler and others? Does being ready to "lose your life" permit one, in Jesus' scheme of things, to kill others?

would do; whom to marry, what occupation to have, and what socio-economic status one had were all dependent upon familial relations. Yet, Jesus instructed the crowd not to put family first. A careful reader should note that Jesus also instructed his disciples to "hate" their own lives. In our individualistic society the focus is often placed on Jesus' instructions concerning family, to the extent that readers skip over his instructions concerning the individual. Jesus did not command something that he was not willing to live up to himself. He lived a life in perfect obedience to the ways of God, and forsook the ways of the world. Through his death, Jesus proved that he was willing to give up everything, including his own life. A proverb sums this up well: "If you can't die for something, you can't live deeply for anything."

Literary Context

Next, Jesus speaks about the necessity of "carrying the cross" in order to be a true disciple. The wording of this phrase in the Greek is ambiguous: does a disciple carry the cross of Jesus, or his or her own cross? The context indicates that we follow him, bearing his cross with him. Jesus is not calling the disciples to carry some abstract cross, or symbol of suffering entirely distinct from the one he carried. Rather, he issues the call to his true disciples to be yoked to him in his death, and through his resurrection, to his life. This "hard saying" builds off of the previous saying, expounding on what it means to "hate" life itself. Ultimately, the life of a believer follows the way of the cross, and Jesus wanted his disciples to be aware of the cost of following him.

Jesus issues a final call that seems somewhat out of place with what comes before it. In verse 33, Jesus speaks about the literal cost of discipleship: giving up all one's possessions (a common Lukan theme of Jesus' preferential option for the poor; see Session 12 below). The Greek word for "possessions" (*hyparchousin*) literally means "what one has," and usually refers to material goods. However, the structure of this pericope indicates that "hating family" and "carrying the cross" are both a part of giving up all one has.

Discipleship costs everything, not just the things that are convenient for us to give up.

To the point of this pericope, all of Luke 14 is set in a dinner scene at a Pharisee's house. Although Luke introduces a change of scene and a new audience—"large crowds"—the material in this pericope has strong links with Luke 14:1-24. For example, the parable of the Great Feast in 14:15-24 teaches that some people use possessions (vv. 18-19) and family relationships (v. 20) to avoid entering the kingdom of God. Likewise, Jesus instructs those at the table not to seek out the prominent places at a banquet; the guests should invite the disadvantaged to take the honorable places. The two teachings of Jesus and the parable of the Great Feast point to the instructions to come on counting nothing above the kingdom of God.

Luke frequently uses table/banquet scenes as venues for addressing the rich with the Good News for the poor. All the Synoptics present Jesus as one who enjoyed eating and drinking, and who made a point about God's kingdom while doing so. Willi Braun has argued that the writer of Luke, especially in Luke 14, presents Jesus in the familiar Greco-Roman role of the "dinner sage," one who uses conversation at formal banquets called "symposia" to persuade others of the need for change. In this banquet scene, Jesus presents Luke's vision of a society that mirrors the values of God's kingdom. Luke 14 is directed especially at the wealthy urban elite, who are most in need of transformation to become a part of this society. Luke 14:25-33 is addressed to these well-off persons, but is also a call to all people to give up what they have, be it great or small, in order to follow Jesus.

Book-Ending with Grace

In any portion of Scripture that contains strong moral demands, it is easy to lose sight of grace. A study of such a passage—actually, of any part of Scripture—needs to be "book-ended" with grace. The only way a student of the Bible can put into practice the principles of Scripture is by first having an encounter with the gracious call of Jesus. Without such an encounter, the practice of Christian living is hopeless.

Resource

For a short description of Willi Braun's interpretation of the table scene in Luke 14, see Van Voorst, *Reading the New Testament Today*, p. 240. For Braun's book itself, see *Feasting and Social Rhetoric in Luke 14* (Cambridge: Cambridge University Press, 1995).

Study Bible

Read the comments about "dropsy" in Luke 14:1-6 in the *NISB*, and relate them to attitudes to possessions in 14:25-33.

All readings of Scripture, especially passages with strict moral guidelines, must begin with grace. Next, with grace in mind, the student must wrestle with the calls to obedience within the text. The principles in the Bible are not merely concepts to toss out or keep on a whim, but instructions with which to wrestle. Finally, all study of the Bible should end with grace. This same pattern is quite useful for preaching and teaching: grace, obedience, grace. Without obedience, discipleship becomes cheap; but without grace, all attempts at obedience are irrelevant.

Resources

Dietrich Bonhoeffer, *The Cost of Discipleship* (New York, Macmillan, 1959); Joel Green, "'Let them take up the Cross Daily': the Way of Discipleship," in his *Theology of Luke* (Cambridge: Cambridge University Press, 1995), 102-120; John T. Carroll and James R. Carroll, *Preaching the Hard Sayings of Jesus* (Peabody, Mass.: Hendrickson, 1996).

Who is the Real Prodigal Here?

Lectionary Loop
Fourth Sunday in Lent, Year C

Literary Setting of the Parable

The names given to stories have a great influence on how we understand them. The context of this parable, following parables featuring a the losing and finding of a sheep and a coin, suggests that if Luke had a name in mind, it may have been the "Lost and Found Son." In Christian tradition, this parable has gone down as the "Prodigal Son." This is a misleading title, because it calls attention to the son as a wastrel ("prodigal" means "squandering," not "wandering") and ignores his repentance, his brother's reaction, and his father's love. The NISB calls it in a caption the "Parable of the Prodigal and His Brother," which gets closer to the center of the parable. Helmut Thielecke called it the "Waiting Father" in his book by that title, and Joachim Jeremias proposed the "Father's Love." These two suggestions name the parable by its central character, and give an indication of its theological point. I would propose a title that draws on the traditional name and more recent scholarship: the "Prodigal Father." His prodigious love, not the sinful prodigality or even the repentance of his younger son, is the point of this parable.

Luke 15:1-3, the introduction to the parable of the Prodigal, looks back to the opening of the last chapter (14:1). Jesus' opponents are scandalized that he actively seeks out religiously marginalized members of Israel, welcoming and even eating with them when they turn to him. A later rabbinic tradition states a position evidently held by some of Jesus' opponents, "No one should associate with sinners, even in order to bring them near to the Torah" (*Mekilta* 57b). Fellowship with sinners is ritually defiling and morally dangerous. The Pharisees are quite happy to see sinners come on their own back to God, but Jesus' close association and love for sinners as persons implied in Jesus' table fellowship with sinners outrages the religious leaders. "So he told them this parable," Luke says (15:3), and the parable of the "Lost Sheep" begins. That the next parable, the "Lost Coin," is also aimed at this situation is clearly implied by its opening word, "Or" (15:8). These parables, as Joachim Jeremias pointed out, positive and grace-filled as they are, contain Jesus' sharp attacks on his opponents. Reading the parable of the Prodigal in light of 15:1-3 is an excellent exegetical strategy.

However, by skipping over the two parables in 15:3-10, the reader of the parable of the Prodigal does not read it in light of the striking pattern set up in these two parables. They both mention the main character first (shepherd, woman); then something important is lost (sheep, coin); the character goes in search of it and finds it; he/she calls together friends and neighbors to celebrate. Jesus concludes both parables with a statement that heaven rejoices over one repentant sinner more than many righteous people who need not repent. By placing these parables with their remarkably parallel structure before the parable of the Prodigal, Luke most probably intends that we read the Prodigal in light of this pattern.

The Story Begins

As the story begins, Jesus introduces us to the main character first, the father who had two sons. The second son asks for his inheritance early. Although this is debated by contemporary scholars, it is likely that a son born after the first son could ask for his inheritance early, while the father was still alive. (The first-born, who gets the lion's share of the inheritance, must wait until his father's death.) A prosperous person like the father of the parable could sell off some of his possessions in order to convey this to the younger son. The codification of this procedure in later rabbinic law, some of which certainly reaches back to the first century CE, indicates that the request of the younger son does not necessarily mean that the younger son "hated"

Sources

Scholarship on the parables is voluminous.

For teaching and preaching the parables, I recommend a classic of parables scholarship, Jeremias, Joachim, *The Parables of Jesus* (2nd ed.; Englewood, N.J.: Prentice-Hall, 1972).

Hultgren, Arland, *The Parables of Jesus: A Commentary* (Grand Rapids, Mich.: Eerdmans, 2002).

Thielecke, Helmut, *The Waiting Father* (New York: Harper, 1959)

Barbara Reid, *Parables for Preachers: The Gospel of Luke, Year C* (Collegeville, Minn.: Liturgical Press, 2000).

Bailey, Kenneth E., *Poet and Peasant* (Grand Rapids, Mich.: Eerdmans, 1976).

Source

For a poignant retelling of this parable, see the highly-praised novel by Ron Hansen, *Atticus* (NY: HarperCollins, 1996). A film adaptation of this novel was done in 2000 by the Hallmark Hall of Fame under the title "Missing Pieces," but its connection to the parable is downplayed.

the father and "wished him dead," as some social-scientific criticism has argued. What the younger son actually *does* with his inheritance indicates his rejection of his father and his father's faith: he moves to a Gentile land, breaking the kinship bond based on religion, and spends his inheritance "dissolutely." He is truly lost, like the sheep (15:3-7) and the coin (15:8-10).

Repentance

Things turn sour suddenly for this younger son; when "the plot thickens," it thickens quickly! He parties away his money, a famine arises making the price of food skyrocket, and he finds himself in the most elemental form of human need—hunger. He attaches himself to a farmer just to stay alive. This young Jewish man now finds himself in the lowest of situations, tending a Gentile's pigs! What is worse, his condition continues to deteriorate; he gazes pathetically at the pig food, but he is not allowed to eat it, and what he is paid cannot sustain his life. Finally, in this bleak situation the young man "comes to himself," that is, he begins a process of repentance. In line with the previous two parables of the lost sheep and coin in this chapter, we might say that he "finds himself." He remembers his past family ties, speaking again of "my father." He realizes that his behavior has broken those family ties, so that he should only live on his father's farm in a new relationship. In social-scientific terms, he wishes to move from the highest kinship status, that of a son, to that of the lowest form of a client, an employee. Note a theological item often passed by: "I have sinned *against* heaven and *before* you" follows the profound Jewish concept that all human behavior—obedience and disobedience—is primarily directed toward God, rather than being just a matter of human social relationships.

Welcome Home!

The "waiting father" has not gone in search of his son, but has done something even harder: he has waited at home, continually watching the road leading to the gate of his property. He could not have stopped his son from wandering, but he had given him something to come back to. He now sees his son coming "from a distance,"

Reflections

"Lost Sheep" Today

1. In contemporary Protestant church life, we face a problem: in significant numbers, as never before, people are defecting from the church and even the Christian faith itself. How can this parable, set in its context of Luke 15, direct us about going after our own "lost sheep" and welcoming back our "prodigal sons (and daughters!)?"

2. I have a friend in upstate New York whose teenage son cleared out his bank account and went to the big city, where he lived contrary to the faith in which he was brought up. Almost a year later, the son suddenly reappeared at his parents' front door broken in body and spirit, asking to come home. As his father was relating this story to me, it was obvious that he was framing it after the parable of the Prodigal. When he reached its happy conclusion of a family reunited, I asked him, "Well, did you kill the fatted calf?" "No," he replied, "but for a moment I wanted to kill the prodigal son!" Reflect on how his tongue-in-cheek answer shows how difficult it is for even Christians to practice the point of this parable. Discuss the nuances of unconditional love: does this sort of love preclude feelings of anger? What do you think God "feels" toward us when we are prodigal sons and daughters?

and contrary to all convention of gentlemanly dignified behavior, runs to meet him. The supposition by some social-scientific interpreters that the father is running to protect the son from the wrath of the neighbors, who supposedly also see him coming and are bent on driving him away or worse, is possible, but not supported by the parable itself. The father, in a gracious act, lets the son speak first, but then cuts him off mid-speech. (Readers of Luke 15 who remember the pattern of the two previous parables have been prepared for this: a party, not a humiliation is in the works.) He commands the servants, probably his two most trusted slaves who must attend him at a respectful distance, to bring the finest clothing and ring for him and prepare a big party.

The Elder Brother

As common experience and developmental psychology have taught us, first-born children are typically dutiful achievers. The "elder brother" of the parable is no different, but of course he also personifies the wrong attitude of the Pharisees. When he hears the noise of the party as he returns at the end of the day from a far field, and finds out what is going on, he refuses to go in. This refusal of table fellowship, especially in the family, is such serious breach of family ties that the father goes out to him and pleads for him to reconsider. Particularly objectionable to the elder brother is that the father has given rich possessions to the younger son, items that by law should have been are a part of the older son's inheritance. The elder son wants the younger son to be no longer his brother; some see his aim as sending the younger son packing, but perhaps he would like him to stay on as a hired hand, a constant target for his righteous hostility. The father's word at the end settles the issue: it is right to welcome the younger son, because the lost has been found. Not only that, but language that taps the deepest meaning of the gospel is applied: "he was dead, and now is alive." The ending of the two earlier parables in Luke 15 is unspoken here, but it certainly applies: "Just so, I tell you, there is more joy in heaven over one sinner who repents than over ninety-nine righteous people who need no repentance."

Further Reflection

1. Define and discuss the meaning of "prodigal." Reflect on how the misinterpretation of the word "prodigal" as "wandering," has altered the application of this parable in Christian living.
2. Do you think the son has to repent before he can receive the father's love and forgiveness? Does the parable seem to show the father's forgiveness even before the son repents? Consider both the words and actions of the son.

Thanksgiving at the Margins

Giving thanks to God is a critical part of the Christian life. Private prayer and meditation should be infused with it. Corporate worship involves giving thanks, and in particular Holy Communion is known as "thanksgiving" ("Eucharist" is from the Greek "to give thanks"). This session deals with one of the most powerful stories about thankfulness in the Gospel of Luke, the grateful Samaritan leper. We will use a combination of narrative and historical approaches, not only to show the power of these interpretive methods for this story, but as a model of their potential for all narratives in the Bible.

Histgorical/Cultural Background

As Jesus journeys to Jerusalem in the "center section" of Luke, he travels through the area on the border between the more Jewish section of Galilee and the more Samaritan section of Samaria. Actually, since 17:11-19 comes near the end of Jesus' journey to Jerusalem, one would think that Jesus would now be on the border of Samaria and *Judea*, but this does not impact the religious meaning of the passage significantly. Wherever this border area was, differences between Jews and Samaritans would be more readily seen, and this locale also explains why this group of ten lepers had at least one Samaritan in it. Observant Jews traveling in these areas would be at some physical risk from Samaritans; the mutual hostility between them in Jesus' day was akin to modern hostility between many Israeli Jews and many Palestinian Muslims. It is "on the way to Jerusalem," as Luke reiterates in 17:11 as this story begins, that Jesus goes through this area.

Lectionary Loop

Proper 23 (28), Year C

Gospel for the Marginalized

On the outskirts of a village, just as he is entering it, Jesus is met by the voices of "ten leprous men" who keep the required distance. Lepers typically lived just outside settlements, near enough to for them to beg at a distance for food from people going in and out. Leprosy is a generic term in the Bible for any skin disease that renders one unclean, ranging from the fatal form (Hansen's disease, which is our conception of leprosy today) to more common chronic dermatological and neurological problems. In ancient Israel and early Judaism, leprosy was seen to be a divine punishment for sin. Its social and religious consequences—exile from home, village and the worship assembly (Lev. 14:34-57)—were often more serious than the medical consequences. This explains why the miracle that Jesus works for these ten lepers is twice called "cleansing" (17:15, 17) and only once "healing" (17:15).

Custom dictated that these men call out to Jesus' group, "Unclean, unclean!" to keep warn them away. Instead, they shout to Jesus for his mercy, inviting him to come closer. They call him "master" (Greek *epistata*), a word used here for the sixth and final time in Luke. In all five previous uses (see 5:5; 8:24, 45; 9:33, 49), "master" is used by Jesus' disciples to address him, often in urgent situations. This usage gives this word more than a generic meaning here; it implies that these ten lepers have faith in Jesus. What sort of mercy they want, they do not say; it could be food, money, forgiveness or cleansing. After "he saw them," bridging the distance between them with a mutual eye contact that others usually refused to make for fear of lepers, Jesus replies, "Go and show yourselves to the priests." They know immediately that this means they were going to be cleansed. Off they go—but to what priests? To Jewish priests living in the area, or to Samaritan priests who would likely have had the equivalent ability to certify someone clean to enter their sanctuary? Because the Gospels are read as having a Jewish background, we often assume the former, but the latter is just as likely, given the area Jesus is in.

Source

For the Hebrew Bible regulations on leprosy see Leviticus 13–14. For Rabbinic traditional regulations written down after the year 200 CE, see the *Mishnah*, tractate "Negaim" ("Leprosy Signs").

However, given the point of the story found at its end, this distinction soon becomes meaningless.

Off they go, and somewhere on the way their leprosy vanishes: "as they went, they were made clean" (17:14). The NRSV obscures some of the nuance of the Greek verbs. The verb translated "they went," *hypagein*, primarily means "to depart," especially from someone's presence. This implies that the cleansing took place as they left the outskirts of the village, and had not gotten not too far away from Jesus. Also, the tense of the Greek verb rendered "were cleansed" may imply sudden, not gradual, cleansing as they walked. (Since they probably had not gotten far from Jesus, the cleansing would have been rapid, if not instantaneous.) Whenever it happened, it was a dramatic moment, and the spare narration invites us, as all biblical narratives do in order to draw us into them and work their transforming power on us, to "fill the gaps" in the story. They looked, one first and probably then the others, at their own hands and feet, and they saw that they were clean. Out of sheer joy and hope, they must have moved or even removed their own clothing, socially inappropriate as that was in Semitic cultures, to inspect themselves fully. The leprosy was gone, and they had been completely cleansed! Their faith turned to sight, and their steps quickened as their bodies strengthened. By faith in Jesus and obedience to his instructions they had been healed, and now they continue to obey him as they made their way to the priests.

But one former leper, when he realizes that he had been healed, does not continue on the way. He shouts praise to God and leaves the group, perhaps drawing some sharp questions and comments from the other nine: "Where are you going? Didn't we just get healed by obeying Jesus' command to go and show ourselves to the priests? If your leprosy comes back, you've got nobody to blame but yourself!"

Ignoring them, and shouting loud praises to God for his healing, he turns and goes back to Jesus. "Loud voice" in the Old Testament signifies especially intense, heart-felt emotion usually in the worship of God, and is found in other places in Luke's Gospel (1:42, 4:33, 8:28, 17:15, 19:37, 23:23, 46). In an act of worship, he "falls

Reflection

Turning Back

Do you think that the one leper disobeyed Jesus by turning back? How does Jesus' response validate or invalidate the leper's spontaneous return to give thanks?

on his face" (the NRSV more formally says "prostrates himself") in front of Jesus, putting his formerly "unclean" leprous body right on the dirt. The man on a journey out from Jesus and a journey back to him is now completely motionless, sprawled out in front of Jesus. He gives Jesus thanks, but probably in a much softer voice—people lying on the front of their bodies generally do have the "lungs" for loud shouting. Then, almost in an aside, comes the plot twist that reorients the story toward its true point, a surprise to most readers of this story and those there to see it unfold: "and he was a Samaritan."

Jesus then poses a series of three rhetorical questions that challenge his listeners, disciples and onlookers alike, to understand the truth of what is happening. Each one hammers harder than the last. Yes, ten lepers were indeed cleansed; remarkably, only one has returned; and this one does not belong to the true people of God, the Jews. With rich irony, Jesus notes that this "foreigner," this man who was doubly marginal because of his ethnicity and his disease, "returns to praise God." Jesus thus validates the decision of this Samaritan to disobey his order in order to return to him. The conclusion looks to have standard wording for a gospel miracle story, but in this scene it fairly bristles with meaning: "Rise up," Jesus says to the man who has been lying at his feet as Jesus has been talking to the crowd, "go on your way" (the same Greek verb as earlier in verse 14, "go"). Where will he go – to a Samaritan priest to certify that he is clean, or to his home? Jesus' next statement makes it clear: "your faith"—expressed in all the man's actions in this story—"has made you well/saved you." On Jesus' word, the word that can heal and declare healing done, this Samaritan is certified clean without any formal inspection. We can well imagine that he went directly to his own home still filled with praise to God and thanksgiving to Jesus.

Luke's deep passion for the poor and marginalized shows itself unmistakably in this passage. Not only is the grateful man a former leper, he is a Samaritan—a sort of "anti-hero" for a Jewish audience, someone they

Reflection

Tales of Two Samaritans

Compare this story to Jesus' parable of the Good Samaritan in Luke 10:25-37. What do you think Luke is trying to tell us about people who show great faith and righteousness?

would prefer not to see as a role model. Yet, it is precisely *this* man who shows gratitude for the wonderful thing that was done for him. All of the ten lepers were cleansed, but Jesus pronounces the thankful Samaritan saved by his faith. In a stunning way, Luke foreshadows the mission to the Gentiles, indicating that salvation would extend beyond the Jews. The other nine lepers were not disobedient; they heeded Jesus' words and were headed to the priest to present themselves. However, Luke clearly praises the behavior of the one who returned to Jesus with overflowing gratitude. Obedience to God is expected and commendable, but gratitude completes the picture. In Luke and in our world, the humble offer the best lessons in gratitude.

An Illustrative Story

The congregation to which my family and I belong is very traditional, with classical music, high liturgy (for a church in the Presbyterian-Reformed tradition, at least), and first-rate preaching. Its large congregation is predominantly professional, upper-middle class, almost completely white, and perfectly proper—and despite all that homogeneity, it is a wonderful church. A few years ago, a new hearing loop induction system was installed in the church to help hearing-impaired people listen to the church service "loud and clear." When my family and I sat down before the service, we saw a hearing-impaired man—a man who is distinctive in our church because of his "foreign" name and the trace of an ethnic accent—being helped at the back sound console to tune his own hearing aid into the new system. Then he took his place a few pews ahead of us. This man was severely wounded in the Vietnam War, and has a hearing loss and other disabilities from his wounds. Despite the "weakness of his flesh," he is very strong in the Spirit.

When the organ prelude ended and the service began with the first words spoken from the chancel over the new sound system, he sat bolt upright in his pew. A look of joy and astonishment came over his face, as he was hearing perhaps the first clear words in church in more than thirty years. He looked from the right to the left, not knowing what to do with his joy.

Reflections

Gratitude

1. Sometimes people use the expression "Thank God!" too lightly, even flippantly. A former colleague of mine at Lycoming College in Pennsylvania, when he heard this, often said, "I do, everyday." What do you think of this clever rejoinder?
2. Why might gratitude be more readily found in those who are marginalized? How does this story compare to the story of the anointing woman in Luke 7, whose forgiveness was great, so her gratitude was also great?

From the Margins

1. Was the thankful Samaritan one of many Samaritans in the group of lepers, or was he the only "foreigner?" Does the ethnic makeup of the group have any bearing upon the theological interpretation of the narrative?
2. Why, in your opinion, would a "foreigner" like this Samaritan be more thankful than the (Jewish) true people of God?

Then, despite the fact that the liturgy was going on, he jumped to his feet, let out a "Hallelujah" to God, and ran as fast as his legs would allow him back to the man at the sound console. After a brief pause there, he grabbed the fellow and embraced him so hard that he lifted him off the ground for a moment. Then, his thanks rendered, he made his way back, happily and quietly, to his pew. It seemed to me that everyone in the church who could see this man smiled at what happened, but wondered what it meant that such joy and thankfulness came from someone who was in so many ways "different" than the rest of us.

Resources

Joel Green, "To Proclaim Good News to the Poor: Mission and Salvation" in his *The Theology of the Gospel of Luke* (Cambridge: Cambridge University Press, 1995), 76-100.

Thomas Lane, *Luke and the Gentile Mission: Gospel Anticipates Acts* (Zurich: Peter Lang, 1996).

John C. Wilson, *The Gentiles and the Gentile Mission in Luke-Acts* (Cambridge: Cambridge University Press, 2005).

Teaching Tip

Discuss: How does the story of the hearing-impaired man remind you of the story of the Samaritan leper? Do you know stories of people who were on the margins of society who showed similar gratitude? What might these stories contribute to understanding the story of the Samaritan leper?

Jesus' Option for the Poor—and Ours

As we have seen in our encounter with Luke, this Gospel has a particularly strong concern that the Good News of God's Reign be brought to the marginalized. In this session, we will look more specifically at this concern, especially in terms of what in recent times is called the "preferential option for the poor."

Reflection

A Rich Ruler Today

What would happen if a rich ruler today, let's say a "ruler" of a business, heard the call of Jesus to "sell all you have and give it to the poor?" What might the reaction of his friends, family, and co-workers be?

The Rich Ruler

Luke 18:18-30 is composed of two main items: the story of a rich ruler's encounter with Jesus, and Jesus' follow-up conversation with his disciples by which Luke shapes the meaning of this encounter for the reader. In the story, a rich man (not called "young" here or in Mark 10:17-22, as in Matt 19:22) approaches Jesus. He is a "ruler," which more likely refers to a religious ruler than a Roman ruler or one of their Herodian allies in Palestine. He asks a question almost universal in its relevance, to paraphrase it: "What must I do to live forever?" After rebuffing the man's wrongly proffered compliment that prefaces his question, Jesus reminds him of the second half of the Ten Commandments (but note that the command against covetousness is conspicuously absent). The man replies that he has kept all them "from my youth," a biblical expression denoting life-long service to God, the best kind. Then Jesus, accepting his answer at face value but sensing the emptiness in him, replies, "You still lack one thing [to live forever]. Sell everything you own and give it to the poor, and you will have treasure in heaven. Then come, follow me." This invitation to sacrifice and discipleship makes the man sad, "for he was very rich" and unwilling to meet Jesus' demand. Mark 10 has the man leaving and Jesus speaking when he is gone, but Luke keeps him there to hear Jesus' concluding comment in this section, spoken to everyone while he is looking at this rich man: "How hard it is for those who have wealth to enter the kingdom of God! Indeed, it is easier for a camel to go through the eye of a needle than for someone who is rich to enter the kingdom of God."

A two-stage conversation then ensues, with the inquiring man now out of the picture. "Those who heard it," probably the saying of Jesus in verses 24-25, said with some astonishment, "Then who can be saved?" This question presupposes that working past undue attachment to the things of this earth to salvation is difficult for everyone, not just for the rich. As such, it seems to disregard the point of what Jesus has just said. Even so, Jesus responds with an aphorism that covers salvation for rich and poor alike: "What is impossible for humans is possible for God." That is to say, only with divine empowerment can the sacrifice of leaving possessions and family take place. Peter, speaking for the other disciples, is eager to show that he and the others have made this sacrifice: "We have left our homes to follow you." This is true as far as it goes, but after Jesus' death, they seem to have family businesses such as fishing boats to go back to! Jesus commends their level of sacrifice: those who have left house and family—strengthened by the mention of "wife, brothers, parents or children"—for the sake of the kingdom of God "will get back very much more in this age," probably in the new families they find in their new life, "and in the age to come eternal life." They will find what the rich ruler could not.

A brief look at the literary context of this passage shows a deep connection with its surroundings. The end of Jesus' journey to Jerusalem has two concurrent themes, the marginalized recipients of the Reign of God and the messiahship of Jesus. Those who inherit the kingdom are like the tax collector who was humbly repentant (18:9-14); they are like trusting children (18:15-17); they are committed people who, like the disciples, leave everything for the sake of the kingdom (18:18-30); they are like the blind man, calling on the Lord in faith when others tell him to keep quiet (18:35-43); finally, they are like Zacchaeus, the tax collector who repents and repairs his fraud (19:1-9). In the middle of these passages lies its christological heart: Jesus, the archetypal marginalized person, who goes faithfully forward to his suffering and death knowing that God will vindicate him in his resurrection. His disciples cannot grasp the idea of a marginalized Messiah, probably wondering how this could be a fulfillment of the scriptures (18:31-34). By omitting Mark's introduction to this passion and resurrection prediction (Mark 10:32a), Luke may be making this prediction the conclusion to the story of the rich ruler; at the least we can say that they are closely tied together.

The story of the blind beggar in the next main narrative, in 18:35-43, provides pointed contrasts with the story of the rich ruler. A blind man approaches Jesus by means of his voice; no one will get out of the way for him, as they did for the rich ruler! He calls Jesus "Son of David," and asks for mercy, keeping up his shouting even as others tell him to keep quiet. Jesus did not accept the descriptor "good" from the rich ruler, but evidently this messianic phrase meets with his approval. After the blind beggar is healed, he follows Jesus. What the rich ruler could not see in Jesus, the blind man could; although the blind man followed Jesus even unbidden, the rich man could not even with a special invitation. Luke's point is clear: riches militate against understanding Jesus and his message and responding to it, but the poor and the blind are more likely to receive Good News from Jesus and follow him.

Social-Scientific Setting

The social-scientific reading of this passage sheds light on its background and its meaning for the reader. In Mediterranean antiquity, social status was determined by where one fell on the social hierarchy. The ruler such as this man was on top, followed by his assistants in the elite class (scribes, soldiers, priests and prosperous merchants). Together, they represented

Resource

For more on social-scientific understanding of the New Testament, see R. E. Van Voorst, *Reading the New Testament Today*, 36–40.

only about 2–5 percent of the population, and they controlled most of society's wealth, either directly or indirectly. They alone could use their wealth to assure their future in the world; to give up such wealth and leave one's social class was unthinkable. The rest of society was composed of people who lived almost from day to day, and could not assure their future: peasants, artisans, shop-keepers and even more marginalized people (slaves, prostitutes, beggars, cripples).

Mediterraneans believed in "limited goods"—in contrast to the modern American myth, it was not assumed in antiquity that one should rise "from rags to riches." If one did manage to improve one's status significantly, it was typically at the expense of someone else. Money, commodities and honor itself were seen as limited in antiquity; and the goods are finite, someone is bound to lose when someone else gains. As a result, people normally sought to maintain their status rather than to gain or lose. Wealth also has a connection to kinship. One's wealth or social position came from one's ancestors, one used it in one's lifetime for the honor of family, and at death all possessions were passed along to one's main male heir. These factors made it even more difficult in Jesus' time to give up all one's wealth than it is for us today.

Jesus' Preferential Option for the Poor

The "preferential option for the poor" is a term first used in the 1970s by Roman Catholic liberation theologians to describe God's special concern for those subjected to poverty and oppression, or otherwise marginalized. Now it is used widely in theological and church circles beyond Roman Catholicism, and has become almost a maxim in recent Christian social ethics. (Even the present Pope Benedict XVI, for many years as Cardinal Joseph Ratzinger an opponent of some forms of Liberation Theology, has written positively about the preferential option for the poor as being firmly grounded in the Bible and especially in the ministry and teaching of Jesus.) We cannot do justice here to the broad meaning of the "preferential option." I would raise several brief issues for consideration.

Study Bible

Discuss Joel Green's comment, "Is the rich ruler's final response a negative one? Luke does not tell us, and this suggests that Luke's own readers must respond to Jesus' directive to declare their friendship with the poor" (*NISB*, 1889).

Discussion

Some interpreters have suggested that the rich ruler could rightly say that he has kept the second half of the Ten Commandments, but not the first, especially the command to serve the Lord alone. What do you think of this suggestion?

1. Like any programmatic slogan, it needs nuance so that it is not misunderstood and then dismissed. For most people who use this expression, it does not mean that God loves the marginalized more than God loves others; Christians believe that God loves all people equally. Neither should it lead to a "works-righteousness" system where the poor merit salvation by virtue of the spiritual value of their poverty. It does mean that God intends that their marginalization, in its physical, social and spiritual aspects, be ended. It also means that the poor have significant spiritual resources to share with others.

2. "The poor" should be broadly understood in its biblical sense as all marginalized persons, regardless of financial status, for example, children and youth who have no voice and are powerless to protect themselves. Roman Catholic teaching has included those wrongfully deprived of life—the unborn, criminals sentenced to death, and those subject to "euthanasia"—in the preferential option. However, understanding it in a full sense should not lead to watering down its commitment to those who are literally poor.

3. The preferential option sends us in direction of radical generosity that promotes a fuller degree of social justice. We cannot "opt for the poor" with our leftover income and castoff clothing. This does not follow Jesus' example of giving his life for others. Think of the difference that would be made in the world if all Christians gave ten percent of their income to the church (and the church spent more of its income to build a more just society rather than on itself)!

4. The preferential option should lead to systemic changes in our economic life. Most of the world has (in my opinion, rightly) concluded that the free market/capitalist system is the best system, despite its significant faults. Perhaps we can say of capitalism what Winston Churchill once said about democracy, that it is the worst system in the world, except for all the others. Nevertheless, we who participate in the capitalist/free market system and benefit from it are called by God to strengthen its best features and ameliorate its negatives, among them its promotion of lux-

Teaching Tip

The ancient Mediterranean world used the terms "rich" and "poor" much differently than we do today. Then, people who could guarantee their material future from their present wealth were "rich"; the "poor" could not, and lived from day to day. Only about 5 percent of people were "rich," and there was no middle class to speak of, only some people who were a little less poor than others. By today's standards, in most liberal democracies that are more or less "welfare states," our poor are relatively well-off compared to the poor of the Third World. This doesn't mean that the poor in North America are not included in the "preferential option," or that we do not have a special obligation to the relatively poor in our own nation. It does bear discussion, however.

Discussion

Compare the meaning of Luke 18:22, ". . . you will have treasure in heaven," with the saying, "You can't take it with you, but you can send it on ahead."

uries as necessities, its relentless consumerism that implies that a person's life "consists in the abundance of possessions" (see Luke 12:15), and the constant temptation of those in control of it not to play by the rules of the market, but resort to crime and corruption to improve profits.

5. Although the preferential option for the poor is not an option for followers of Jesus, it is subject to Christian freedom. Jesus did not lay down a detailed program to build a new society, but called all his followers, as individuals and as a group, to work creatively and responsibly for the poor.

6. Practicing a preferential option overcomes topical and temporary concern for the poor. Giving should not be governed by the latest storm or famine crisis in the television news! Rather, it leads to a continual and firm relationship with the poor that endures all sorts of weather.

7. Reinhold Niebuhr would remind us here that good and evil are always mixed together in our world. The world being what it is, solving one problem usually leads to another. For example, rising prosperity in India and China in the last twenty years has moved hundreds of millions of people from poverty into a "middle" class, but this growth has contributed to world-wide energy shortages and more rapid environmental damage (the poor go easier on the earth and its atmosphere than the middle class).

8. Marxist ideology and practice that comes with some forms of liberation theology should be avoided. With its atheism, anti-Semitism and totalitarianism, Marxism is a poor partner with Christianity. Class conflict and armed violence are not a part of the teaching of Jesus, who was—and still is—a friend of sinners rich and poor, bringing the Good News of God's Reign to all. The symbol of the Christian faith is the cross, not a clenched fist.

9. Finally, preferential option is for *all* the poor, not just the poor of our area or even our nation. The world is our neighborhood, and all its people are the neighbors we are called to love.

Resources

In the excellent 2004 film "Millions," directed by Danny Boyle, two young boys come into possession of a large bag of money from a botched robbery, but have only a short time to spend it or give it away before the UK switches to the Euro. This PG-rated film shows the temptations and other difficulties that come with the possession of wealth. (For another film on this subject, see the same director's 1994 "Shallow Grave," rated R.)

Resources

For a Roman Catholic biblical approach, see Norbert F. Lohfink, S.J., *Option for the Poor: The Basic Principle of Liberation Theology in the Light of the Bible* (second edition; Dallas: D & F Scott, 1996). For an evangelical Protestant approach, see Craig L. Blomberg, *Neither Poverty Nor Riches: A Biblical Theology of Possessions* (Downer's Grove, Il.: InterVarsity, 2001). For a social-scientific view, see Philip F. Esler, *Community and Gospel in Luke-Acts: The Social and Political Motivations of Lucan Theology* (Cambridge: Cambridge University Press, 1987), 164–199.

Faithful to the End

Lectionary Loop

First Sunday of Advent, Year C

Eschatology Today

The first Sunday in Advent typically deals with eschatology. As Christians prepare for Christmas in four weeks, the lectionary points their vision much farther, to the end of time. This may be jarring to many people forced by relentless consumerism into the "Christmas season" before their Thanksgiving Day dinner is fully digested, but this orientation to the future has biblical precedent. In the New Testament, the understanding of the present comes by way of the end, when the kingdom of God will come in its fullness and all God's enemies will be vanquished. In fact, the word "coming" (Greek *parousia*, Latin *adventus*, from which we get "Advent") consistently means in the NT what we call the "second coming" of Christ, not the "first." The first Advent is known through the second, so the lectionary's summons to look to the beginning of the New Age is fully appropriate.

Many North American Christians today have one of two main attitudes about the NT teachings of eschatology: either they feel little concern about the coming of the Reign of God at the end of time, or they are preoccupied with it. Although recent church history has shaped this bifurcated approach, especially the struggle between premillenial-dispensational churches and churches with a more "mainstream" eschatology, its roots reach all the way back to the New Testament's diverse eschatology. In some parts of the New Testament, such as the early Pauline letters, the Gospel of Mark and the book of Revelation, the end is imminent and shapes life in the present strongly. In other parts, such as the Gospel of John and later Pauline letters such as Ephesians and the Pastorals, eschatology is more "realized" in the present, although the hope of Christ's coming has not been abandoned. Luke's balanced eschatology, with its lively hope in the coming of Christ without seeing it as imminent or predictable, can help us to steer a middle course between these two poles. It can help the modern Christian to appreciate the importance of eschatology without getting "hung up" on its difficulties.

Literary Context

The literary context of Luke 21 is entirely given to eschatology, and is set in the Temple. The setting of this chapter looks back to 20:1, where Jesus teaches the people in the Temple and speaks "the Good News." Jesus had cleansed the Temple and tried to reclaim it with his teaching there, but the rulers of that place did not recognize him (20:41-44). In the two stories about finances that connect our chapters 20 and 21, the Temple's leaders are portrayed as neglectful, even abusive, toward the poor (20:45 – 21:4). After this lectionary passage, chapter 22 presents Jesus as the exemplar of faithfulness in trial and temptation. In the face of betrayal by one of the twelve, Jesus instituted the Lord's Supper and continued his journey to the cross.

Coming of the Son of Man

Luke's eschatological message in chapter 21 is overall a positive one. The Day of the Lord brings salvation: "redemption is drawing near." Here traditional Jewish apocalyptic imagery is adapted to early Christian expectations, which are Christocentric. The literary chiasm of this imagery in vv. 25-26—signs in heaven/distress among the nations/signs in heaven—serves even subconsciously to assure the reader that God is guiding the world to its end. Cosmic signs signify a cosmic redemption. The culmination of this end, which makes a new beginning for the world, is the coming of the Son of Man. The "coming of the Son of Man" language is Danielic (Dan 7:13 where the meaning is uncertain), but the meaning in Luke is Christocentric. For the people of God, the end is to be faced

Reflection

Is it possible for Christians to keep "one foot in heaven and the other on earth," as a common saying goes? How can you live between these two poles of NT eschatology?

Study Bible

Discuss Joel Green's remarks in the *NISB*, p. 1895 that "this generation" in Luke has a special meaning: it refers "not to a certain number of decades or to people living at such-and-such a time, but to a category of persons known for their recalcitrance to the purpose of God," as in Luke 7:31; 9:41; 11:29-32, 50-51; and 17:25.

Reflection

Discuss the disciples' inability to stay awake and watchful with Jesus (Luke 22:45-46). What does this say about the task of being alert for the kingdom of God today?

with hope, not fear: "When these things begin to take place, stand up and raise your heads, because your redemption is drawing near" (21:28).

Luke appends a parable to illustrate this teaching. Jesus' short saying about the fig tree is not a typical "parable" as we usually understand them, short stories. In particular, this saying is a "likeness" or illustration. Just as the sprouting of fig leaves is a sign of summer, the signs Jesus has just spoken of are signal the coming kingdom. Jesus has already told a parable with eschatological connotations about a fig tree (Luke 13:6-9). In the Mediterranean climate, summer comes quickly after winter dormancy of trees; no lengthy spring intervenes, as in temperate climes. The theme of watchfulness for the end is reinforced here: people can read natural signs, so God's people should read the supernatural signs found in the teaching of Jesus.

The final section in Luke's "Little Apocalypse," 21:34-36, is the command to "be alert/watch." Verse 34 commands moral watchfulness. Even the people of God are subject to an unholy triad of temptations: "dissipation, drunkenness and the worries of this life." These temptations can blind one to the coming of the Kingdom of God. Jesus urges readiness (21: 34-35). In Luke, this readiness is gained through prayer; this is echoed in the passion narrative as Jesus prays to escape his time of trial, that is, to be preserved through it (Luke 22:40,46). The command is for watchfulness "at all times" (verse 36): the end may come at any time. Despite signs, and despite the command to read the signs, the end will be sudden and unexpected by most, even most of Jesus' followers. This adds greater urgency to moral preparation for the end. In the grand culmination of the chapter, we will "stand before the Son of Man," that is, come into his presence and dwell there forever.

Moral Alertness

This moral readiness for the coming of God's Reign raises the question: In light of all the varied teachings of Jesus, and the example he set, how are Christians today to focus on what is important? In his magisterial book, *Jesus Remembered*, James D. G. Dunn gives

Source

James D. G. Dunn, *Jesus Remembered* (Grand Rapids, Mich. / Cambridge, England: Eerdmans, 2003), especially pages 607-611.

Reflections

Thoughts on Judgment

1. How does Luke's eschatology help us to avoid two common extremes: thinking we can know the timing and details of the end on the one hand, and on the other supposing that there will be no end at all?
2. In medieval and Renaissance churches, paintings of the Last Judgment were typically put inside the main door, so that the people would see them going out of church. (Michelangelo's "Last Judgment" in the Sistine Chapel is a striking exception to this, painted as it is on the front wall over the main altar.) What do you think of this use of promised blessings and punishments to motivate Christians today?

Poetry and Hymns

1. "The Second Coming" by William Butler Yeats and "Once by the Pacific" by Robert Frost are powerful modern expressions of eschatology. You can find them in standard poetry collections, or on the Web.

(Continued on page 90)

a helpful outline. First, Christian discipleship is oriented to God as Father and King. God's radical love and transforming grace are the pattern for Jesus' followers. Second, Jesus' followers, now predominantly Gentiles, follow Jesus' call to Israel to return to the Lord in view of the coming of God's Reign. The values Christians live by are nothing more and nothing less than God's word in Torah and the prophets; all Christians are called to live as Israel should before God. Third, although Jesus' teaching "amounts to no blueprint for a complete social order," as for example we have in the Dead Sea Scrolls, Jesus expects his followers to (like him) be deeply involved in social affairs—he taught no distinction between "personal" and "social" ethics. In this, Jesus was a "transformative sage," and his wisdom should still transform society to prepare for the coming of the Kingdom. Finally, although Jesus did not "establish the church," he did envisage his disciples functioning as an "assembly" gathered in the presence of the Lord. In sum, Dunn says, Jesus' vision for the present is "living in the light of the coming kingdom," in a sacramental universe where God's people receive and extend forgiveness, are constantly surprised by God's grace, and celebrate God's goodness in open table-fellowship and love of neighbor.

(Continued from page 89)

Read them for mood and emotional effect, and compare them to this passage in Luke.

2. In many Latin requiems, there is a hymn about judgment, commonly called "Dies Irae," or Day of Wrath. This hymn, both text and music, is often frightening, and meant to strike fear into the hearts of the listeners. Listen to this hymn as set to music, for example by Mozart or Fauré. How does the concept of "Dies Irae" differ with Luke's portrait of eschatology? How is it similar?
3. Reflect on the meaning of the words of the famous African-American spiritual, "My Lord, What a Morning" (refrain and verse 1):

My Lord, what a morning, when
the stars begin to fall.
You'll hear the trumpet sound to
wake the nations underground,
looking to my God's right hand,
when the stars begin to fall.

Resources

"My Lord, What a Morning," public domain.

Hans Conzelmann, *Theology of St. Luke* (New York: Harper & Row, 1960).

John T. Carroll, *Response to the End of History: Eschatology and Situation in Luke-Acts* (Atlanta: Society of Biblical Literature, 1989).

E. Earle Ellis, *Eschatology in Luke* (Facet Books; Philadelphia: Fortress, 1972).

The Risen Christ Encounters his Disciples

Probably the most important event in the New Testament is the resurrection of Jesus. The resurrection serves as a seal of what Jesus accomplished on the cross, presents Christ as victor over death, and inaugurates more than any other event in Jesus' life the Reign of God. Many writers of the New Testament write with passion about Jesus' resurrection. For example, when responding to those who denied the resurrection, the apostle Paul writes that without Jesus' resurrection, "your faith is futile and you are still in your sins" (1 Cor. 15:17). Yet for all its importance, the resurrection itself is not narrated! This beginning of a new age occurs in a holy silence. What the New Testament does narrate is its sequel: empty tomb narratives (e.g., Luke 24:1-12) and appearance narratives (e.g., Luke 24:13-53). In the first, the disciples (both females and males) find the tomb of Jesus empty and hear the news of his resurrection from angels; in the second, Jesus reveals himself as the resurrected Lord to his disciples. Both are necessary elements of the Gospel's treatment of Jesus' resurrection, but the emphasis, especially in Luke, falls on the appearance narratives. In this session, we will examine the first of the two appearance narratives in Luke, the powerful Emmaus story (Luke 24:13-35).

The context of Luke 24:12-25 is important for its interpretation. The first part of chapter 24 narrates a scene at the empty tomb. An interpreting angel reminds those who had gathered at the tomb about resurrection after three days; the "must" here suggests biblical warrant for Jesus' death and resurrection. In

Lectionary Loop

Easter Evening, Year C

Source

For the first extant narration of the resurrection itself, told with many popular and legendary touches, see the second-century *Gospel of Peter* 9:34–10:38.

each subsequent section of chapter 24, the concept of Jesus' resurrection is paired against the Old Testament understanding of the Messiah. Through this running theme, Luke 24 explains how Jesus' suffering and resurrection were completely in line with what was prophesied before. Understanding this is a vital necessity for the transformation of Jesus' disciples.

Journey Motif

The careful reader of Luke notes that its important journey motif continues to its end. Here in chapter 24, the disciples are repeatedly journeying (24:13-15, 33-35, 47). As they walk along the road, Jesus gives them a faithful interpretation of the Scripture, but their eyes are not fully opened until they share in the breaking of bread. Along this journey with Jesus, they receive an understanding of who Jesus is, what happened to him, and why it happened. Jesus' death and resurrection did not run contrary to the prophetic tradition. Rather, Jesus showed them that it was necessary that "the Messiah should suffer these things and then enter into his glory." Through this encounter, they are transformed into competent disciples, changed people embarking on a journey. Luke continues the journey theme throughout Acts as the disciples are "journeying for Jesus." Verse 47 of this passage points to the journey to come.

God Gives Understanding

Two disciples were headed for Emmaus, on a journey from Jerusalem, discussing the events concerning Jesus' crucifixion. Jesus comes near to them, notices that they are sad, and explains to the two disciples that the things that happened to him were in complete accordance with Scripture. The two invite Jesus to come with them, and when they recline around the table together Jesus makes himself known through the breaking of bread. (It would have been unusual for a guest to offer the blessing and distribute the food instead of the head of the family.) Jesus shows the disciples that he is really alive, even commenting that he has "flesh and bones." This account, unique to Luke, is the longest, most sophisticated narrative of the appearance of the risen Jesus that

Reflection

On the Road

Note the reference to "on the road," the journey motif. Why is it significant that this encounter with the risen Lord occurs "on the road," going away from Jerusalem? What is the significance of their return to Jerusalem after they recognize Jesus?

we have in the Gospels. Thematically, this passage hinges on the tenet that God gives understanding. Verse 16—"their eyes were kept from recognizing him"—is in the passive, a technique often used in the Bible to indirectly refer to something that God is doing. This technique is often referred to as "divine passive." Clearly, Luke intends the reader to see God's work in the shutting of the disciples' eyes. Again, when their eyes are opened in verse 31, the divine passive is used, an indicator that the understanding gained was given by God. Even though God's presence in this story is not directly cited, Luke writes in such a way that a Greek-language reader—or a careful reader of English—would have known that God was present.

The Nature of Jesus' Body

When Christ breaks bread in this pericope, is it an allusion to the Eucharistic meal? This may seem obvious to us, but we cannot be certain that Luke intended this. The language used here—took, blessed, broke, gave—is common to any and every formal meal in ancient Judaism; this is what the host does, and Luke has used this language in non-Eucharistic contexts (e.g., 9:16). Also, drink/wine is not mentioned. From the modern Christian reader's perspective, the meaning we construe is often Eucharistic. While this story brings a fresh perspective on the Eucharist as a means of grace and especially understanding, this may not have been the author's intention.

The conclusion of this narrative in 24:31-35 is a fitting ending for a remarkable story. During the meal "they recognized him," that is, they recognized that this was Jesus, and that he was alive. There is no thought of a phantasm here! Then, given this "aha!" moment, they looked back on their experience and said, "So that is why our hearts were deeply stirred when this man talked to us on the road and explained these scriptures to us! He was talking about himself!" (Author's paraphrase).

They quickly returned to Jerusalem, even though the darkness of night had completely fallen. They go to "the Eleven and their companions," where we expect them to recount their experience. Instead, the first

Reflections

On the Journey with Jesus

1. The Western Theological Seminary, where I teach, decided to name its new center for continuing education of clergy and laity "Journey." In the context of this story about the resurrection appearance on the road to Emmaus, why might the name "Journey" be particularly appropriate?
2. Some scholarly circles characterize Jesus as a "wandering prophet," who roamed about preaching to whomever would listen. How does Luke's description of Jesus' journey to Jerusalem, and his journey alongside his disciples, challenge this understanding of Jesus? What do you think might be Luke's purpose in setting much of the ministry of Jesus in this journey section?
3. This extended account of the Road to Emmaus appears only in Luke. Reflect on the importance of including a section in this gospel as a journey to Jerusalem. Discuss the significance of how the story continues—away from Jerusalem and out into the world—in Luke's Acts of the Apostles.

word is not their report to the Eleven, as one might expect in the narrative, but a word from the Eleven to them: "The Lord has risen indeed, and he has appeared to Simon [Peter]!" This revelation points to a resurrection appearance that otherwise falls outside the narrative view of Luke; no such story is narrated. Yet, without narrating the story, the gospel lets the reader know that Jesus has appeared to more than one group of disciples. However, the two disciples from Emmaus have the final word: "Then they told what had happened on the road, and how he had been made known to them in the breaking of the bread."

Resources

Hymns

1. Consider the meaning of the first and fourth stanzas of the classic Eucharistic hymn, "Come, Risen Lord," Hymn #503, in the *Presbyterian Hymnal* (Louisville: Westminster/John Knox Press, 1990), in the light of this passage.
2. The well-known African American spiritual, "Were You There," deals movingly with our trembling over the death and burial of Jesus. But the hearts of his followers also trembled in a variety of ways after Jesus was raised from the dead. How appropriate, in your opinion, would it be to add the following proposed stanzas:

   "Were you there when they found the empty tomb?"
   "Where you there when they met him on the road?"
   "Where you there when they saw him in the meal?"

Consider also the words of the hymn "On the Day of Resurrection," based on the Emmaus story, Hymn #309, in the *United Methodist Hymnal* (Nashville: United Methodist Publishing House, 1989).

Transformation Complete

Our journey with Jesus through the Gospel of Luke is completed with this passage. Yet the journey with Jesus in his Spirit will go on, as the Gospel of Luke continues in the Acts of the Apostles. The narrative of the ascension is reiterated in Acts 1 in an overlap that ties these two books together like two tightly-spliced ropes. Therefore, although this session will focus on Luke 24:36-53, we will often glance forward to Acts 1.

Literary Context

For readers using the historical method, Luke 24:36-53 appears to be a narrative unconnected to the previous narration of an appearance of the risen Jesus, the Emmaus story. In fact, if one takes away the transitional "While they were talking about this" in verse 36, the story has no explicit or even implicit reference to Emmaus, even though the two disciples from Emmaus are present in 24:36-53. This passage looks like an independent resurrection appearance narrative of a type common in the Synoptics. However, for readers using narrative method, this tension between them disappears. Even though the two disciples from Emmaus were there and told the others what had happened, they all are surprised and then frightened when Jesus appears among them (as one might expect!). This appearance may be supernaturally sudden, just as Jesus had "vanished from sight" at table in Emmaus (24:31). Jesus then stays with this group, probably the larger group of disciples with men and women (24:10, although Acts 1:1-11 speaks of the male "apostles" until the larger group returns to view.) Then he departs

Lectionary Loop

Ascension of the Lord/Seventh Sunday of Easter, Year C, Luke 24:44-53

again, this time to heaven (24:51); his exodus is now complete. Jesus has accomplished his mission in faithfulness to God. His transformation to an eternally living being leads to his exaltation at God's right hand, where he will rule until the end of time.

The Greek text of this pericope contains an unusual amount of textual variants, with eleven variant readings in eighteen verses. The basic meaning of the passage is clear and certain enough, but its original wording is nearly impossible to determine. However, the basic sequence of events in Luke is not duplicated in the other gospel accounts. In Matthew, Jesus is taken up into heaven from a mountain in Galilee (Matt. 28:16). The "Longer Ending" of Mark implies that the ascension occurs in the same place as the meal of the risen Jesus with his disciples (Mark 16:19). John has Jesus breathe the Holy Spirit out upon the disciples after his resurrection but before his departure (John 20:22), whereas Luke indicates that the disciples had to wait in Jerusalem for the outpouring of the Spirit. Thus all four gospels (and Acts) include part of this Lukan pericope, though only Luke narrates an ascension.

Jesus' greeting in v. 36, "Peace be with you," is a common greeting, yet it takes on an ironic meaning in light of how terrified the disciples must have been. They did not have a peaceful reaction to his appearance! At first they were startled, and when the meaning began to sink in, they were terrified. The word "ghost" refers to a person's spirit disembodied by death (the Greek word is *pneuma*, the common word for "spirit"), and the disciples were probably afraid that this "ghost" had come to "haunt" or damage them. The next saying of Jesus attempts to convince the disciples that he is not a spirit, but a resurrected, embodied person. First, Jesus established his identity: "See that it is I myself." Next, Jesus established that he was not simply there in spirit: "Touch me and see." Luke gives a curious description of Jesus' body in the words of Jesus: ". . . for a ghost does not have flesh and bones as you see that I have."

It is interesting to note that Jesus speaks first. When he does show himself to the disciples, the marks are on his "hands" and "feet."

Teaching Tip

Variant Readings

The NRSV text notes six of the eleven variant readings found in the United Bible Societies' *Greek New Testament*, and careful Bible study groups will want to consider them, at least briefly.

Reflection

"Flesh and Blood?"

On the surface, Jesus' words about having "flesh and bones" seem to make sense; Jesus is trying to convince the disciples that he has been physically raised. Yet, this description is complicated by Paul's "flesh and blood cannot inherit the kingdom of God" (1 Cor. 15:50). What do you make of this?

Jesus does one more convincing act to prove that he is who he claims to be: he eats fish in front of them. This action serves to illustrate and prove in the narrative that he is embodied. He is not a ghost.

What Kind of Body Will We Have?

"What kind of body will we have in heaven?" This is probably one of the most common questions Christians today have about "the afterlife," only less common than one other, more generic question, "What is heaven like?" Evidently it was common in the first century as well: "With what sort of body do they (the resurrected ones) come?" (1 Cor 15:35). The New Testament's answer is "Look at Jesus." His resurrected body is a contiguous with the old body, but now eternal and fit for heaven, as ours will be. Jesus' body is not merely a resuscitated corpse. However, when we look at the resurrected Jesus, his body has some particular features. The wounds on the body of the risen Jesus are there for an apologetic reason in the Gospels, to make identification certain. But they have a deeper theological significance: they forever remind us that the Lord is the Crucified One. To use the term made famous by Henri Nouwen in his book by this title, Jesus is forever a "wounded healer."

What does this resurrection embodiment mean? The "big issue" here concerns not just our bodies, but a Reign of God complete, a Kingdom of God fully come to earth. This is nothing less than a "new heaven *and a new earth*," to use the language of the book of Revelation (Rev 21:1). Most Christians today have a hard time with this concept, especially the "new earth" part. In some ways, the Gnostics and their devaluation of the material world won, and our view of the afterlife is often purely spiritualized. Cartoons display the saints as winged spirits on clouds, playing harps for eternity. Such a spiritualization of heaven does not do justice to the physical reality of the coming kingdom. How could God's next, perfect world be less embodied, less real and rich, than this one?

The Coming of the Spirit

The disciples' witnessing of "these things" is to be empowered and directed by the Spirit, as is suggested

Teaching Tip

Placement of Nails

Christian tradition understands "hands and feet" (v. 39) as the palms of the hands and the top of the feet. Much more likely, the marks would have been on his wrists and ankles; the Greek word for "hands" can also refer to the forearm as well, and the word for "feet" to the entire lowest part of the leg. As archaeological evidence shows, the nails used in crucifixion typically went in the wrists and ankles, where the body could bear weight, without the nails ripping out as they would from the palms or the feet proper.

Resource

Henri J. M. Nouwen, *The Wounded Healer: Ministry in Contemporary Society* (Garden City, NY: Doubleday, 1972).

Reflection

Hymn

Consider these mystical words from the 1851 hymn, "Crown Him with Many Crowns," by Matthew Bridges (#151, as found in *The Presbyterian Hymnal* [Louisville: Westminster/John Knox, 1990]; words in the public domain):

"Crown Him the Lord of love!
Behold His hands and side,
Rich wounds, yet visible above,
In beauty glorified.
No angel in the sky
Can fully bear that sight,

(Continued on page 98)

in verse 49. In his lifetime, and in resurrection, Jesus is in main possession of the Spirit. As he prepares to depart, he reminds the disciples that they are in need of the Spirit before they can go out into the world. The Greek verb for "I send" (*apostellō*, from which we get our word "apostle") is present active, which indicates a continuous kind of action. Acts 1:8 reiterates the Jesus is the sender of the Spirit, but only from heaven after his ascension.

This connection between the departure of Jesus and the sending of the Spirit raises a creedal question that has troubled the whole Church for a long time. The Nicene Creed originally stated the Holy Spirit proceeds from the Father. In the West, however, this was edited to include the phrase "and from the Son" (the so-called "filioque [Latin, "and the son"] clause"). This addition was not meant to be historical, but rather, ontological. It was to serve as a description of a relationship within the Godhead, not a statement about "Who sent the Spirit to the church after Jesus left the earth." We can affirm both the truth of the original Nicene Creed, that the Spirit proceeds from the Father, and the perspective of the New Testament, that the Spirit was sent to the Church by Jesus (Luke 24:49).

Ascension Narrated

Finally, we must consider the issue of Luke's narration of the ascension. None of the other Gospels narrates an ascension; Jesus is simply is gone. (Matthew comes close, but still does not narrate the ascension as an event.) Luke narrates the event twice – in Luke and in Acts. However, in Acts the Spirit comes 40 days after Easter Sunday, and in Luke is comes on Easter Sunday itself (24:13 "that same day," which seems to cover the whole chapter). In verse 50, the disciples embark on a short final journey with Jesus in person. The act of "lifting up hands" is customary in departing blessing. In artistic depictions of the ascension, Jesus frequently is depicted with his hands palms up, as if in prayer, open to the direction to which he is going (for example, Rembrandt's painting of the Ascension). This is a misunderstanding of the text. His hands are not up in prayer; they are palms-toward-disciples, in priestly

(Continued from page 97)

But downward bends his burning eye
At mysteries so bright."

Reflection

It can be difficult, however, to keep together both the death of Jesus and the life of Jesus, just as it is unfeasible for an (empty) cross to be a crucifix at the same time. For us, it's one or the other. When I lead tours to Italy, I generally take my groups on a tour of St. Peter's Basilica in Rome with the official Vatican guides, to give them a more traditional Roman Catholic view of this church. Before one such tour, one of the guides said that they had just been in their annual audience with the Pope, then John Paul II. She told our group that she had finally gotten up the courage to ask him why there were only empty crosses in the prominent places in that church, not crucifixes, as is typical for Roman Catholic churches. Instead of giving an explanation from art and architectural history, which would have been more historically accurate, the Pope responded to her, "Because Jesus is alive!"

Reflection

An Advocate

Consider Jesus' sending an "Advocate" in John 15. What are the similarities and differences with the Spirit Luke-Acts?

blessing. Once again, and here for the last time, the disciples see on earth his wounded hands. He goes and disappears as he blesses (the Greek verb for blessing has a continuous aspect). The disciples respond: they worship him, go to Jerusalem "with great joy," and are continually in the temple "worshipping God," although the Greek verb (*eulogeo*) is the same "blessing."

In conclusion, we see the transformation of the disciples throughout this narrative in a series of snapshots. Verse 37 depicts them as "startled and terrified," but by verse 41, they are joyful but still disbelieving and wondering. Verse 52 serves as an indicator of complete transformation; they are worshipful, full of great joy. They are poised at the end of Luke for their final transformation that will come occur in Acts 2: the coming of the Holy Spirit.

Reflection

Considering Luke-Acts

1. What effect does the interposition of the Gospel of John between Luke and Acts have on how we read and use Luke-Acts today?
2. Make a chart of the similarities and differences of the end of Luke and the beginning of Acts. What common themes do you see?

Considering Heaven

1. How might a spiritualized vision of the afterlife detract from the physical reality of the world to come or of this world?
2. In 1 Corinthians 15, Paul calls the resurrection body "a spiritual body." How might this term help to understand Jesus' body as portrayed in Luke 24?
3. Discuss what you believe about resurrection. Consider what you have been taught, what you have imagined, what you have heard at funerals, what you have seen in art and literature. How does this study of Luke inform or complicate your understanding?

Resources

Mikeal C. Parsons, *The Departure of Jesus in Luke-Acts: The Ascension Narratives in Context* (Sheffield: Sheffield Academic Press, 1988); A. W. Swipe, *The Ascension of the Messiah in Lukan Christology* (Leiden: Brill, 1997).

THE BOOK OF GENESIS

A STUDY BY
WILDA C.M. GAFNEY

Wilda C.M. Gafney is Assistant Professor of Old Testament and Homiletics at Lutheran Theological Seminary at Philadelphia.

GENESIS

Outline

I. Introduction
   A. The First Word
   B. Faulty Assumptions
   C. What Is Genesis About?

II. Session I—A Snake in Paradise: Genesis 3:1-7, 14-20
   A. The Crafty Serpent
   B. Why Are Things This Way?

III. Session 2—Two Portraits of Noah's Family: Genesis 9:8-27
   A. God's Covenant with All Creatures
   B. The Best and Worst of Human Possibilities

IV. Session 3—God's Promises to Abram: Genesis 15:1-21
   A. Abraham's Fear
   B. God's Covenant with Abram

V. Session 4—Hagar, Mother of Many Nations: Genesis 16:1-14
   A. Sarai Gives Hagar to Abram
   B. Divine Annunciation to a Slave Woman

VI. Session 5—The Courtship of Rebekah: Genesis 24:10-67
   A. A Strong Matriarch is Introduced
   B. Rebekah Chooses Isaac

VII. Session 6—A Blended Family: Genesis 30:1-24
   A. Family Conflict
   B. All Jacob's Children

VIII. Session 7—Return to Bethel: Genesis 35:1-29
   A. Deborah's Honor
   B. Jacob's New Name
   C. Rachel's Sorrow
   D. Esau and Jacob Reconcile

IX. Session 8—Judah's Sexual Ethics: Genesis 38:1-30
   A. Tamar and Levirate Law
   B. Tamar Takes Things into Her Own Hands
   C. Tamar is More Righeous than Judah

X. Session 9—Prince of Egypt: Genesis 41:1-57
   A. Joseph Interprets Pharaoh's Dreams
   B. Joseph Becomes a Leader
   C. Joseph's Brothers

XI. Session 10—Joseph's Family Reunion, Finally: Genesis 45:1-28
   A. Fulfillment of God's Blessing
   B. Sibling Revalry Continues

XII. Conclusion
   A. Israel's Blessings
   B. The Story Ends, but also Begins

Introduction

The Pastor's Bible Study on Genesis

The First Word

The first word of the Hebrew Scriptures is an enigma. Is it "When-beginning" or "In-antiquity?" We know it is not "In-the-beginning," at least when translated from Hebrew. There is no definite article. The Hebrew equivalent for the word "the" is absent. The traditional, "In the beginning," is an English translation that does not translate the Hebrew literally. (Nor does it follow the Greek version of the Hebrew Scriptures, the Septuagint, where the phrase is "In-beginning" or "in a beginning," with no definite article.) Perhaps we should not so quickly abandon the ancestral Hebrew text because it does not say what we want it to say. Here are just a few of the ways in which the first two verses of Genesis can be translated:

New Revised Standard Version:

In the beginning when God created* the heavens and the earth, the earth was a formless void and darkness covered the face of the deep, while a wind from God swept over the face of the waters. (*or "When God created" or "When God began to create")

Jewish Publication Society:

When God began to create heaven and earth—the earth being unformed and void, with darkness over the surface of the deep and a wind from God sweeping over the water...

Schocken Bible:

At the beginning of God's creating of the heavens and the earth,

Study Bible

See Excursus on "Creation: Ordering Chaos," in the *New Interpreter's Study Bible (NISB)*, p. 5, for discussion of "beginning."

when the earth was wild and waste, darkness over the face of Ocean,
rushing-spirit of God hovering over the face of the waters…

Revised English Bible:
In the beginning God created the heavens and the earth. The earth was a vast waste, darkness covered the deep, and the Spirit of God hovered over the surface of the water.

New American Bible:
In the beginning, when God created the heavens and the earth, the earth was a formless wasteland and darkness covered the abyss, while a mighty wind swept over the waters.

New Jerusalem Bible:
In the beginning God created heaven and the earth. Now the earth was a formless void, there was darkness over the deep, with a divine wind sweeping over the waters.

Friedman, in *Commentary on the Torah:*
In the beginning of God's creating the skies and the earth, when the earth had been shapeless and formless and darkness was on the face of the deep, and God's spirit was hovering the face of the water…

**My Translation:*
When beginning, He, God created the heavens and the earth. The earth was formless and shapeless; darkness covered the face of the deep, while the Spirit of God, She, was fluttering over the face of the waters. (*Unless otherwise noted, all subsequent translations are the author's.)

These translations demonstrate how that mysterious first word *bereshit,* is an invitation to deeper engagement with the scriptures. The first word is also a reminder that the scriptures do not always say what we think they say, or even what we have always "known" they say. The last translation also demonstrates that

Teaching Tip

God is called by many names in Genesis. One of these names spelled with the Hebrew equivalent of the letters YHWH is the Most Holy Name of God and has no certain pronunciation or exact translation. (It is most probably related to the Hebrew and Aramaic verbs for being—e. g. "I AM"—but is not an exact match for either language.) Due to its holiness, the Divine Name was traditionally replaced (for pronunciation purposes) with a common title for male human dignitaries, "adonai." The NRSV capitalizes "LORD" when translating God's most holy name to distinguish it from other lords in the scriptures. (I will only use "Lord" when it actually appears in the scriptures and indicate the Most Holy Name as I have done here.) Some of the names of God that appear in the book of Genesis are:

YHWH — Too Holy to Be Pronounced
Elohim — God
Shaddai — Nurturer
God of Ancestors
El Elyon — God Most High
El Olam — Everlasting God
El Roi — God Who Sees Me
The Maker of the Heavens and the Earth
The Fear of Isaac
The God of Israel
The Mighty One of Jacob

Teaching Tip

Because the Hebrew names of biblical characters are sometimes quite different from the more familiar English names, I will provide the Hebrew names in some cases. Abel's name is "*Hevel,*" and Cain's name is "*Qayin.*"

while virtually all biblical names for God are grammatically masculine, the Spirit of God is grammatically feminine in Hebrew, recalling that human beings, created in the divine image, are male and female.

Faulty Assumptions

Many readers of Genesis are surprised to find that a great number of our cultural traditions about the text have no basis in the text. For example, there is no apple in Genesis; the forbidden fruit in the garden is not identified. There is no "fall" of humanity in the biblical account; the "fall"is a later interpretive strategy, forcefully advocated by John Milton in Paradise Lost, among others. The humans disobeyed God by eating the fruit, but the text does not say that eating the fruit is a sin. The first mention of sin in the bible is the murder of Abel (*Hevel*) by Cain (*Qayin*) (4:7).

We also assume that the serpent in the garden is Satan, but the serpent is a wild animal, not Satan. The first use of the word "*satan*" in the Bible describes the divine messenger sent to Balaam (*Bil'am*), who stands in the path of his donkey as a "*satan*," an "adversary" (Num 22:22).

Many people think that the woman was cursed for her disobedience. God does not curse the as-yet-unnamed woman in the garden. Instead, God curses the ground and the serpent. Many more examples from the Bible invite us to deeper study. In the Bible, 50 chapters of Genesis are replete with rhymes, puns and intricate literary devices. We cannot hope to address all of it here. We will focus on some of the texts that appear in the lectionary in addition to some, perhaps lesser known, stories.

We will find that the narratives contained in the biblical text are regularly, surprisingly gritty and intimate. The language is open and frank, sometimes challenging our notions about what a sacred, authoritative text should and should not say. We will not shy away from difficult passages.

What is Genesis About?

From where did we come? Why are we here? Genesis answers these questions, explains why things are

Study Bible

Shepherd
Redeeming Angel

Skim through your Bible to see if you can find these and other names for God. If you like, keep your own list of the names as you come across them in the course of this study. Which names speak most meaningfully to you? Which reflect your experience of God?

Study Bible

See "Genesis Introduction" for an overview and outline of Genesis, *NISB*, pp.1-4.

Reflections

What do we bring to our study of the bible?

1. How did I first learn these stories? Are they new to me?
2. What does the text mean to me? Is it a good story? History? Instructional?
3. What do I have in common with the people of the text? How am I different?
4. What do I know about the world (and the bible) that the people in the text didn't know?

the way they are and how the world has changed from an Israelite perspective. In Genesis we are introduced to a God of many names who handcrafts human beings like pottery and develops a particular affection for some of them, more so than others.

It is helpful to remember that Genesis is shaped by the reflections of an Iron Age people on their Stone Age ancestors. It is also useful to recall that Genesis was not historically read on its own, but always served as an introduction to the Torah, the first five books. Now we roll the scroll (or turn the pages) back to the beginning of a text whose first word gives us pause. Let us begin.

Sources

Nahum Sarna, *The JPS Torah Commentary: Genesis*. (Philadelphia: Jewish Publication Society, 1989).

The Schocken Bible: The Five Books of Moses, Edward Fox, translator, (New York: Schocken Books, 1995).

The Complete Parallel Bible. (Includes NRSV, REB, NAB and NJB) Oxford, New York, 1993.

Commentary on the Torah, Richard E. Friedman, translator, (Harper San Francisco, 2003).

Hebrew Names Bible on www.crosswalk.com.

A Snake in Paradise

The first three chapters of Genesis occupy a prominent place in popular culture and imagination. But this was not always the case. There are no quotations of Genesis 1-3 in anywhere in the Hebrew Scriptures. Yet these chapters have figured prominently in Christian interpretive practices; there are direct quotations of Gen 1-3 in Matt 19:4-5, Mark 10:6-8, 1 Cor 6:16, 15:45, Eph 5:31 and Hebrews 4:4. Misreadings of Gen 3 in particular have led to a number of false assumptions of the roles and status of women and men in the later biblical world and its interpretive communities.

The Crafty Serpent

Gen 3 also has one of the more interesting characters in the scriptures. Its first words are, "Did God really say…?" Our introduction to the serpent is three-fold: It is particularly crafty, it is a wild animal, and God created it. And unlike every other serpent in the scriptures (and in our experience) it can speak, presumably Hebrew. Now, evidently, before the creation of the first woman the snake has overhead God's conversation with the first human being in 2:16-17: "Of every tree of the garden you may eat; but of the tree of the knowledge of good and evil, you shall not eat of it. For in the day that you eat of it you shall certainly die." The serpent asks the woman what God *really* said, proving to the reader that it is indeed quite crafty. The woman's response adds a new element to God's instructions concerning the tree: not only should the fruit not be eaten, it should not even be touched! There is a Jewish tradition that identifies the woman as the first Rabbi

Lectionary Loop

First Sunday in Lent, Year A, Genesis 3:1-7

Teaching Tip

As you read the scriptures, ask yourself:

1. What doest the text actually say?
2. What did the text mean in its ancient context?
3. What does the text mean today? To me? To my community?

Sources

See Phyllis Trible's discussion on p. 10 of the chapter "A Love Story Gone Awry" in *God and The Rhetoric of Sexuality*. Philadelphia: Fortress Press, 1978. pp. 72–143.

Athalya Brenner (ed.), *A Feminist Companion to Genesis* Sheffield: Sheffield Academic Press, 1993. pp. 24–201.

Dana Nolan Fewell and David M. Gunn, "Shifting the Blame," in their *Gender, Power and Promise: the Subject of the Bible's First Story*. Nashville: Abingdon Press, 1993. pp. 22–38.

because she developed and taught a system for complying with the divine command. This is based on the rabbinic principle of "building a fence around the Torah, found in the Talmud to describe interpretive practices which make it easier for humankind to comply with divine instructions

The snake contradicts God. "You certainly will not die." The serpent now offers new possibilities; the unnamed fruit is transformative. The first humans will become like their Creator; here that means that they will be educated. They will know all good, all evil, and everything in between. (Paired terms of this sort in Hebrew indicate a range between and including the two separate notions.) This eye-opening conversation transforms the woman who now sees the fruit in a new light. The fact that the fruit would make them wise makes it irresistible.

The woman took some of the fruit and ate it first. We do not know what effect it had on her, but we know that she did not change her mind. She gave some of the fruit to her man—there is no specific word for husband in Hebrew; the word for "man" (*ish*) is used here—he was apparently there and silent during the entire conversation. After eating the fruit, the first insight that they gain is that they are naked, and they clothe themselves with fig leaves.

God responds to these things in verses 14 and following. God curses the serpent; it will now crawl on its belly (apparently a new development), eat dirt, and be the enemy of future generations of humanity. God informs the woman that her childbirth will now be more painful (would it have been painless before the fruit?). In spite of this she will desire her man, and he will rule over her. God informs the man that the ground will be cursed because he listened to his woman instead of God; he will now have to toil and sweat in order to feed himself. And one day (but not today) he, "the *adam*" (here, "*adam*" means "human being;" the "the" means this is not yet a name) will crumble into the earth, the *adamah*, from which he, the first earthling, was made. Then the human who had been handcrafted from the humus named his woman "Life" (*Chavah*/Eve).

Why Are Things This Way?

Among other things, this story teaches us how hard life was in ancient Israel. And it gives at least one explanation to the complaint: "It shouldn't be this hard to feed a family. It shouldn't be this hard to have a family. Someone, somewhere must have done something wrong. It wasn't us. It must have been our ancestors." And this story offers us a glimpse of paradise through the eyes of this people who knew both desert living and the hardships of agrarian life: a lush garden, abundantly watered, with an endless food supply. While there are lush gardens and rainforests on this earth, there are also vast deserts, lava fields and glaciers. Even in arable land, natural weather patterns and ecological disasters still wipe out entire harvests and plunge nations into famine. At one level the Garden stories remind us that we are vulnerable to nature, whether to serpents or the unyielding ground.

Study Bible

For discussion of the people's relationship to the land, see "The Ancestors in Their Environment," *NISB*, p. 28.

Sources

Phyllis Trible, *God and the Rhetoric of Sexuality* (Philadelphia: Fortress Press, 1978).

For an excellent overview, see Clair Amos, "Genesis," in the *Global Bible Commentary* (Nashville: Abingdon. 2004).

For an excellent in depth treatment, see Nahum Sarna, *Genesis*. (Philadelphia: Jewish Publication Society, 1989).

Reflections

Reading Between the Lines

1. How does the serpent's craftiness reflect on its Creator?
2. How should we understand the walking, talking snake?
3. How does the snake know so much?
4. How did the woman learn God's instructions?
5. Was the serpent right? (Did they die? Were their eyes opened? Did they become like God?)
6. What does it mean to be God-like?
7. What do you think of the man's silence in this lesson?
8. What is your idea of paradise?

Two Portraits of Noah's Family

The stories of human origins, civilization formation, deluge and restoration found in the book of Genesis have some counterparts in the Ancient Near East. But the story of the proto-Israelite Noah is markedly different than that of the Babylonian Utnapishtim. Each man builds an ark and survives a flood, but Noah survives because of his God where Utnapishtim survives in spite of his.

God's Covenant with all Creatures

After bringing Noah and his family safely through the flood, God says, "I, I am the One who is establishing this my covenant with you all…" This covenant is not just with Noah's immediate family, but also with all of his descendants, and, more than that, with every living creature on earth. As a part of this covenant God promises never again to destroy the land with a flood. As the sign of this promise, enduring throughout all human generations is God's bow. The weapon of divine warfare has now become a promise of survival. (One wonders, if God's bow was the rainbow, what were God's arrows? Zechariah 9:14 says they are like lightening.)

It is difficult for modern readers to know what to make of this since we know about devastating floods and tsunamis all over the earth. One way of understanding this text is that it is about covenant, and that it provides reassurance that no matter how devastating the hurricane, flood or tsunami, humankind will survive.

The Best and Worst of Human Possibilities

The stories of Noah's descendants teach us something else about God's covenant with humanity. God's

Lectionary Loop

First Sunday in Lent, Year A, Genesis 9:8-17

Resources

A wonderful resource for many of these ancient flood stories is *Old Testament Parallels: Laws and Stories from the Ancient Near East*, edited by Victor Matthews and Don Benjamin, (New York: Paulist Press, 1997).

Study Bible

See excursus titled: "Two Flood Narratives," *NISB*, 17. What do you make of these two versions, plus the parallel stories from the Ancient Near East?

Study Bible

See excursus on "Covenant," *NISB*, 113-114.

loving kindness is not dependant on human behavior. The verses following the covenant story are typically not read in lectionary-based services but have figured prominently in the history of the United States. This story begins with a return to a land-based life after so much time on the ark. Noah plants what we are to believe is the first cultivated vineyard in the land. Mysteriously he also apparently ferments his harvest, and becomes drunk. (The text doesn't tell us how he learns the art of winemaking, and the requisite time passes in a single verse.) Noah passes out dead drunk, and his "nakedness is uncovered."

The expressions "to cover" and "uncover" nakedness in Hebrew always have a sexualized connotation. This may help to explain what is a very cryptic and perplexing narrative. Noah's son Ham sees his father's nakedness. Many ancient and contemporary, Jewish and Christian commentators have articulated the possibility that there was inappropriate contact between Ham and his father based on the vocabulary of this passage. The intoxication of Noah supports this reading; alcohol consumption by victims and perpetrators is frequently linked to sexual assault. Ham tells his brothers, Shem and Yapheth, that their father is lying naked in the tent. They enter in such a manner as to avoid looking at their father or uncovering his nakedness themselves and throw a garment over their unconscious father.

When Noah awakes, covered in the garment, he curses his grandson, Canaan, the son of Ham. Notice the text in v. 24: "When Noah awoke from his wine he knew what his youngest son had done to him." This verse may indicate that either Ham did something inappropriate with Noah or that Ham revealed what Noah did to him when he told his brothers what happened in their father's tent. The curse is an unwarranted reaction if the only thing that had happened was that Ham had seen his father exposed and arranged for his brothers to preserve his dignity. In any case, whatever happened should have been between Noah and Ham; the grandson, Canaan, was never implicated.

However, Noah curses Canaan, making him the

Teaching Tip

The Shape of the Earth

It may be helpful to remember that the authors of the bible, like all pre-modern peoples, believed that the earth was flat and had four corners (Job 37:3; Isa 11:12, 41:9; Ezek 7:2; Rev 7:1, 20:8). The word "earth" in the scriptures refers to soil, not a globe, and the term could refer only to the land of Israel or all land everywhere. In Israelite cosmology pillars supported the land, which was over a great and watery abyss (1 Sam 2:8, Job 9:6, 38:16-17; Pss 69:15, 75:3; many others). Over the land was the dome of the sky, also called the heavens. Beyond the dome were the upper waters that fell as rain through windows in the "heavens."

Study Bible

See "Excursus: Israel Among the Nations: The Political Map in Genesis," *NISB*, 21–22.

Reflections

Ecological Disasters

1. How do we understand the devastation of continuing floods on the earth in light of the Noah story?
2. What biblical covenants do you consider to be binding?
3. How does your understanding of contemporary, planetary science affect the way you read Genesis?

slave of his uncles, Shem and Yapheth. In addition, Noah blesses Shem and reiterates that Canaan is to be his slave. Noah blesses Yapheth to dwell in the tents of his brother Shem and repeats for a third time that Canaan is to be their slave. Whether or not this story contains a memory of domestic violence, it serves to reinforce the Israelite view that Israel was favored by God who granted them the land and service of Canaan.

It is difficult to comprehend the power of this narrative on slave-holding people, especially those in the 19th and 20th century American South. The exegetical tradition pre- and post-Civil War was that since Ham was the ancestor of African peoples including Egypt and Nubia (Gen 10:2), the cursing of his son, Canaan, meant that the enslavement of Africans was the will of God. In addition, the tradition of interpreting Ham's name as "hot" (thus representing the African continent) had the result of including all African peoples in the misnamed "Curse of Ham." This does not take into account that Ham also means "father-in-law" as it does in Gen 38:13, 25 and 1 Sam 4:19, 21.

In these two narratives Noah's family represents the best and worst of human possibilities. In the best possibility, the one lifted up by many churches, Noah and his descendants are the recipients of a divine promise. In the worst, there is a painful reminder of a brutal history. Noah's family represents the evil that human beings are capable of doing to each other.

Reflection

Slavery

How did American slavery differ from Israelite slavery? The following verses offer a few glimpses:

1. Israelite slaves did not work on the Sabbath (Exod 20:10).
2. All Hebrew slaves had the option of being freed every seven years (Exod 21:2).
3. Anyone who kidnaps a person to sell that person must be put to death (Exod 21:16).
4. A slave-owner who kills a slave must be punished (Exod 21:20).
5. A slave who is maimed by his or her owner must be set free (Exod 21:26).
6. Freed slaves must receive liberally from their previous owner's livestock and other income, which he or she helped produce prior to being freed (Deut 15:13).
7. Female captives must be treated as wives and cannot be sold as slaves if they have had sexual relations with their captor (Deut 21:13).

Sources

Cain Hope Felder, "Race, Racism and Biblical Narratives" in his *Stony the Road We Trod,* (Minneapolis: Fortress Press, 1991).

Peter T. Nash, *Reading Race, Rereading the Bible,* (Minneapolis: Fortress Press, 2003).

Musa Dube,"The Postcolonial Condition" in her *Postcolonial Feminist Interpretation of the Bible,* (St. Louis: Chalice Press, 2000).

God's Promises to Abram

After calling Abram the Chaldean from his home city of Ur on the Euphrates—Chaldea would later become part of Babylonia and eventually Iraq—God initiated a relationship with Abram and his descendants. For his part, Abram abandoned the god of his ancestors, Nanna, the Sumerian moon-god (also known as the Babylonian god "Sin") and patron of Ur. God has promised to bless Abram, magnify his name, bless those who bless him, curse those who curse him and bless all the peoples of earth through him (Gen 12:2-3). Abram begins to worship the God who appeared to him and whose name, YHWH, is Too-Holy-To-Be-Uttered. Abram had many adventures including losing Sarai to Pharaoh (12:15) and getting her back (12:19), becoming a wealthy man (13:2), waging war to rescue his nephew Lot and his family (14:16), meeting and being blessed by the enigmatic Priest of El Elyon (God Most High) and King of Salem, Melchizadek (14:18).

Abraham's Fear

After all of these things, God appears to Abram again and greets him with a standard divine assurance: "Fear not!" This greeting occurs frequently in the Hebrew Scriptures and in the literature of the Ancient Near East (ANE). Of what was Abram afraid? He has been victorious in all his undertakings. As soon as he opens his mouth, Abram reveals his greatest fear. Abram's first speech to God is about his continuing childlessness, which does not make sense to him in light of God's earlier promise. This is God's third appearance to Abram, but it is the first time that Abram speaks to God. This time, they have a conversation.

Lectionary Loop

Tenth Sunday After Pentecost, Year C, Genesis 15:1-6

Study Bible

See excursus on "God Most High and Melchizadek," *NISB*, p. 31.

Abram: "Lord God-of-the-Holy-Name, what will you give me? I am going around childless! Eliezer of Damascus is the only heir of my house! Look! You have given me no offspring! And now look! One born in my house will inherit it!"

God-of-the-Holy-Name: "This man shall not be your heir; only one from your own body shall be your heir. Now then, look heavenwards and count the stars, if you are able to count them. So shall your offspring be."

God's "Fear not!" precedes Abram's lament. God knows what Abram is going to say before he opens his mouth. And Abram's first speech to God is quite a lament. God's subsequent reassurance is effective and timely. There are many surviving ANE texts that detail the adoption of servants who cannot be later disinherited, even if biological children are subsequently born to the adoptive parents. The God-of-the-Holy-Name has convinced Abram not to adopt Eliezer. Abram believes God, and God deems Abram's belief as righteousness.

God's Covenant with Abram

As we saw in the last lesson, the lectionary portion ends before things get too messy (in this case, v. 6). But human life is messy and complicated. And the scriptures are a treasure because they speak to us in all our complexities. God and Abram have another conversation.

God-of-the-Holy-Name: "I am The-One-Whose-Name-is-Holy who brought you from Ur of the Chaldeans, to give you this land to possess."

Abram: "Lord God-of-the-Holy-Name, how will I know that I shall possess it?"

God makes a covenant with Abram, and appears as a smoldering furnace and a fiery torch to act out the covenant. The divided carcasses of the ceremonial animals indicate what will happen to either party who breaks the covenant (Jer 34:17-20). God is putting Godself at risk to reassure Abram, but only if God breaks the covenant, which God will not do.

God promises Abram the lands of many peoples, but does not specify what will happen to all of those peoples. The geographic boundaries described here were

Teaching Tip

Abraham Speaks to God

Each time that he addresses God, Abram uses the human title "lord" before he invokes the name of God. (A partial list of names of God in Genesis is found on p. 4 in the Introduction.) When the word for lord, *adonai*, precedes the sacred letters of the Divine Name, rather than read "Lord LORD," the tradition is to read "Lord GOD," with the capital letters indicating the Most Holy Name. To minimize confusion, I am only using "Lord" in translation when it actually appears in the text.

never realized, even during the time of David and Solomon, who controlled only some of that land. The Israelite kings did not displace all the indigenous inhabitants. One way of reading this story is that God's promise to Abram and his descendants was not based on the extermination of any other people or culture, but rather on the expectation that there was enough room for many nations to coexist. This is an especially important vision in times when some people think that there is only room for one nation in the contested and deeply divided Holy Land.

Reflections

God and Promises

1. What does it mean that the land God promises to Abram is already occupied?
2. What happens when two groups of people claim the same land?
3. Can a divine claim in a sacred text resolve a land dispute?
4. How is this story useful to us today?
5. How can this story help us understand the promises of God?
6. Are there any divine promises for which you are waiting?
7. How can this story help us understand promises made to God?
8. Are there any promises that God is waiting for you to fulfill?
9. What do you make of Abraham's being blessed so that by him all families of the earth will be blessed? (Gen 12:3)

Resources

While written as a reflection of the Book of Exodus, Robert Allen Warrior's "Canaanites, Cowboys and Indians" in R. S. Sugitharajah's *Voices From the Margin,* examines the implications of the gift of an inhabited Promised Land. Also see Naim S. Ateek's "Palestinian Perspective" in the same book.

Hagar, Mother of Many Nations

Genesis chapter 16 does not appear in the Revised Common Lectionary. It is, however, a significant text in the cultural lectionary of many African American Christians, particularly women. This lesson provides us insights to the perils and possibilities of human relationships along gender, class and ethnic lines.

At the beginning of this chapter we find that in spite of God's reassurance to Abram, he is still "going about childless" as he lamented in 15:2. Now Sarai is identified as the cause of his childlessness; she is barren. And she has an Egyptian slave-girl called Hagar. I say that she is "called Hagar" and not "named Hagar" (reading against the biblical text) because Hagar is a masculine Hebrew name meaning "foreign thing" from the root *gur* that means "to sojourn." I very much doubt that her Egyptian parents gave her such a name. It is more likely that Hagar is what she was called after she entered a Hebrew-speaking household. I find it note-worthy that her name is not even "foreign woman" even though it was her female body, her womb, that would be colonized to gestate the hopes of Abram, the potential patriarch.

Sarai Gives Hagar to Abram

As we saw with the potential adoption of Eliezer, the social and cultural practices of Abram and Sarai are shaped by the practices of their cultures of origin and neighboring peoples in the Ancient Near East. In a well-attested practice, Sarai gives Hagar to Abram as a surrogate. In v. 3, even though she is a slave, Hagar is the same category wife as is Sarah in verse 1; the word

Resources

Renita Weems, *Just A Sister Away*, (San Diego: LuraMedia, 1988).

Reflection

Polygamy

In the polygyny (the practice of marrying multiple wives) of ancient Israel, there were two types of wives, primary and secondary. A primary wife, *ishah* (the same word as "woman") had full societal recognition as well as legal status, and her children had full inheritance rights. A secondary wife, *pilegesh,* also had full societal recognition and legal status, but her children had limited or no inheritance rights. Some translators have called secondary wives "concubines." This is incorrect because these women were also wives. The type of marriage agreement, not the order of the marriages, determined the status of the wife. Judges 19:1, 2 Samuel 15:16, and 2 Samuel 20:3 all use both terms together, with *pilegesh* as secondary in rank to modify wife, *ishah*, making the relationship clear. Some translators fail to translate *ishah*, woman/wife when it is

(continued on page 120)

for woman *ishah,* is also used for a primary wife. (The word *pilegesh* means auxiliary wife in terms of status, but is never used for Hagar.) The biblical text has compressed ten years into one verse. It has been ten years since Abram has settled in Canaan. This does not include the first leg of his journey or his stay in Egypt. They have waited for God for more than ten years; they are desperate.

We do not know under what circumstances Hagar initially entered servitude; we do know that she has no say over her body being given to Abram or her child being given to Sarai. Hagar is on the underside of all of the power curves in operation at that time; she is female, foreign, enslaved. Yet she has one source of power. She is fertile; Sarai is not and as a result, Hagar held Sarai in low esteem. Sarai is free; she has some societal privilege as Abram's wife and Hagar's mistress, but she is still an infertile woman in a male-dominated world, which imperils her status. And she is angry. First Sarai takes her anger out on Abram. She calls on God-of-the-Holy-Name to do justice on her behalf. When Abram removes himself from the fray Sarai takes her anger out on Hagar. Sarai brutalized Hagar. The standard translations—dealt harshly (NRSV) and treated harshly (JPS)—do not capture the physical violence that is represented by this word. In fact, Sarai's oppression of Hagar in v. 6, is the same as Egypt's oppression of Israel in Exod 1:11, ultimately leading to God's liberating intervention.

Divine Annunciation to a Slave Woman

But Hagar liberates herself; she runs away. A messenger of God-of-the-Holy-Name finds Hagar in the wilderness. This messenger of God-of-the-Holy-Name functions as God in disguise. The holy messenger uses the first person in verse 10, speaking as God, and Hagar realizes that she has seen God in v. 14. (Compare with Gen 18:1-8 in which God appears as three persons who use both singular—in verses 1 and 13—and plural—in vv. 5 and 9—verbs.)

God's message to Hagar is disturbing. She must return to Sarai and submit to her abuse. (This reminds me of Paul's return of Onesimus the slave to his owner

(continued from page 119)

combined with *pilegesh,* secondary. I have translated both terms when they occur together:

- *Judges 19:1* "... a certain Levite... took a wife (*ishah*) for himself of secondary status (*pilegesh*)..."
- *2 Samuel 15:16* "The king left, followed by all his household, except ten wives (*nashim* is the plural of *ishah*) of secondary status (*pilegeshim*, plural form)..."
- *2 Samuel 20:3* "David ... took the ten wives (*ishah*) of secondary status (*pilegeshim*)..."

Abraham had three primary wives:

- Sarah—Gen 11:29 "the name of Abram's wife (*ishah*) was Sarai"
- Hagar—Gen 16:1 "Sarai, Abram's wife (*ishah*), took Hagar the Egyptian, her slave-girl, and gave her to her husband Abram as a wife (*ishah*)."
- Keturah after Sarah's death—Gen 25:1 "Abraham took another wife (*ishah*), whose name was Keturah"

Abraham also had an unknown number of secondary wives:

- Gen 25:5-6 "Abraham gave all he had to Isaac. But to the children of his secondary wives (*pilegeshim*) Abraham gave gifts, while he was still living, and he sent them away..."

in Phil 12-16. In both cases the biblical text affirms their enslavement.)

God's words may be unwelcome, but there is hope. Sarai will not destroy Hagar; she will survive. In v. 10 we find the first divine annunciation and promise of a dynasty to a woman in the canon. Hagar will become the Mother of Many Peoples. (See Ps 83:7, "the tents of Edom and the Ishmaelites, Moab and the Hagrites." The Hagrites also appear several times in 2 Chronicles.)

This chapter of Hagar's story contains an episode without peer in all of scripture. In verse 13, Hagar names God: *El Ro'i*—God of seeing—"Have I seen the One who sees me and lived to tell of it?") She is the only person in the canon to give God a name.

Teaching Tip

Human and Divine Messengers

Biblical Hebrew uses the same word to describe the messengers of God (*malak*—singular/*malakim*—plural) as it does human messengers. For example Jacob sends messengers to his brother Esau in Gen 32; the spies that Rahab hides are called messengers (*malakim*) in Josh 6. On the other hand, the same word (*malakim*) is used for the messengers of God who ascend and descend the ladder in Jacob's dream in Gen 32. The word "angel" is (from the Greek term *angelos,* meaning "messenger") is misleading, because modern readers think of an "angel" as a supernatural or divine being. But *malak*/*malakim* simply means "one who bears a message." In addition, the iconography that we associate with angels was not associated with the *malak* of the Hebrew Scriptures. The best illustration of this is that the divine messengers Jacob saw had to traverse the distance between the heavens and the earth on a ladder because they did not have wings and could not fly. (The winged seraphs and cherubs that appear later in the Bible are never called messengers.)

Reflections

Infertility

1. What are the implications of this story for difficulties surrounding fertility and potential solutions, such as surrogacy? What are the economic and political implications of passing along inheritence?

(continued on page 122)

(continued from page 121)

2. How can this story help us think about the intersection between race and class?
3. What did Sarai and Hagar have in common?
4. What do Hagar and Abram have in common?
5. What does the name Ishmael ("God hears") suggest about God's intentions for and relationship with his descendants?

What does God's treatment of Hagar and Ishmael model for our own relationships with their Arab (both Christian and Muslim) descendants? Discuss the significance of this Egyptian slave woman's receiving help from Abraham's God and being the only person in the Bible to give God a name.

Resources

Phyllis Trible, "Hagar: The Desolation of Rejection" in *Texts of Terror* (Philadelphia: Fortress Press, 1984).

Delores S. Williams, "Hagar's Story: A Route to Black Women's Issues" in her "Sisters in the Wilderness: The Challenge of Womanist God-Talk." (Maryknoll: Orbis, 1993).

Savina J. Teubal, "Sarah and Hagar: Matriarchs and Visionaries," in Athalya Brenner (ed.), *A Feminist Companion to Genesis*. (Sheffield: Sheffield Academic Press, 1993).

Athalya Brenner, "Female Social Behavior: Two Descriptive Patterns Within the 'Birth of the Hero' Paradigm," in *A Feminist Companion to Genesis,* (Sheffield Academic Press, 1988).

Dana Nolan Fewell and David M. Gunn, "Keeping the Promise," in their *Gender, Power, and Promise*. (Nashville: Abingdon, 1993).

The Courtship of Rebekah

> **Lectionary Loop**
> **Seventh Sunday after Pentecost, Year A, Genesis 24:34-38**

This is such a large story that we cannot give it all equal, thorough coverage. There are significant elements throughout the chapter, so we will skip about.

A Strong Matriarch is Introduced

Rebekah (*Rivkah*) is one of the most dominant matriarchs in Israelite history. A close reading of her story indicates that she is also one of the most active. There are at least 20 verbs devoted to her actions in chapters 24-27. The sixty-seven verses that comprise chapter 24 are full of her comings and goings. Listen to some of the verbs describing her in the beginning of the narrative:

- "she went down, she filled, she went up" (24:16)
- "she said, she hurried, she lowered, she caused to drink" (24:18)
- "she finished, she said 'I will draw'"(24:19)
- "she hurried, she emptied, she ran, she drew" (24:20)
- "she said 'I am' " (24:24)
- "she said" (24:25)
- "she ran, she told." (24:28)

We know that Isaac is from a family that reckons its identity along paternal lines. They are the family of Avraham, Yitzhak and Ya'akov—Abraham, Isaac and eventually Jacob. But Rebekah's father is identified by a matronymic (maternal name); he is Bethuel the son of Milcah (Gen 24:15, 24), his mother. (Other persons in the scriptures identified by their mother's names include Jacob, who identifies himself as the son of Rebekah (*ben Rivkah*) but does not mention Isaac or even Abraham in Gen 29:12, and David's chief warriors—and nephews—Joab, Abner and Abishai, the sons of Zeruiah, their mother, in 1 and 2 Samuel.) Rebekah's household is also matrilineal; it is identified as part of her mother's household in 24:28. (Other matrilineal households in the scriptures include the families of origin of Ruth and Orpah in Ruth 1:8 and the bride in the Song 3:4 and 8:2.)

Abraham's servant repeats the narration of meeting Rebekah and repeats a number of her actions (along with his entire conversation with Abraham and God) when he meets her family. (Narrative repetition is a common feature of Hebrew prose.) At the end of the chapter, during the family conversations, Rebekah agrees to marry Isaac. In v. 50, Bethuel, Rebekah's father, and Laban, her brother, tell the servant to take her and go. Laban making all the decisions may appear to be patriarchal but Bethuel and Laban do not have the final say, even though the servant of Abraham now gives betrothal presents to the family.

Rebekah Chooses Isaac

Notice how the decision is actually reached. When Milcah, Rebekah's mother is consulted, she and Laban first ask the servant to delay his return for ten days in 24:55. Then in 24:58, Milcah and Laban make sure that Rebekah's wishes are honored; when asked whether she will return with the servant and marry Isaac, Rebekah said, "I will." Rebekah rides off into the sunset in a narrative in which she will continue to be active. She is not alone when she journeys to meet her new husband; she takes women-servants from her parents' household with her, including her nurse from her infancy, Deborah (whose name is given in 35:8), who may have been like a second mother to her. There is no word for "marriage" in biblical Hebrew, and there is no description of any civil or religious ceremoney for Rebekah and Isaac's union. Rather, the marriage is constituted by their mutual acceptance of each other as marriage partners along with the agreement of their families. Although he is from a patrilineal family, we see in v. 67 that Isaac practices matrilocation: Isaac and Rebekah reside in the tent of his mother. (See Gen

Teaching Tip

A Male-Focused Text and World-View

The biblical text is regularly presumed to be patriarchal. A common understanding is that all males held power and authority over all females with the highest concentration of power in the hands of the family father or patriarch. It is true that the scriptures are male-focused (or androcentric) and that they do not accurately reflect the religious experiences of all ancient Israelite women and men through the time periods that they describe. But it is not the case that all men always had power over all women. Many men were subject to other men, particularly the kings, and there were queens (like Athaliah who ruled Judah for more than five years) to whom both men and women were subject. In addition, some households were matrilineal (descent traced through the mother) and some were patrilineal (descent traced from the father) in ancient Israel. The two types of households are described in the text as "mother's household" and "father's household" respectively. We will see the convergence of these two types of households in the courtship of Rebekah (*Rivkah*), who is from a matrilineal family, and Isaac (*Yitzhak*), who is from a patrilineal family.

2:24 for the earliest evidence of matrilocation.) The end of this chapter is quite tender. Isaac loves Rebekah, and she comforts him after his mother's death.

Reflections

Family Structures

1. What can we learn from Rebekah's hospitality?
2. What kind of blessing do Milcah and Laban bestow on Rebekah in 24:60?
3. Do you believe in love at first sight? Do you believe that God acts as a matchmaker?
4. A modern version "matrilocal" and "patrilocal" family organization might be witnessed at holidays. Which set of grandparents get to see the children for which holidays: the mother's parents or father's parents? How does your family decide? What determines whether your family is matrilocal, patrilocal, or evenly divided? Religious or cultural custom? Geography? Quality of family relations? Number of relatives on each side? Politics?
5. What makes a marriage valid in your eyes?
6. How does Rebekah's story challenge or illuminate your perceptions of ancient household structures and marriage customs?

Resource

Carol Meyers' chapter "The Family in Early Israel" in *Families in Ancient Israel*, Leo G. Perdue, et al., eds., (Louisville: Westminster/John Knox Press, 1997).

A Blended Family

We have come to another story of a barren woman. Barrenness was a common feature in the literature of the Ancient Near East. Like their neighbors, biblical authors used this theme to illustrate both the power of God (who alone gives life) and the prominence of one who is eventually conceived against all odds.

Family Conflict

In desperation, Rachel demands that Jacob (*Ya'akov*) provide her with children, or she will die. Jacob "becomes furious..." The expression denotes a snorting bull. Jacob (correctly) blames God for Rachel infertility, because God is the author of life. Like her mother-in-law Sarai before her, and many women of means in her culture, Rachel chooses the option of surrogacy. Rachel gives Jacob her servant, Bilhah, and tells him to "go into her," meaning to have sexual intercourse with her.

Jacob fathers two sons, and Rachel names them with reference to her conflict with her sister: Dan (Judge) and Naphtali (Struggle). The name "Judge" could refer to the way in which Jacob judged between the two sisters. He loved Rachel more than Leah (Gen 29:30). The story tells us that: "Leah had peculiar eyes, and Rachel was beautiful in form and had a beautiful face," (29:17). "Jacob served seven years for Rachel" that were "just a few days in his eyes because of the love he had for her" (29:20). The name "Struggle" could refer to the story aboutJacob's being tricked into marrying Leah and having to serve another seven years for Rachel (29:21-30).

Teaching Tip

The Hebrew literally means "enter her," or "go into her." I translate this more explicitly as "penetrate her," since the desired result is that he impregnate her. We have no way of knowing if people living thousands of years ago thought that this statement was a euphemism or if it was unabashedly descriptive. What are some other ways the Bible describes sexual relations? Are these any more or less explicit (from our modern point of view)? When you read this story, what impression to you get of the people's attitude or values toward sexual relations and reproduction? Do you find the biblical account refreshingly honest, horrifyingly blunt, or somewhere in between? How does it differ from or instruct your own attitudes or values?

The now infertile Leah competes with Rachel for Jacob's attention by ordering him to marry her maid, Zilpah, as her surrogate (30:9-13). Zilpah gives birth to two sons, whom Leah names Gad ("Fortune") and Asher ("Blessed"). This time Leah is hoping to be vindicated by her peers; when naming Asher she says, "Women and their daughters will call me blessed." These verses account for several years, anywhere from the two required to conceive and birth two babies to six, allowing for five years in which the first child was being nursed before the second child was conceived.

A similar pattern occurs in verses 30:14-18, but there is a twist: Leah's son Reuben found mandrakes, a plantused medicinally and believed to treat infertility. In exchange for some of the mandrakes, Rachel barters with Leah for a night with Jacob. Jacob complies, and Leah conceives and gives birth to Issachar ("Payment," perhaps in reference to the bartered mandrakes). Leah's pregnancy may have followed Zilpah's closely but still represents several years in the narrative.

We find that in spite of his professed preference for Rachel, Jacob continues to sleep with Leah (30:19-20). Monogamy as a modern romantic ideal is not part of this portrayal of Iron Age polygamy. Jacob fathers another son whom Leah names Zebulun ("Cohabitation"). Finally, Leah gives birth to a daughter whom she names Dinah ("Judgment"), without explaining

Study Bible

See notes on 29:17. The meaning of the word *rakkot*, when used to describe Leah's eyes, is uncertain. The word literally means "delicate" or "weak." *The New Revised Standard Version* (NRSV) and *New American Bible* (NAB) choose to interpret this term as "lovely." *The Jewish Bible* (TANAKH) and *New International Version* (NIV) translate "weak." *The King James Version* (KJV) renders it "tender." My translation is "peculiar." How does the choice of translation influence the interpretation of the story? How would you interpret "delicate eyes" or "weak eyes?" Does Leah compare favorably to Rachel, who is described as "graceful and beautiful" (NRSV)? Why do you suppose Jacob loved Rachel and not Leah?

Teaching Tip

Birth-Mothers and Birth-Order of the 12 Tribes

Leah	**(Rachel' s Maid) Bilhah**	**(Leah's Maid) Zilpah**	**Rachel**
1 Reuben	**5** Dan	**7** Gad	**11** Joseph
2 Simeon	**6** Naphtali	**8** Asher	**12** Benjamin
3 Levi			
4 Judah			
9 Issachar			
10 Zebulun			
Dinah			

her name as was done for each of Jacob's sons (30:21). Then God remembers Rachel; Jacob returns to her bed—a point which is not mentioned in the text. God opens her womb, and she has a son whom she names Joseph (*Yosef*, "Addition") in hopes that she will have another son (30:22-24).

Jacob's Children

This list of Jacob's children (along with Benjamin, who has yet to be born), account for the legendary Twelve Tribes through whom Israel's identity will be constructed. Dinah, Jacob's daughter, is also named, because the next chapter is about her abduction and rape and the vengeance of her brothers that lead to their possession of the land of Shechem. But did Jacob have any other children whose stories were not deemed crucial to the overall narrative? Surprisingly, yes.

In Gen 46:26 we find: "Those who came into Egypt, who were his own offspring, not including the wives of his sons, were 66 persons in all." The Hebrew actually says "who went out of his loin." "Loins" is usually plural; here it is singular, specifying the male procreative organ. The total number of persons that Israel is credited with fathering is 66. If we subtract 12 for the Patriarchs and one for Dinah, that leaves 53 unnamed children. The text is careful to stipulate this number does not include Israel's grandchildren. Some of Jacob's unnamed children appear several places in Gen. In 37:35, after being told of Joseph's (orchestrated) demise, the text reads "All his sons and all his daughters sought to comfort Jacob; but he refused to be comforted…" And in Gen 46:7 we are told that Israel brings at least three generations with him to Egypt—himself, his daughters, his sons and their sons and daughters. (There are no grandchildren attributed to his daughters.)

This is a touching story with many familiar overtones. While most Western Christians do not practice polygamy, there are many blended families as a result of widowhood and divorce, and many people enter into marriage with children from previous relationships. The elements of sibling rivalry, jealousy, infertility and

Study Bible

See the excursus on "Sibling Rivalry in Genesis," *NISB*, p. 13. Other stories of sibling rivalry in the Bible include Cain and Abel (Gen 4:1-16), Noah's sons (9:20-27), Isaac and Ishmael (21:8-21), Jacob and Esau (25:19-25; 27:1-45), Joseph and his brothers (chapters 37-50), and the brothers in the Parable of the Prodigal Son (Luke 15:11-32). Can you think of other such rivalries?

desperation transcend time and location. Yet God loves this family and has promised fidelity to them throughout all their generations. God is the God of Abraham, Isaac and Jacob. But God is also the God of Hagar and Sarah, Rebekah, Rachel and Leah, Bilhah and Zilpah.

Reflections

1. How do women compete with each other for male attention today?
2. How can conflicts within a blended family be eased?
3. What causes sibling rivalries? Are sibling rivalries inevitable?
4. In our culture, do we hold women without children in lower esteem than women with children? If so, in what ways?
5. Do we value men by whether or not they have children?
6. This story carefully records the name given for each child. How are names significant? How do we choose names for our children today?

Resources

For a discussion of women's roles in the family, see Dana Nolan Fewell and David M. Gunn, "The Way of Women," in their *Gender, Power, and Promise*, (Nashville: Abingdon, 1993), and Carol Meyers, "The Family in Early Israel" in *Families in Ancient Israel*, Leo G. Perdue et al. eds. (Louisville: Westminster/John Knox Press, 1997).

Return to Bethel

God calls Jacob back to Bethel, where he dreamed of the ladder in 12:6; it was there that Ya'akov the "Heel-Grabbing-Sneak" became Israel the "God-Wrestler." For the first time Jacob insists that his family and servants abandon their devotion to other gods, such as those Rachel stole from her father in 31:19. It appears that some wore earrings with images of symbols of other gods; polytheism was not a secretive practice. After demonstrating their fidelity to the God of Jacob's ancestors, everyone in Jacob's company, his family and servants, was prepared for an encounter with God. Jacob built a new altar at Bethel for the occasion.

Deborah's Honor

The inclusion of Deborah's burial in (35:8) seems like an interruption, but it indicates that she was held in high esteem. (The death of Rebekah, whom Deborah served as a nurse and woman-servant, is not recorded.) Deborah was buried under a tree at Bethel-El that was named "the Oak of Weeping," in her memory.

Jacob's New Name

As a sign of their new beginning, God blesses Jacob (35:11). Just as in 17:1, God reveals Godself as *El Shaddai*, a God of sustenance, or God of Breasts, whose breasts never run dry. Jacob's renaming is reiterated; he is now "Israel"—the one who wrestles with God—no longer is he the sneak-thief *Ya'akov,* who trips his victims by grabbing their heels.

Reflections

Evolution of Monotheism

While ancient Israel is regularly described as monotheistic (belief in one god), Israel was actually henotheistic (belief in one's own god while recognizing the existence of other gods). The scriptures bear witness to the Israelites' widespread belief in the existence of gods of others who lived in the surrounding territory. (Deut 6:14: "Do not follow other gods, any of the gods of the peoples who are all around you, because the Holy One your God, who is present with you, is a jealous God.")

Eventually these beliefs would be supplanted by orthodox monotheism. (Isa 45:5: "I am the Holy One, and there is no other; besides me there is no god.") The practice of worshipping household gods would continue for thousands of years and would eventually be actively prosecuted by King Josiah (Judg 17-18; 1 Sam 19:13-16; 2 Kings 23:24).

Rachel's Sorrow

Suddenly Rachel is pregnant and in hard labor. The first we hear of Rachel's pregnancy is when it has reached its end. Another year of her life has ended without comment; now her life is coming to an end. With her last breath Rachel names her son "*Benoni*, Son-of-my-sorrow" (35:18). Ignoring his wife's dying wish, Israel changed the baby's name to "*Binyamin*, Son-of-the-right-hand." Rachel's death and burial are recorded (here and in 48:7); the death of Leah is not. But Rachel will not be interred in the family tomb at Macphelah; she is buried where she died and her remains are never retrieved. Leah will be buried with Israel, a small victory after a life of struggle (49:31).

In a disturbing episode in verse 22, Reuben sleeps with Bilhah, his father's wife and his mother's surrogate, who would have been like an aunt to him and may have helped raise him. The text does not say if the act was consensual. It is clear that he waited until his father was out of town. This story may explain why Reuben does not enjoy the status of a firstborn son.

Esau and Jacob Reconcile

The chapter ends with the death of Isaac, who is buried by his once estranged sons, Esau and Jacob (now Israel).. We have not revisited the story of Jacob's deception and betrayal of his brother, Esau (at the urging of his mother, Rebekah, in chapter 27), or their reconciliation in chapter 33. The brothers seem to have achieved a peace that the sisters, Rachel and Leah, were not able to attain. This is an enduring portrait of the family. Sometimes grief brings together those who were alienated from each other. Sometimes there is reconciliation, and sometimes there is not. This Iron Age family is not so different from our own families.

Teaching Tip

The name "*El Shaddai*" is traditionally translated "God Almighty." However, this is not a literal translation of Shaddai. In Biblical Hebrew a *shad* is a breast. (Contrary to the note on Gen. 17:1 on p. 35 and Excursis on "Shaddai/The Almighty" on p. 386 of the NISB.) Traditional male scholarship has regularly sought an alternative translation; however, the ancient Israelites were not uncomfortable with maternal imagery for the divine. When For example, when Ruth laments in 1:20-21 that Shaddai has dealt harshly with her and YHWH has abandoned, her she is describing God in maternal and paternal language. She is bitter because God has failed to comfort her, either as mother or as father. Because of the root word "*shad*" (breast), many contemporary scholars translate *El Shaddai* as "God of Breasts." We can see the linguistic origin of this translation in blessings that indicate God's ability to nurture and sustain life which were originally composed with this understanding of God. Jacob's blessing of Joseph in Gen 49:25 is the best illustration; (note also the reference to Tehom, "the deep," of Genesis 1:1):

"By the God of your father who will help you
Shaddai (the Breasted One)
who will bless you with blessings of the heavens above
blessings of Tehom (the Deep or She who lies below),
blessings of breast *(shad)* and womb."

The notion God as nurturing mother can be found in the prophet Isaiah: "Can a mother forget her nursing

(continued on page 133)

(continued from page 132)
child, or show no compassion for the child of her womb? Even these may forget, yet I will not forget you" (Isa. 49:15), and, "As a mother comforts her child, I will comfort you" (Isa. 66:13). The theme endures in the New Testament, where immature Christians are urged towards "spiritual milk" and to "taste" that the Lord is good (1 Peter 2:2).

Reflections

1. Discuss how family members endure broken relationships for years.
2. When have you seen reconciliations in situations where all hope seemed lost?
3. How does a death in the family affect relationships in the family?
4. In what ways do we still see henotheism in our culture, that is, how do we profess belief in one God but may believe in the existence of other "gods?" What other "gods" compete for our attention?

Judah's Sexual Ethics

This is a story that does not appear in the lectionary. But like Jacob's deception of Esau, it reveals an Israelite ethical standard with which we are not quite comfortable, that is that "the ends justifies the means." Time is greatly compressed in this story. In one sentence Judah meets, marries and impregnates his wife, resulting in a live birth. Obviously this takes more than nine months. We never learn the name of Judah's wife, only that of her father, Shua. Two to five years later they have a second son (this estimate is based on lactation practices in subsistence and pastoral economies). This also takes place in one verse. Judah's naming of his first child is unusual. In the Hebrew Scriptures, mothers usually name their children. Two to five years later they have a second son; this also takes place in one verse.

Er, the firstborn, reaches adulthood; he may be as young as 13 but may be older. In verse 38:7 we meet the first of three 'Tamars" in the Hebrew Scriptures. Tamar shares her name with the daughter of David who is raped by her brother, and the granddaughter of David, who is named in honor of the raped Tamar. Absalom names his daughter Tamar to "raise up offspring" for his sister. Her naming may also point to this story that hinges on the custom of having children for one's sibling in the event of an untimely demise.

Tamar and Levirate Law

As soon as we met the first Tamar, she is married and widowed in the space of a single verse. We do not know what Er did to merit a divine death sentence. There are of course many wicked people in the scriptures (and in

Study Bible

See study notes for 38:1-11 on p. 67. The story of Tamar is based on the custom of levirate marriage – from the Latin *levir*, brother-in-law –a cultural practice that would later be enshrined in Deut 25:5-10 as statutory. A brother fathers children for his deceased sibling, so that his name will carry on and so that his widow would have economic support. Onan resists levirate marriage to Tamar, possibly because he considered the children he might father to be rivals for his own share of the inheritance.

our experience) who do not drop dead in their youth. Meanwhile, Er's brother Onan reaches adulthood. He is charged with marrying his sister-in-law and having children with her in the name of his deceased brother so that his brother's name will not perish form the earth. Onan practiced some form of birth control; likely possibilities include *coitus interruptus* and non-genital intercourse. As a result of his disobedience, Onan is also sentenced to death. Judah is understandably concerned about the life of his remaining son Shelah and suspicious of Tamar. There is no reason for Judah to send her back to her father while waiting for Shelah to reach marriageable age. Judah is clearly trying to get rid of Tamar while claiming intent to honor tradition.

Tamar Takes Things into Her Own Hands

After all this, Judah's wife dies. She has given birth three times, named two sons and died. In this narrative, she has never spoken a word and has no agency. During his marriage Judah has become friends with his neighbor, Hirah. After mourning his wife he goes for a visit. Someone tells Tamar that her father-in-law has taken a trip. Tamar knows that Shelah has now grown to adulthood and that Judah has not fulfilled his duty to her by giving her to Shelah in levirate marriage. Tamar puts on a veil to disguise herself.

Judah thinks she is a common prostitute because she is hiding her face. (It should be noted that Judah's intent to employ a prostitute is not a transgression of biblical sexual ethics. Only married women and marriageable young women were off-limits.) Tamar begins to negotiate the fee. He offers a goat that he doesn't even have with him; she requires him to leave a guarantee of payment. Tamar exacts a high price: his seal (identity), staff (symbol of authority) and his cord (dignity—it was probably the belt holding his clothes together)! He is apparently desperate, because he gives her all these things. The deed is done; the narrator tells us that she conceived before she dressed herself. She goes home as herself, a widow, undisguised.

Judah sends his friend to pay his debt to the supposed prostitute (38:20). Hirah adds quite a bit of confusion to the text. He says that he could not find a

Teaching Tip

"Sacred Prostitution"

See the "Special Note" on temple prostitution in the *NISB*, p. 68. For centuries biblical scholars have taught that religious personnel in temples in the Ancient Near East practiced religious sexual commerce. E. J. Fisher demonstrated that the traditional translation of the terms *qodesh/ qedesha*, literally "holy man/holy woman" as "temple prostitutes," is based almost entirely on the writings of the first-century historians Herodotus and Lucian and not the biblical texts themselves. Herodotus in particular was known for distorting portraits of non-Greek cultures in his accounts. (Source: "Cultic Prostitution in the Ancient Near East: A reassessment," Biblical Theology Bulletin, 1979, 6: 225-236.)

The one reference to the parallel term in the Code of Hammurabi makes no mention of sexual activity, but merely describes temple service. The tem simply means "religious official," "pure, or consecrated woman," "a woman of special status."

It is likely, given the rhetoric of the prophets, that the Israelites called these temple servants prostitutes because they were serving another god. The Israelites referred to their own relationship with God in marital terms, like fidelity and adultery, and serving other gods was like prostitution (see Ezek 16 and Amos 2-4).

Hebrew has an unambiguous term for sex worker (*zonah*). Both terms, *zonah* (38:15, 24-25) and *qedesha* (38:21-23), are used in this story, leading to more confusion.

"holy woman" (*qedesha*) —but Judah said "prostitute" (*zonah*). He asks the locals if they have seen a holy woman (*qedesha*); they said that they had not seen a holy woman (*qedesha*). Hirah may have been trying to be discrete; he did not want to tell his friend that he was unable to find his harlot, or ask the townsfolk where to find a prostitute (*zonah*). His use of the term "holy woman" (*qedesha*) may have confused the locals. Now Judah is in trouble; he has forfeited his pledged property. How will he explain that?

Tamar is More Righteous than Judah

When Tamar's pregnancy begins to show in v. 24, she is accused of being a prostitute (*zonah*). Without ever speaking to her, Judah pronounces sentence, that she should be burned. As Tamar was being taken to her death, she sent someone to her father-in-law; apparently he was not present. The messenger took Judah the pledges he had given to the woman he thought was a prostitute to identify the father of her child. Judah passes judgment again, with more humility: "She is more righteous than I." The text does not record the suspension of her execution. What a scene that must have been!

Tamar delivers twins (38:27). The first, like Esau, puts forth a hand, which is tied with a scarlet cord, and then withdraws back into her womb. The second emerges completely, and Tamar and the midwife name him Peretz (Breach), saying, "What a breach you have breached for yourself!" The first twin, whose hand is tied with the cord, is named Zerah ("Appearance"), perhaps because he "appeared" first from the womb.

The chapter ends there, but Tamar's story does not. Not only is her name a favorite in biblical and postbiblical tradition, but she makes several more appearances in the canon. In Ruth 4:12, Ruth, who also uses her wits to trick a man into levirate marriage, is blessed in the name of Tamar on the day of her marriage to Boaz. Tamar's story is briefly recounted in 1 Chr 2. A city south of the Dead Sea bears her name. And Tamar is named in the genealogy of Jesus in Matt 1:3.

Reflections

1. Do the ends really justify the means? When?
2. Discuss Onan and Judah's reluctance to follow the levirate law and Tamar's decision to take matters into her own hands. Why does Judah say that she is more righteous than he is? (See the discussion of vv. 38:12-23 in the Study Bible, pages 67-68).
3. Are the sexual ethics expressed in this story compatible with your community's contemporary values?
4. What does this story suggest about the consequences of adopting all biblical ethical standards as our own?
5. In what ways do you see separate ethical standards in operation for women and men?
6. Do you know someone whose identity hinges on one unsavory act from their past?
7. Why do you think the Gospel of Matthew includes Tamar in the genealogy of Jesus? (See Study Bible notes on Matt 1:1-17 on p. 1748).

Resources

Phyllis Trible, "Tamar: The Royal Rape of Wisdom" in *Texts of Terror*, (Minneapolis: Fortress Press, 1984).

Prince of Egypt

The Joseph story covers seven chapters and can be read as an independent narrative. We are going to focus on Joseph's rise to power in Egypt and its implications. When our lesson begins, Joseph has been a victim of the sibling rivalry that we have seen in each generation of his family. He has narrowly escaped being murdered by being sold into slavery. He has just begun to prosper when he is falsely accused of sexual assault and imprisoned. He offers his services to his fellow inmates, one of whom (the king's cupbearer) promptly forgets him upon his release; the other is executed. When our lesson unfolds, Joseph languishes in prison for two more years, which pass in a single verse.

Joseph Interprets Pharaoh's Dreams

Then Pharaoh has the same dream in two versions—thin cattle have consumed fat cattle, and wasted heads of grain have consumed full heads, in groups of seven (41:7). Prompted by Pharaoh's desire to have someone interpret the dreams, the cupbearer finally remembers Joseph, who interpreted his dream while they were imprisoned together. When his liberation was announced, Joseph prepared by changing his clothes and shaving (41:14). We can imagine that there was a bath, based on what we know about Egyptian hygienic standards. Joseph shaved himself not only because it was the Egyptian custom, but also because he was probably filthy and possibly vermin infested, after his stay in prison.

When he meets the Pharaoh and learns why he has been summoned, Joseph declares that God is the one who interprets dreams, not him; but he is certain that once again God will reveal to him the meaning of someone else's dream. In verse 25 Joseph explains that God has revealed God's intentions to Pharaoh (41:25); we have no idea if Pharaoh was familiar with Joseph's God. Joseph explains the dream: The number seven refers to years represented by the cows and corn. There will be seven years of abundance followed by seven years of famine. The duplication means that God will act soon.

Joseph Becomes a Leader

Now, Joseph stops interpreting and starts suggesting. He proposes that Pharaoh designate a new bureaucratic office to manage foodstuffs in Egypt (41:33). "Let Pharaoh oversee the appointment of appointed overseers." The verb *pachad* is an administrative verb that means personally to oversee a situation and remedy any dysfunction. It was translated by *episkope* in the Greek version of the Old Testament (the Septuagint) and was eventually used to describe the Christian office of bishop. (See Acts 1:20 and Psalm 109:8.) Does Joseph have himself in mind for the job he describes?

The Pharaoh agrees to Joseph's proposal because he sees something unique in him. Joseph is the first person described in the scriptures as having the Spirit of God internally. When he assumes the post he designed, Joseph becomes Pharaoh's second-in-command. What happened to the former second-in-command? Joseph gets his chariot, along with a military salute that is no longer clearly understood (41:43). The word translated as "bow-the-knee" has lost its meaning; it could mean "Attention!" if it is a similar-sounding Egyptian word.

Joseph is fully assimilated into Egyptian society, his name is changed to Zaphenath-paneah, "God Speaks and He [Joseph] Lives" (or "Creator and Sustainer of Life") (41:45). Joseph is given an Egyptian wife, Asenath ("She Who Belongs to the Goddess Nieth"), who is the daughter of Pothiphera, the Priest of On (Heliopolis), and a sun-worshipper. Now, all doors in Egypt are open to him. Immediately after the account of his marriage, "Joseph went out from Pharaoh's presence and throughout all the land of Egypt" (41:46). In

Study Bible

See a description of Joseph's administrative role in Egypt in the study notes of the *NISB*, pp. 71–73 and 79–80.

his self-articulated position, Joseph directed the storage of all of Egypt's abundance.

In another episode of compressed time, Asenath and Joseph have two sons, Manasseh ("Causing Forgetfulness") and Ephraim ("Double Fruit"). Eventually they will become patriarchs of two of the 12 tribes. (There was no official tribe of Joseph, and the tribe of Levi had no land, Joseph's sons rounded the number back to 12.) At the end of the chapter Joseph rations food to everyone in need, from Egyptians to the hungry refugees from every known land.

Joseph's Brothers

The severity of the famine eventually brings Joseph face to face with his long-lost brothers. In chapters 42-44 Joseph manipulates his brothers into bringing him Benjamin, holding Simeon hostage and sending them home with the much-needed food. Israel is so reluctant to part with Benjamin that he leaves Simeon in jail until all the food is gone, and they are desperate once again. Now Joseph sets up Benjamin to be imprisoned as a thief, and Judah begs Joseph for 16 verses to take him instead. And the chapter ends!

Reflections

1. Do you think dreams can have predictive or other meanings? How do you interpret dreams?
2. Are you still waiting for someone to keep an unfulfilled promise? Have you ever forgotten a significant commitment you have made?
3. Simeon is left in jail to protect Benjamin. Can you think of situations in your experience where one family member was favored over another or made to suffer for someone else's benefit?
4. Discuss Joseph's creating a position for himself and his success as a ruler. Is his example one to emulate?

Resources

For another ancient literary tradition of foreigners rising to power in Egypt see, "The Annals of Dedumoses"in Victor Matthews and Don Benjamin, *Old Testament Parallels: Laws and Stories from the Ancient Near East*, (New York: Paulist Press, 1997).

Joseph's Family Reunion, Finally

Joseph's family reunion takes place over the course of chapters 42-45. Joseph's brothers come to him for food for their family, and they do not know who he is. Joseph pretends not to recognize his brothers. It has been as many as 20 years since they have seen him; he has grown up and become Egyptian in every way possible. Later, we learn that Joseph has been using an interpreter but still remembers his mother-tongue, which they do not know he understands. At one point (42:17), Joseph has his brothers thrown into the very same prison in which he was imprisoned. When he releases them, they return home, and Simeon rots in jail while his family lives off the rations he and his brothers acquired. After they have run out of food Israel sends the brothers back to Egypt. This time they bring Benjamin with them. When Joseph sees him, he is overcome with emotion; Joseph leaves the room to cry and then washes his face and returns, composed (43:30). He lets them go again, but instructs a servant to plant his cup in Benjamin's sack. The brothers are returned to Joseph's home, terrified that Benjamin will be taken from them and that the loss of Benjamin will kill their father.

Lectionary Loop

Fourteenth Sunday after Pentecost, Genesis 45:1-15

Fulfillment of God's Blessings

Finally, Joseph can't stand it any longer (45:1). He breaks down and puts out all of his servants so he can be alone with his brothers, revealing his true identity and demanding to know if his father is still alive. His brothers could not confirm that their father was still alive; they could not speak at all. More slowly Joseph explains (again) who he is and how he came to be there. He begins equating their actions with God's; God sent him to Egypt. As modern readers we must be careful about attributing all human actions to God. Surely God blessed Joseph; God used him to bless the Egyptians and would use him to bless the Israelites. But that does not justify his brother's hatred of him, their mistreatment of him or any of the abuse he suffered in Potiphar's house or jail. God transformed those experiences, which is not the same as sanctioning them.

Joseph reveals that he intends for the Israelites to live in Egypt with the Egyptians (45:10). This seems to be Plan A. The eventual migration to Canaan (Plan B) becomes necessary later when the Egyptians forget Joseph and mistreat his descendants. At last, Joseph reveals Benjamin to his brothers. Pharaoh unwittingly echoes Joseph's plan for his family to immigrate to Egypt (45:16).

Sibling Rivalry Continues

In addition to supplies for the journey, Joseph gives his brothers gifts. Joseph gives Benjamin more than his other brothers. The lavishing of attention on Benjamin is surprising given the trouble that favoritism has caused in his family. One could argue that his troubles with his brothers started when his father gave him a fancy robe in 37:3. Joseph's special garment is believed to have been a long garment with long sleeves that covered the wrists and ankles. (David's daughter, Tamar, also wore one in 2 Sam 13:18, as did all of the king's daughters who were eligible for marriage. The description of the garment as multicolored comes from the Greek scriptures and is not in the Hebrew text.) Joseph also sends along provisions for his father and the rest of the family.

When the brothers return home in (45:27), Jacob does believe that Joseph was alive, much less lord of Egypt, until he sees the provisions. In the last verse of the chapter, Jacob accepts Joseph's invitation on behalf of the rest of his family and declares that he must see his son again before his eyes close in death.

Reflections

1. What relationship exists between sibling rivalry and favoritism in families?
2. Why does Joseph deceive his brothers? Does he want them to taste the fear and uncertainty that he experienced?
3. Is Joseph's torment of his brothers directed by God? Is it justified?
4. What do you think: if God transforms negative experiences into good, does this mean that God sanctions evil, suffering, and mistreatment?
5. If God is ultimately responsible for Joseph's journey to Egypt, why is it necessary that his brothers suffer at all?

Resources

Susan Niditch, "Jacob and Joseph" in *A Prelude to Biblical Folklore: Underdogs and Tricksters*, (Chicago: University of Illinois, 2000).

Conclusion

Genesis 47–50

The last four chapters of Genesis point more and more towards the inevitable Exodus from Egypt. In 46:4 God promises to bring Israel and his descendants to the land of Canaan, (but doesn't say how or when) and promises that Joseph will bury his father. As Israel's death approached, Joseph swears on his father's (and his own) fertility that he will not bury Jacob in Israel, but will inter him in the ancestral plot in Canaan (47:29). Israel adopts Joseph's sons Manasseh and Ephraim so that he can leave them an inheritance in the Promised Land (48:4).

Study Bible

See the Special Note on the status of Ephraim and Manasseh in *NISB*, 81.

Israel's Blessings

In chapter 49 Israel tells his sons what will happen to them in the days to come. Most are blessed, but a few are rebuked:

- Reuben is the first proof of Jacob's fertility. However, Reuben shall forever be in disgrace for sleeping with his stepmother (perhaps by force, as she is never faulted.)
- Simeon and Levi are undifferentiated; both are cruelly violent. This may be a reference to their ambush of the Shechemites. In addition to "murdering people" (will later be forbidden in the Decalogue specifying this exact verb), they also torture animals for pleasure.
- Judah is praiseworthy and so lives up to and into his name. This blessing provides support for the Lion of Judah imagery that would symbolize the kingdom of Judah and its Messiah-King. The notion that Judah would rule the other tribes is also included in this blessing.

- Zebulon: (According to Genesis 30 Issachar is older; no reason for the inversion is given.) Zebulon is portrayed as a seafaring people here but as a land-locked people in Joshua 19. (In Judges, Dan and Asher are the sea-going tribes.)
- Issachar seems to be destined to serve as forced labor, a beast of burden.
- Dan is skilled both in governing and in covert military action.
- Gad shall raid and be raided.
- Asher shall be prosperous.
- Naphtali is a doe, a symbol of maternity, beauty and grace.
- The attacks on Joseph described here could be references to his troubled relationship with his brothers and his negative experiences in Egypt. There are several rare descriptions of God in this text: "the Mighty one of Jacob," "Shepherd" (a common image, but rare title), "Rock of Israel" (also drawn from a common image, but also a rare title). This section also includes a particularly maternal fertility blessing invoking Shaddai the nurturing provider and Tehom the deep of Genesis 1:2.
- This blessing reflects the military might that the tribe of Benjamin would be remembered for in later texts.

Jacob gives final burial instructions in vv. 29-32 and dies in v. 33.

The Ends but also Begins

Chapter 50 records the burial of Israel and the eventual death and burial of Joseph. Israel is embalmed like an Egyptian so that it will be easier to transport him back to Canaan. The embalming took forty days, which was followed by an official mourning period of seventy days due to Joseph's status in Egypt. An official Egyptian delegation accompanies Joseph to bury Israel in the family tomb at Macphelah. Joseph and the delegation observe another, seven-day, period of mourning at the burial site. Joseph lives to see his great-grandchildren (50:23). For the first time, Joseph acknowledges that the immigration to Egypt is not per-

Reflection

Ethnic Identity

Given that Abraham, the ancestor of the Israelites, was a Chaldean, and that the two tribes of Manasseh and Ephraim were half-Egyptian in their origins, it may not be appropriate to view Israelite identity as ethnic in a biological sense. When Israel departs Egypt in the Exodus, they are accompanied by a mixed multitude (Exod 12:38). The national origins of the "mixed multitude" are not specified. Many are likely Egyptian, or fellow slaves from other ethnic communities. All of them eventually incorporate and assimilate. They will be identified as "whisperers" or "rabble" and blamed for the Israelites' craving for meat. Moses (Moshe), a son of the holy tribe of Levi marries first the Midianite Zipporah (Exod 2:21) and later a Nubian or Kushite woman (Num 12:1).

When Samaria was Israel's capitol after Judah became a sovereign state with Jerusalem as its capitol, the Assyrians attacked and carried away all of the nobility, artisans and skilled laborers that they could. The rest of the folk were left behind. Then the Assyrians transplanted people from Babylon, Cuthah, Avva, Hamath, and Sepharvaim who married what was left of the Samarians (2 Kgs 17:24). Their descendants became known as the Samaritans. They were treated as ethnically and religiously distinct from the Judeans, but they had a shared ancestry.

After the fall of both kingdoms Ezra (9:12) and Neh (13:30) tried to establish a new holy land for an ethnically pure people. They broke up the mar-

(continued on page 147)

manent. God will bring their descendants to the land promised to Abraham. Joseph makes his sons promise to bury him in Canaan. Strikingly, the account of the death of Joseph (50:26), the last verse in the book of Genesis, is not accompanied any account of mourning. Like his father before him Joseph is embalmed so that his remains can be taken to Canaan for interment. Moses took the remains of Joseph with him in the Exodus (Exod 13:19).

Genesis is the book of beginnings. It describes the beginning of human life, the initiation of covenantal relationships between God and humanity, the origins of the family that would become a nation holding a special place in God's heart and the inauguration of a story that leads inexorably to liberation and purification. Genesis is the beginning of the Torah, the Hebrew Scriptures and the Christian Bible. It is an invitation to keep reading.

(continued from page 146)

riages of those who had married foreign women and exiled those Israelites who could not prove their ancestry to Nehemiah's satisfaction (Ezra 10:44, Neh 7:64, 13:25). But by Nehemiah's definition, some of Israel's greatest ancestors and rulers would be prohibited from entering the sanctuary: Joseph (because of his Egyptian wife in Gen 41:45), Simeon (because of the Canaanite mother of his child in Gen 46:10), Moses (because of his Midianite and Nubian wives), and David (because of his Moabite great-grandmother, Ruth). The Book of Ruth shows the other side of the ethnic purity debate, when a Moabite woman is proven to be faithful to Israel and becomes the ancestress of King David.

Reflections

1. How does the Joseph story set the scene for the Exodus?
2. Discuss the diversity of the group of people from many origins that departs from Egypt. Why do you suppose Ezra and Nehemiah later became concerned with "purity?" How does the story of Ruth counter this concern?
3. What do you make of Ruth's presence as an ancestress of Jesus in the Gospel of Matthew?
4. How is Genesis a book of beginnings for you?

PSALMS

A STUDY BY

DEBORAH J. SPINK

Deborah J. Spink, who earned a Ph.D. in religion at Temple University in Philadelphia, is a Biblical Studies adjunct professor at the Palmer Theological Seminary in Pennsylvania.

PSALMS

Outline

I. Introduction
   A. Record of Emotional Responses to God
   B. Hebrew Poetry
   C. Expression of Worship

II. Session 1—Happy or Wicked–Your Choice! Psalm 1
   A. The Choice
   B. Happy/Blessed are Those Who Follow God
   C. They are Like the Tree of Wisdom
   D. The Wicked are Like Chaff

III. Session 2—The Majesty of God and the Role of Humans: Psalm 8
   A. The Superscription of Title: The Director, The Gittith and "For David"
   B. Outline of Psalm 8
   C. Lips of Children vs. the Enemy
   D. Son of Man
   E. Humans Given Honor

IV. Session 3—Something Borrowed: Psalm 29
   A. Liturgical Borrowing
   B. The Title and Psalm Classifications
   C. The Storm
   D. "Sons of Gods"
   E. Yahweh Enthroned

V. Session 4—Forgiveness of Sin: Psalm 32
   A. What Sin Feels Like
   B. The Need for Forgiveness
   C. The Need for Prayer
   D. Trust in the Lord
   E. *Maskil*, *Selah*, and Psalm Classifications

VI. Session 5—A Psalm of the Aged: Psalm 71
   A. The Problems of Aging
   B. The Title
   C. Rock, Refuge, Fortress
   D. Lament Structure
   E. Our Hope

VII. Session 6—A City Lament: Psalm 79
   A. The Title
   B. City Lament Genre
   C. Seventy-Seven Times

VIII. Session 7—The Justice of God: Psalm 82
   A. Just Judges
   B. Divine Council
   C. Standards for Judges
   D. Shaken Foundations
   E. Monotheism
   F. The New Judge of the Earth

IX. Session 8—God's Dwelling Place: Psalm 84
   A. Layers of Meaning: Lovely/Beloved
   B. Pilgrimage to Zion
   C. Psalm Classification

X. Session 9—Revenge! Psalm 137
   A. No "Sanitizing"
   B. Communal Lament Over Zion
   C. Vows
   D. Revenge
   E. Psalm Outline
   F. Honest Prayers
   G. The Law of Love

XI. Session 10—I Will Praise God: Psalm 146
   A. Hallel Psalms
   B. Son of Man
   C. Reasons to Praise God

Introduction

Psalms

Record of Emotional Response

Have you ever wondered if there really is a God and if God cares for you? Have you ever wondered why, if God exists, why God would allow evil to triumph so often? Have you ever had to make a choice in your life but were not sure which path to choose? Have you ever reflected on the beauty and power of nature and how infinitesimally small humans are in the scheme of things? Ever messed up so bad that you knew you deserved to be punished but instead were overwhelmed by an act of forgiveness and love? Ever been so depressed you wondered if life was worth living? Ever been so happy you praised God in every way you knew how? Ever get so angry at someone you wanted to kill them? Ever been so relieved at how something turned out you could not stop thanking God? Ever feel so young and full of energy you felt you could take on the world? Ever feel so old and achy you felt you could not get out of bed in the morning? Ever wake up in the middle of the night worrying? Ever feel you could do no wrong or that you could do nothing right? Ever been overwhelmed by the power and love of God? If you have ever felt or experienced any of these things, then the book of Psalms is for you. All of these questions and emotions are honestly expressed and explored in the book of Psalms.

You will not read, "…thus saith the Lord," in the book of Psalms. The book of Psalms is *not* the recorded commandments of God; rather the book of Psalms is the record of human reaction to God's words and actions or,

Sources

For more background information on the Psalms see "The Psalms," *NISB*, 749–752; Gillingham, S.E., *The Oxford Bible Series The Poems and Psalms of the Hebrew Bible*, eds. P. R. Ackroyd and G. N. Stanton. (Oxford University Press, 1994); and Longman III, Tremper, *How to Read the Psalms*. (Grove, Ill.: Inter-Varsity Press, 1988).

Reflections

1. What is it you use as a guide to help you make the "right" choices in your life? Who or what do you turn to for advice?
2. What is your definition of "happy" or "blessed?" Do you feel blessed/happy to be in relationship with God knowing that God will guide you no matter where life takes you?
3. What is the fruit you want to bear in this world? What is it you want to "prosper" in? Do you take the time to meditate on God's law? Do you believe following God's law will help you to bear the fruit you want or God wants?

sometimes, the perceived lack of action. They are honest, raw human emotions written in poetic form. It is not clear if these poems were written only to be used in worship, or if they were personal prayers expressing the deepest feelings of those trying to find and follow God in their lives and later adapted for liturgical use. There is evidence that the canonical book of Psalms did not take its final form until the 1st century CE and that the psalms were meant to be sung. The book of Psalms is divided into five books probably mimicking the five books of the Torah. Each book ends with a benediction praising God.

Book 1: Psalms 1-41
Book 2: Psalms 42-72
Book 3: Psalms 73-89
Book 4: Psalms 90-106
Book 5: Psalms 107-150

Hebrew Poetry

It is interesting that some of the most emotional expressions in the Bible are written in some of its most structured language—Hebrew poetry. It is as if the depths of emotions explored had to be boundaried in some way. These boundaries are seen in the use of various Hebrew poetic techniques: parallelism, acrostic, *inclusio*, chiastic, etc. The psalms can also be identified by various forms of classification. Although there are variations as to the types of classifications of psalms, the general ones are: hymns of praise, thanksgiving, Zion, and kingship; laments and petitions; trust and confidence; wisdom or didactic; and liturgical.

Expression of Worship

These sessions explore ten psalms found in lectionary C. The psalms were meant to be experienced. Some sessions come with music for the psalm to be sung in worship as you are studying it. Some sessions also provide the general form classification of the psalm being studied. I encourage you to use that form to write a psalm based on the experiences of the group studying the psalm or your own personal experiences. These forms are tools to help us worship and express

Teaching Tip

For different hymns based on the Psalms go to Web site: www.cyberhymnal.org

our emotions to God and can be very moving when used to respond to situations today. (See Session 5, Ps 71.) These psalms are far from a "dead" medium and hold keys to help us express our emotions and deepest desires to God and to each other.

Happy or Wicked—Your Choice!

The Choice

In *Harry Potter and the Chamber of Secrets*, Harry Potter realizes how much he and his arch rival, Tom Riddle (alias the evil Lord Voldemort), are alike. Professor Dumbledore agrees with Harry as he notes they are both resourceful, determined, can speak Parseltongue, and have a certain disregard for rules, but there is one huge difference between Harry Potter and Lord Voldemort—the choices they've made. Harry chose to be in Gryffindor school house instead of Slytherin, the house identified with the evil Lord Voldemort. Dumbledore brings home the point, "It is our choices, Harry, that show what we truly are, far more than our abilities" (Rowling, 333). Psalm 1 is about the most importance choice of all, whether to follow God or not.

Happy/Blessed are Those Who Follow God

Psalm 1 is known as a wisdom or didactic psalm. It is purposely placed at the beginning of the Psalter to help readers/hearers understand that the choice to follow or not to follow God is always before them. The consequences of that choice can be read throughout the biblical text. Brueggemann (39) identifies Ps 1 as a psalm of orientation where "the well-oriented life fixed on torah expectations is one of happiness and well-being. The violation of that orientation is a sure way to diminishment and disintegration."

Ps 1 is structured in two sections. Verses 1–3 describe the ones who are "happy" and "blessed" when they follow God's laws or torah (the verb form of the Hebrew word *'shr*, means "to go straight on in the way

Sources

J. K. Rowling, *Harry Potter and the Chamber of Secrets* (New York: Arthur A. Levine Books/Scholastic Press).

of understanding"). Those who follow God's laws delight in them for they understand how to live life correctly.

The righteous are those who know how to make the right decision, to choose the right path in life. They know not to associate with the wicked. The parallel structure in the Hebrew verses emphasized what the wise person does not do. The wise person does not walk (*halak*), stand (*'amadh*), or sit (*yashav*) with those who refuse to follow God's laws, i.e. the wicked (*rasha'*, those who have already acted against God's law), the sinners (*khatta'iym*, those who "miss the mark" and make the wrong decisions by not following God's law), and the scorners (*le'iym*, those who mock those who do follow God).

The Hebrew paints the picture of someone trying to lure people into doing something that is against God's law by enticing them into a conversation as they walk and talk together. As the conversation becomes more serious, someone stops walking and stands face to face with the detractor in order to talk about the ramifications of that decision, as the sinner literally tries to get the person to "miss the mark," to make the wrong choice. As the person gets pulled into the conversation, she or he and the sinner sit conspiring together. They actually begin to mock those whom they will scam, those who still follow the law of God.

The Psalm teaches, in contrast, that those who are happy are blessed because they are in a "right" relationship with God as they sit and meditate, take a stand in, and walk daily in God's law through the everyday choices of their lives.

The simile the Psalmist used to illustrate what it is like to follow God's law—a tree—was full of historical imagery for the Hebraic hearer/reader. In the book of Genesis, Adam and Eve had a choice to make about a tree. The serpent questioned them, "Are you allowed to eat from all of the trees in the garden?" Eve replied they could eat from any of the trees except the tree in the middle of the garden, and so the choice was set before them. Do they eat of the fruit from the one tree God told them to avoid, one which according to the

Study Bible

See the Excursus: "*'Ashre*," *NISB*, 754.

biblical text was good for food, a delight to the eyes, and desired because it helped make one wise? They chose against God, and so the consequences followed. Curses were invoked, and Adam and Eve were banned from the Garden of Eden because they delighted in the tree rather than God's word.

Study Bible

See the Excursus: "Wisdom and Life," *NISB*, 905.

They are Like the Tree of Wisdom

According to the Psalmist, those who now delight in God's law are like a tree of wisdom. These trees are planted by streams of water. One need only visit the Middle East for a short stay to appreciate its hot, dry, barren climate and water as a very precious a commodity. Throughout the Old Testament, starting with the book of Genesis, we have examples of people fighting over the rights to wells, the right to have water. The trees of Ps 1 have no concern about the water that nourishes them, for their roots are nourished and fed not by one stream, but by *streams* of water.

From the Christian perspective, it is hard not to hear Jesus' words to the Samaritan woman at the well who came looking for water.

> Jesus said to her, "Everyone who drinks of this water will be thirsty again, but those who drink of the water that I will give them will never be thirsty. The water that I will give will become in them a spring of water gushing up to eternal life" (John 4:13-15, NRSV).

Or Jesus' words at the end of one of the festivals in Jerusalem:

> Let anyone who is thirsty come to me, and let the one who believes in me drink. As the scripture has said, "out of the believer's heart shall flow rivers of living water" (John 7:37-38, NRSV).

These streams of water allow the trees to bear fruit in season, and their leaves do not wither; instead, they prosper in all they do.

Throughout the biblical tradition, you only needed to look at the fruit a tree bore to tell if the tree was good or bad. One could argue the first commandment given in the book of Genesis was for humankind to be "fruitful" and multiply (Gen 1:22).

> A good tree cannot bear bad fruit, nor can a bad tree bear good fruit. Every tree that does not bear good fruit is cut down and thrown into the fire. Thus you will know them by their fruits (Matt 7:18-20, NRSV).

The Wicked are Like Chaff

Section two, vv. 4-6, outlines what happens to the wicked or those who choose not to follow God's laws. The Psalmist uses the simile of chaff in the wind to represent the wicked. During the process of harvesting, usually in the afternoon when the wind picked up, the winnower would throw what was harvested into the air, and the wind would blow away the chaff (that which was of no value). The grain (the fruit of the crop) would drop at the winnower's feet.

John the Baptist combines the imagery of fruit and chaff when he warned the Pharisees and Sadducees.

> Even now the ax is lying at the root of the trees; every tree therefore that does not bear good fruit is cut down and thrown into the fire. "I baptize you with water for repentance, but one who is more powerful than I is coming after me; I am not worthy to carry his sandals. He will baptize you with the Holy Spirit and fire. His winnowing fork is in his hand, and he will clear his threshing floor and will gather his wheat into the granary; but the chaff he will burn with unquenchable fire" (Matt 3:-12, NRSV).

And the prophet Jeremiah used the imagery of a dry shrub in the desert and a fruitful tree planted by water when he warned:

> Thus says the LORD: Cursed are those who trust in mere mortals and make mere flesh their strength, whose hearts turn away from the LORD. They shall be like a shrub in the desert, and shall not see when relief comes. They shall live in the parched places of the wilderness, in an uninhabited salt land. Blessed are those who trust in the LORD, whose trust is the LORD. They shall be like a tree planted by water, sending out its roots by the stream. It shall not fear when heat comes, and its leaves shall stay green; in the year of drought it is not anxious, and it does not cease to bear fruit (Jer 17:5-8, NRSV).

Dorsey outlines Ps 1 with four part symmetry:

a the righteous keep separate from the wicked (1:1-2)

b the fruitful, secure state of the righteous (1:3)

b' the barren, insecure state of wicked (1:4)

a' the wicked kept separate from the (blessed) righteous on judgment day (1:5-6)

The Psalm ends with a chiasm where the thought pattern is a b b'a'.

> Therefore the wicked will not stand in the judgment,
> nor sinners in the congregation of the righteous;
> for the LORD watches over the way of the righteous,
> but the way of the wicked will perish.

Now it is the wicked who will not be able to stand with the righteous, nor sit in the congregation of the righteous, for their walk will lead to destruction.

Who are you walking, standing and sitting with in your life? Are you more like chaff blowing in the wind or a fruitful well watered tree? The choice is yours.

Sources

David A. Dorsey, *The Literary Structure of the Old Testament: a Commentary on Genesis-Malachi* (Grand Rapids, MI: Baker Academic, 1999).

The Majesty of God and the Role of Humans

Lectionary Loop

Trinity Sunday, Year A, C, Psalm 8
New Year's Day, Year A, B, C, Psalm 8
Thursday of Easter Week, Year A, B, C, Psalm 8
Proper 22, Year B, Psalm 8

The Superscription or Title: The Director, the Gittith and "For David"

One summer when I was a kid and we were vacationing at the shore, my father got us up in the middle of the night to go to the beach to watch a meteor shower. It was while lying on the beach looking up at those "shooting stars" that I got my first taste of how small our planet really is, how great God's universe is, and how awesome it is that God cares for us. Those are the feelings I believe the author of Ps 8 was trying to convey.

Outline of Psalm 8

Psalm 8 contains a superscription or title, and although the titles were added later, they still give insight into how the psalms were used. This title gives the instructions: "for the director of music according to the *gittith*." There are fifty-five other psalms also written to "the director of music." Psalm 8 was probably used by the guilds of singers during the second temple period.

No one is quite sure what the word *gittith* means. It could indicate the type of musical instrument the music of the psalm was to be played upon, like a lyre. Or, it could be a wine press indicating the time of year the psalm was to be used, for example at the end of the autumn harvest possibly during the festival of the booths or tabernacles. Or, *gittith* could mean the music associated with the Philistine city of Gath, or it could be the name of the psalm's tune.

It is interesting that these directions are also found in Pss 81 and 84. In the structure of the book of

Psalms, Pss 8, 81and 84 are psalms of praise that follow a series of lament or complaint psalms. It could be that "according to the *gittith*" indicates music or a ceremony of praise and joy needed to follow mournful psalms, just like the structure of lament psalms almost always end with thanksgiving and praise to God.

The Hebrew title also indicates Ps 8 is "*ldavid,*" meaning "to David." The Hebrew preposition "l" contains within its breadth of meanings that these psalms could have been written "for David," "to David," or "in regard to David." The name "David" can also stand for the person David or the household of David. There are seventy-two psalms in the Psalter that include the same Davidic heading. Scripture teaches that David was a singer of songs (1 Sam 16:14-23; 18:10; 2 Sam 1:17-27; Amos 6:5; the Dead Sea Scrolls indicated David wrote 4,050 psalms in 11QPs2); however, there is not enough evidence in the psalm to know if it were written by David or for David.

Psalm 8 is a hymn of praise to the majesty of God the creator and the distinct role of humans in God's creation. It contains an *inclusio* where the psalm begins and ends with the same phrase, "O Lord, our Sovereign, how majestic is your name in all the earth!" This sets the whole tone of the psalm as the psalmist lifts up the majesty of God's name in all the earth. The psalmist moves through the psalm declaring God's glory in the heavens, considering the worth of humankind, showing how God cares enough for human beings to place them over all the earth, and ends once again lifting up the majesty of the name of God in all the earth.

Dorsey (177) outlines Ps 8 as having four part symmetry:

a **refrain:** "O Yahweh, our Lord, how majestic is your name in all the earth!" (8:1a[8:2a])

- **b** **question:** In light of Yahweh's <u>glory</u> (*hôd*) revealed in the creation of the heavens and in the <u>works</u> (*ma'asê*) <u>of your fingers</u> of what value is humankind to Yahweh? (8:1b-4[8:2b-5])

    - **b5** **answer:** Humankind is valuable because Yahweh has given human beings glory (*kabôd*) and has put them in charge of "the works (*ma'asê*) of your hands" (8:5-8[8:6-9])

a5 refrain: "O Yahweh, our Lord, how majestic is your name in all the earth!" (8:9[8:10])

Lips of Children Versus the Enemy

As we move through the psalm, v. 2 in the Hebrew reads:

> From the lips of children and infants you ordained strength because of your enemies to silence the enemy and the avenger.

The parallelism with the verse sets up the irony of the situation. God will strengthen the weak, children and infants, because of God's enemies. It is the sound from the lips of children and infants that will silence the enemy and avenger. In the New Testament, Jesus uses this verse to silence his skeptics.

> The blind and the lame came to him (Jesus) in the temple, and he cured them. But when the chief priests and the scribes saw the amazing things that he did, and heard the children crying out in the temple, "Hosanna to the Son of David," they became angry and said to him, "Do you hear what these are saying?" Jesus said to them, "Yes; have you never read, 'Out of the mouths of infants and nursing babies you have prepared praise for yourself'?' " (Matt 21:14-16, NRS).

In our culture we have the proverbial saying, "out of the mouths of babes," meaning that children in their innocence often speak truth in a way that adults will not. The strength of that truth has a way of silencing people.

The irony of the sound of the children silencing the enemy sets up verse 3's irony that despite the grandeur of God's created universe, God cares for mere mortals and has put them in charge of the earth. The psalmist used language ("son of man") that came to have deep symbolic meaning in very different ways. For example in Ps 8:5 the Hebrew reads,

> What is man that you are mindful of him, the son of man that you care for him?

"Son of Man" (*ben adam*) is a term used 80 times in the book of Ezekiel to refer to the human being named Ezekiel. In the book of Daniel, the term takes on new meaning as it is used in a simile.

> In my vision at night I looked, and there before me was one like a *son of man*, coming with the clouds of heaven. He approached the Ancient of Days and was led into his presence. He was given authority, glory and sovereign power; all peoples, nations and men of every language worshiped him. His dominion is an everlasting dominion that will not pass away, and his kingdom is one that will never be destroyed" (Dan 7:13-14, NIV).

Son of Man

In the book of Daniel, the term of "Son of Man" can mean *messiah, faithful Jews*, or an angelic being, usually referring to either Gabriel or Michael. By the time of the New Testament Gospels, the title becomes associated with Jesus. The biblical translations of the rest of Ps 8 are dependent on which interpretation is used for son of man: humankind/mortals or messiah. Notice the use of the term "son of man" contrasted with "mortals" and the singular and plural pronouns associated with each.

> When I consider your heavens, the work of your fingers, the moon and the stars, which you have set in place, what is man that you are mindful of him, the *son of man* that you care for *him*? You made him a little lower than the heavenly beings and crowned *him* with glory and honor. You made *him* ruler over the works of your hands; you put everything under his feet (Ps 8:3-6, NIV).

> When I look at your heavens, the work of your fingers, the moon and the stars that you have established; what are human beings that you are mindful of them, *mortals* that you care for *them*? Yet you have made *them* a little lower than God, and crowned *them* with glory and honor. You have given *them* dominion over the works of your hands; you have put all things under *their* feet (Ps 8:3-6, NRSV).

The Hebrew text actually says "son of man" and uses singular masculine pronouns. At the time the psalm was written, the sense of the term "son of man" probably meant mortal human beings as the psalmist wondered how such a majestic creator God could possibly have cared so much for mere human beings to be willing to give them dominion over all the earth.

By the time of the Gospels, Jesus identifies himself with the title, "son of man," and after Jesus' resurrection, the writer of the Book of Hebrews identifies Jesus with Ps 8.

> Now God did not subject the coming world, about which we are speaking, to angels. But someone has testified somewhere, "What are human beings that you are mindful of them, or mortals, that you care for them? You have made them for a little while lower than the angels; you have crowned them with glory and honor, subjecting all things under their feet." Now in subjecting all things to them, God left nothing outside their control. As it is, we do not yet see everything in subjection to them, but we do see Jesus, who for a little while was made lower than the angels, now crowned with glory and honor because of the suffering of death, so that by the grace of God he might taste death for everyone (Heb 2:5-9 NRSV).

Notice the difference in translation of Ps 8:5 in the Book of Hebrews. That is because the Hebrew text reads, "a little lower than God" sometimes read as "less than the gods" or "heavenly beings," while the writer of Hebrews followed the Greek translation of Ps 8:5 that uses the word "angels." Both translations stress the incredible responsibility God has placed on humanity. The writer of Hebrews argues that humans are not crowned with glory, nor do they have everything in subjection to them; but Jesus, since his resurrection, is crowned with glory and honor, and everything is in subjection to him.

In vv. 7-8, the psalmist then lists all of the works of God's hands over which humans now have dominion: sheep, oxen, beasts of the field, birds of the air, and fish of the sea, recalling God's original decree in Gen 1:26,

> Then God said, "Let us make humankind in our image, according to our likeness; and let them have dominion over the fish of the sea, and over the birds of the air, and over the cattle, and over all the wild animals of the earth, and over every creeping thing that creeps upon the earth" (Gen 1:26, NRS).

Study Bible

See the "Excursus": Dominion or Dependence?" *NISB*, 8.

Humans Given Honor

The psalmist has now defended and explicated the psalm's opening statement, "O Lord, our Sovereign, how majestic is your name in all the earth!" This psalm is a psalm of orientation that exudes confidence in the created order and stability of God's universe. God made everything on the earth and above in the heavens. This majestic God gave humans dominion over all that God created and, in doing that, also gave humans a place of honor and glory. The psalm ends as it began:

> O Lord, our Sovereign, how majestic is your name in all the earth!

Reflections

1. Does the fact that some of the Psalms may have been written *for* David rather than *by* David change the value of what they teach us?
2. What experiences have yoiu had where children have said "the darnedest things" and spoken the truth in the situation?
3. Do you view this Psalm as a treatise on why humans are important or a prophecy of the "son of man" as a messiah figure yet to come and fulfilled in Jesus, or both?

"Something Borrowed"

Liturgical Borrowing

Throughout the history of the church, followers of Jesus Christ have "borrowed" from the popular media of their cultures in order to convey the Good News of Jesus Christ. In the New Testament, some scholars suggest 1 Cor 13 and Phil 2:1-11 might have been borrowed hymns of their day. In Acts 17 in his address on the Areopagus, Paul, in order to get his point across, freely quoted from Epimenides and Aratus, whose writings would have been familiar to the Athenians in that time period. Some of the church hymn lyrics from the 1500's were put to the popular secular songs of their day; and in the movie "Sister Act" the nuns use popular songs with a Christian twist, and the attendance at their church services soars. In my own church, we use the tune "Mary Had a Little Lamb" with words of welcome that our children sing every time a child is baptized.

Psalm 29 is an indication that this "borrowing" from the surrounding culture of the day has been going on for thousands of years because it has been identified as a Yahwistic adaptation of an older Canaanite hymn for liturgical use. We see evidence of this when we look at the geography of the psalm as it moves from the Mediterranean, over Lebanon, and Sirion and then down through the wilderness of Kadesh; the vocabulary and grammar used (i.e., *bny 'lym*, "sons of the gods"); the structure of the repetitive parallelism common to Ugaritic (the language of the Canaanites) epics (abc:abd:abe in vv. 1-2, and 4-5); the concept of Yahweh (not Baal) overcoming the

Lectionary Loop

Baptism of the Lord, Year A, B, C, Psalm 29
Trinity Sunday, Year B, Psalm 29

forces of chaos and being enthroned Lord over the earth and sea.

The Title and Psalm Classifications

The title indicates that Ps 29 is "*ldavid,*" (to or for David). This raises the question of whether David adapted the Canaanite hymn, using the form of hymns common in his day, or whether an unknown psalmist adapted it in honor of David.

Psalm 29 is considered a hymn of praise, a victory hymn and an enthronement psalm. It starts off with a call to worship telling the heavenly court to give praise to Yahweh. The reason for that praise is the thundering power of the voice of Yahweh, depicted in a thunder storm blowing in off the sea, over the mountains in the north, and down through the wilderness in the south. The psalm ends with the victorious Yahweh being enthroned over the resulting flood and with a hope that Yahweh will strengthen his people and bless them with peace.

The Storm

Have you ever watched a thunderstorm come in? I have vivid memories as a child playing on the beach watching a thunderstorm roll in over the ocean. First the sky turns gray while the water begins to churn. White caps form on the water as the wind picks up. Beach umbrellas and chairs start to fly. People scramble inland as the thunder rolls and the lightening strikes at the sea.

The psalmist does a beautiful job of painting the thunderstorm rolling in. The voice of the Lord is over the waters; then it thunders, and the water becomes "mighty waters" as the storm grows. The storm moves inland, and the wind of the storm makes things fly and skip about. The voice of the Lord thunders (seven times in this psalm, the Hebrew number of completion), and the lightening begins to flash. The wilderness shakes, and the trees dance in the wind; suddenly the storm is over.

The Lord now sits enthroned upon the flood. Some scholars believe this represents the ancient fight of creation where Yahweh once again defeats Yam, the god

Reflections

1. What difference does it make if the material we use to worship God is "borrowed" or adapted from the popular culture of our day? Is it acceptable to worship God with bar tunes, rock, rap, hip-hop, poets of our day? What are the criteria for "acceptable" borrowing?
2. How do we ascribe to God the honor due his name?
3. Most of the surrounding cultures of the Israelites believed there were many gods and they were polytheistic in nature. Throughout the Old Testament the Israelites are warned not to follow other gods. Does it make a difference if the ancient Israelite religion was first henotheistic and then monotheistic in faith? How do you view the concept of God presiding over his court of angels or as Romans puts it "powers and principalities"?
4. Is God the God of nature? Does God control thunder storms, tsunamis, earthquakes, hurricanes? Does nature show he power of the wrath of God or is nature simply a metaphor of what God's power is like? Should we pray to God to help control the power of the natural world aound us?

of chaotic waters. It is Yahweh who is more powerful than the storm and brings order out of the chaos of the storm, or as Brueggemann would say, brings a "new orientation," a new beginning.

"Sons of Gods"

The opening verse of Ps 29 in the Hebrew text begins, "Ascribe to Yahweh, sons of gods . . ." The reference to other gods or divine beings can also be found in Pss 82, 86, 95, 96, 135, 136, and 138. It is one of the phrases that has raised the interesting question, "How soon did the religion of the Israelites become monotheistic (a belief in one and only one God)?" Was the religion of the Israelites at first henotheistic (a belief in a ruling god over lesser gods) and/or monolatry (a belief in worshiping one specific god among all the gods)?

The term *bny 'lym* has been translated as "sons of gods," (NJB), "heavenly beings," (NRSV) "mighty ones," (NKJV, NIV) and "sons of the mighty" (NAU). The term may refer to the pantheon of gods originally thought to have surrounded the Canaanite god El, or to the divine beings that minister in the heavenly world. In any case, it is this pantheon of heavenly beings called to worship Yahweh.

Study Bible

See the Excursus: "Creation: Ordering Chaos," *NISB*, 5.

Yahweh Enthroned

The court of heavenly beings now cries, "Glory," at the recognition of Yahweh's power. Yahweh is enthroned as King over the flood, over the chaos of the natural world divinely subdued. Yahweh is now King forever.

Psalm 29 ends with a desire for God to bless his people with strength and to grant them peace in the midst of the chaotic world they live in. In the New Testament it is Jesus who is able to bring order out of the storm, peace out of chaos, and have his disciples questioning in awe, "Who was this that even the wind and sea obeyed?" (Mark 4:35-41).

Forgiveness of Sin

> **Lectionary Loop**
> **Lent 4, Proper 2, 6, and 26, Year C, Psalm 32**
> **Lent 1, Year A, Psalm 32**

What Sin Feels Like

When I was a child, my older teenaged sister went out and bought her own brand of shampoo instead of using the family's communal bottle. One day I purposely washed my hair with her shampoo. When she found what I had done, steam started coming out of her ears. She came to my room and told me she knew I had used her shampoo, and further she wasn't going to tell our parents because they would know in the morning by looking at me: since I had used her shampoo without asking her permission, my hair was now going to turn bright green and fall out by morning!

I spent all night wide awake checking to see if my hair had started changing color or was even on my head. The next morning, I was very relieved to find my own hair still on my head and its normal color. Certainly I should not have taken my sister's shampoo without asking, but her "curse" upon me, as childlike as it was, gave me a taste of what it feels like when we sin against someone else by betraying their trust or taking what is theirs. Forty years later I still remember that sleepless night worrying about what would happen to my hair and what my parents would do to me when they found out, sorry that what I had done had affected my relationship with my sister. It was a long time before she trusted me again. If you have ever done something you know you were not supposed to do, ever hurt someone you did not mean to hurt and felt the fear and pain of that error, then you understand the emotions behind Ps 32.

The Need for Forgiveness

Psalm 32 addresses the need for the forgiveness of sins. The psalmist starts out in vv. 1-2 by reminding us what it feels like to be free of sin. A literal interpretation of the Hebrew paints a picture of sin as if it were a great weight being lifted off of us. The sin is then hidden, concealed, covered over, never to be seen again. God does not hold the sin against us, and our spirit no longer has any deceit within it—we are truly free.

In vv. 3-4, the psalmist reminded us what it is like to have sin remain within us. We worry day and night so much so that we can't eat, we can't sleep, and our bodies start to waste away. Because of his secret sin, the psalmist believed God's hand was upon him day and night sapping his strength. These verses have been interpreted to refer variously to the psychological and physiological effects sin can have upon us.

Teaching Tip

Work through "Session 1 'Moments of Truth' Psalm 32" in *The Pastor's Bible Study*, 1:165-168.

The Need for Prayer

In v. 5 the psalmist confessed his sin to God, and the psalmist immediately felt God's forgiveness from the guilt of his sin. Now that the psalmist is feeling the relief he outlined in vv. 1-2, he addresses all people of faith who turn to God in prayer. The Hebrew of v. 6 is unclear and can be read in two different ways. On the one hand, it can mean the faithful need to pray to God while God may still be found for there will be a time when they cannot reach God. The psalmist used familiar imagery: when the rains come and suddenly cause a "rush of mighty waters," possibly symbolizing a time of great distress or even death. On the other hand, v. 6 may mean the faithful are to pray to God so that the "rush of mighty waters" will not reach them. Perhaps it was even written in such a way so that both meanings apply. The faithful have only a certain amount of time when they will be able to call upon God. If they reach God in time, God will save them from the "rush of the mighty waters." Based on vv. 3-4 where the psalmist described what happens when you hold sin in and do not confess it, it is best to turn to God as quickly as possible before the sin becomes so great it overwhelms. Thus, those who are faithful in prayer as a constant in their lives will be prepared for the time of distress whenever it comes.

Trust in the Lord

In v. 7 the psalmist acknowledges God as his hiding place, his protection in times of trouble. (In session 5, we will consider Ps 71:3 where God is referred to as a "rock, refuge, fortress.") When the psalmist is in God's care, songs and shouts of deliverance and salvation are sure to surround him no matter what the situation.

In v. 8 it is unclear whether it is the psalmist or God who will be doing the teaching and keeping an eye upon the student. In v. 9 the student is warned not to be like a stubborn mule whose temper has to be tamed and who acts without understanding, and v. 10 ends with the psalmist telling those who have confessed their sins and are once again in right relationship with God and neighbor to rejoice, be glad and sing to the Lord.

Maskil, *Selah*, and Psalm Classifications

The title attributes this as a psalm of David, although there is not enough evidence within the psalm to know if it was written by David or for David. The title identifies this psalm as a *Maskil* (along with Pss 42; 44; 45; 52-55; 74; 78; 88; 89; and 142). The Hebrew participle Maskil can mean either a didactic poem, and/or a skillful, artistic song. Since the music of the Psalms has not survived, we have no way of knowing.

We can surmise that Ps 32 is a didactic poem. We learned in Ps 1 (Session 1) that everyone has a choice in life, either to follow God or not to follow God. Ps 32 gives hope to those who, for whatever reason, have chosen not to follow God and have allowed sin to enter their lives; it offers the good news that when a sinner confesses sin to God, God forgives, and the sinner is once again in communion with God, surrounded by God's love, shouting with joy at the salvation God offers. Bruggemann (94–98) identifies Ps 32 as a psalm that identifies the disorientation and guilt that sin causes as well as the reorientation of what it means to be in relationship with God once again.

Reflections

1. Talk about a time when you know you did something wrong and tried to keep it a secret from everyone else. Were you successful? How did you feel while you were keeping the secret? How did you make amends if you ever did? How did you feel once the secret was known?
2. Are there times today when it is appropriate to keep a sin a secret? What might be the benefits of confessing your sin to another person?
3. Is there a need for a more public confession of our sins as in the Roman Catholic practice of confession, or is praing to God at home alone sufficient?
4. Using the formula provided, write a Thanksgiving psalm.

Psalm 32 also includes the word *Selah* at the end of vv. 4, 5, and 7. No one is really sure what the word means. Based on the Hebrew root of the word, cognate languages, and the Targums, some have speculated that it means: a pause or interlude in the performance of the psalm, a notation about the musical accompaniment, a change in instruments or voices, a prompt to begin the voices or instruments at that point, an indication to repeat or go to a refrain, possibly an indication that the word "forever" be said or that the worshipper should prostrate herself or himself at that point in the psalm.

Ps 32 is classified by some scholars as a Thanksgiving psalm:

1. It begins with the psalmist's intention to praise God or with a blessing (as in the case of Ps 32 vv. 1-2).
2. There is the lament or the reason why the psalmist called on the name of God (because of the unnamed sin of vv. 3-5).
3. The psalmist thanks God for answering the prayers (v. 7),
4. The congregation is called on to thank God too, (vv. 6, 8-11) (Longman: 30-31).

Study Bible

See the "Excursus: Penitential Psalms," *NISB*, 797.

Ps 32 is also known as one of the six classic penitential psalms identified by the Christian liturgical tradition (along with Pss 6; 38; 51; 102; 130; and 143). "Confession and divine compassion, mortality and salvation, repentance and forgiveness lie at the heart of the Christian appropriation of all seven penitential psalms" (*NISB*, 797).

A Psalm of the Aged

The Problems of Aging

There is a saying in our culture that the only two things we have to do in life are pay taxes and die. I would like to add one more thing to this list—grow old. From the moment we are born we begin to grow old. Some may argue we grow better or stronger at least until our late teens and early twenties, but should you live into your thirties and beyond, you begin to feel the tell tale signs of growing older. You cannot run quite as fast or jump quite as high. It begins to get a littler harder to take off weight and keep it off. At night your vision isn't quite what it used to be, and in a crowded room you find yourself asking, "What did you say?" "Senior moments" begin to occur as you try to remember what it was you were looking for or where it was you were heading. The aches and pains begin, and one begins to feel his or her mortality and wonder, "What does life hold for me now?" and, "Where is God in this equation?" Now that the gray hairs are starting to show and the strength isn't what it used to be, how do I live my life? Will the God I trusted in my youth be there in my old age? Psalm 71 is an individual lament psalm written by a person who had followed God since birth but now questioned if God would be there as he grows old.

The Title

Although Ps 71 has no title, we know the psalmist was a musician since vv. 22-23 allude to his ability to play the harp and the lyre and since v. 25 conveys the psalmist's ability to sing. The psalmist is also well versed in the other psalms as many of the verses of Ps 71 are found elsewhere in the collection:

Lectionary Loop

Epiphany 4, Proper 16, Year C, Psalm 71:1-6
Tuesday of Holy Week, Year A, B, C, Psalm 71:1-14

vv. 1-3, are found in Ps 31:1-3a
vv. 5-6, are found in Ps 22:9-10
v. 12a, is found in Ps 22:1b, 11, 19
v. 12b, is found in Pss 38:22; 40:13
v. 13, is found in Pss 35:4, 26; 22:30
v. 18, is found in Ps 22:30-31
v. 19, is found in Ps 36:6

The psalmist is someone who has known God since birth (v. 6) and has worshiped God throughout his youth (vv. 5-6, 17). The psalmist is also someone who is beginning to feel the problems of an aging body (vv. 9, 18) and who has the wisdom of maturity to be able to look back on how God has saved him in the past with the hope that God will help him now (vv. 20-21). Because of this, readers often speculate Ps 71 may have been written by David in his later life although there is no conclusive evidence for this view within the psalm. There is evidence that the Davidic title from Ps 70 should apply to Ps 71 (since the LXX gives Ps 71 a Davidic title), as well as semantic and manuscript evidence supporting the idea that Pss 70 and 71 were meant to be read together.

Rock, Refuge, Fortress

In v. 3, the terms "rock," "refuge," "fortress," are metaphors used throughout the Old Testament to describe the character of God.

The term "rock" (as found in Gen 49:24; Deut 32:4; 1 Sam 2:2; 2 Sam 22:2; Pss 18:2; 19:14; 61:2; 92:15; and Isa 26:4) refers to God who should be the very foundation of our lives. Jesus used this imagery in Matt 7:24-27 and Luke 6:46-49 when he taught the parable about the wise man who built his house on the rock and the foolish man who built his house on the sand. It was the house built on the rock—on the solid strength, dependability, security, and protection of God—that would be able to withstand all the storms of life. Likewise, it is evident within the psalm that God had been the "rock" for the psalmist.

The term "refuge" (as found in 2 Sam 22:3, 31; Pss 2:12; 5:11; 16:1; 17:7; 18:2; 31:2; 34:8; 36:7; 46:1; 59:16; 62:8; 91:2; 144:2; Prov 30:5; and Nah 1:7) refers to God as a place or stronghold of safety and protection. Taking refuge in Yahweh probably referred to an ancient custom of seeking asylum and protection in the sanctuary. All who seek God for refuge, no matter what the upheaval in their lives, will find God a safe haven who provides for their every need. The psalmist is now looking for God to be his refuge as he grows older.

And the term "fortress" (as found in 2 Sam 22:2; Pss 18:2; 31:2; 59:16) uses military imagery to show God as the source of safety, protection and rest for all those in need. The psalmist is looking for God to be a fortress who will keep those who are wicked, cruel and unjust, away from him.

Lament Structure

Psalm 71 is an untitled individual lament found in book two of the book of Psalms. All laments have a basic form that can include:

- calling upon the name of God or the invocation
- a plea asking God for help
- the reason why the psalmist needs help often called the lament or the complaint
- a confession of sin or an assertion of innocence
- calling upon God to deal with the enemy (revenge)
- confidence that God will help
- voicing a hymn of praise, thanksgiving, or blessing

The psalmist has done a masterful job of interweaving the basic form of the individual lament:

- calling upon God: v. 1a
- asking for God's help: vv. 1b-4, 12, 18a
- expressing the complaint or lament: is God rejecting the psalmist in old age?: vv. 9-11
- reminding God of the times the psalmist has praised God since birth: vv. 5-8, 14-17, 18b-19
- asking God to disgrace the psalmist's accusers: vv. 13, 24b
- confiding in God's response: vv. 20-21, 24
- voicing a hymn of praise: vv. 22-24

Dorsey (180) analyzes Ps 71 as having five part symmetry:

a plea to God for help (71:1-4)
b statement of trust (71:5-9)
c prayer for help from the enemies (71:10-13)
b' ? statement of trust (71:14-19)
a' vow to praise God for God's help (71:20-24)

Since there is no information within Ps 71 that helps us place it historically, there are a variety of suggestions as to how this psalm may have been used. It has been variously identified as a psalm read by the king during the autumn festival in pre-exilic Israel; as a "protective psalm" read when there was an impending crisis, asking God for protection from danger and various enemies; as a prayer in post-exilic Israel since there was always an impending crisis; as a psalm read by those literally taking refuge in the temple for various reasons; as a prayer for the sick; and as a prayer after the temple was rebuilt used on fast days by those waiting for "a new glory from Yahweh" (Tate: 212).

Our Hope

It is so easy to praise God in your youth when life is going well. You are strong and able; you have your whole life ahead of you and all of your family around you. In some ways it gets harder as your body starts to fail, as loved ones die, and as you realize your time here on earth is growing short. Mid-life crises occur as you begin to ponder what it is you thought you would do with your life, but, for whatever reason, you haven't done, and what it is you have actually done with your life. You begin to wonder, where is God in all of this and will God still be there for me as I grow old? Your faith begins to be tested no matter who you are. Psalm 71 gives us the assurance that no matter how bad things get, God will revive us and bring us "out of the depths" to continue to praise God's name. God will help us deal with the wicked, the cruel and the unjust in our lives. The New Testament takes it a step further. God will not just revive us daily to fight the battles of life, but when we die, through Jesus Christ, we will be resurrected from the dead. Our battles with the wicked,

Reflections

Describe times in your life you know God has been there for you. Was there ever a time you felt God was not there for you? How do you know God will be there for you in the future?

Teaching Tip

Using the basic form of a lament, write a lament about something that is of concern in your life.

the cruel, the unjust and even our own bodies on this earth will finally be over. We know that as we grow older, our bodies grow weaker, but as we walk with God, our spirits are renewed day by day, preparing us for the day we are finally called home to eternal glory (2 Cor 4:16).

A City Lament

Lectionary Loop

Proper 20, Psalm 79:1-9, Year C

The Title

On September 11, 2001, planes controlled by terrorists flew into the World Trade Centers in New York City and the Pentagon, and one plane crash-landed in Pennsylvania before reaching its intended target. Approximately 3,000 people died that day. A national lament went up wondering where was God? How could God allow this to happen? What did the United States do to deserve this? This is not the first time these questions have been raised when a national disaster has occurred. These questions can be traced in the ancient writings of the Mesoptamian city laments, the biblical book of Lamentations, the Pseudipigraphal book the Psalms of Solomon, and in the Hebrew canonical communal lament Ps 79.

In its title, Ps 79 is attributed to Asaph. King David appointed the Levites to carry the ark from the house of Obededom and asked them to appoint their kindred as the singers to play on musical instruments and make loud sounds of joy as the ark was moved. Aspah, son of Berechiah, from the line of Gershom, son of Levi was appointed as a singer who was to sound the bronze cymbals as the ark was moved (1 Chr 15:11- 25). When the ark was moved to the tent David had pitched for it, Aspah was appointed to minister before the ark (1 Chr 16:4-6). After King Hezekiah restored the temple, he ordered the Levites to sing praise to God using the words of David and the seer Aspah (2 Chr 29:30). Aspah's name also appears on Pss 50; 73-83. Given its historical time frame, Ps 79 was probably written to honor Asaph or possibly to be performed in the style of Asaph.

Psalm 79 is believed to have been written after the unthinkable had happened. The Israelites thought they had it made. Despite the prophets' words of warning, the Israelites figured it did not matter if they took advantage of the poor, the needy, the widow, the orphan, or the foreigner within their midst. After all, they had the temple and the ark of the covenant; hence, they had the very presence of God to protect and provide for them. So it was with horrified surprise that they watched the King of Babylon come in, deport the leadership class of Jerusalem, loot the Temple and utterly destroy Jerusalem in 597 BCE while the Edomites cheered them on. Brueggemann (71–74) identifies Ps 79 as a psalm of disorientation as the people of Israel are dealing with the realization of the destruction of Jerusalem and the temple and their desire for restoration or "new orientation" in the vengeance and healing power of Yahweh.

Psalm 79 contains characteristics of a city-lament genre. These works raise the question of Divine Abandonment. Where was God? How could God have allowed this to happen? The authors believed that a city could only be destroyed if God left the city and that God must have been angry with them in order for God to have abandoned them:

79:4 We have become a taunt to our neighbors,
mocked and derided by those around us.
79:5 How long, O LORD? Will you be angry forever?
Will your jealous wrath burn like fire?
79:10a Why should the nations say, "Where is their God?"

They begin to assign responsibility as they question what they must have done wrong for God to be angry:

79:8a Do not remember against us the iniquities of our ancestors:
79:9b deliver us, and forgive our sins,
for your name sake.

City Lament Genre

The city-lament genre identifies the Divine Agent of Destruction, the means by which God allowed the city to be destroyed, whether it was an enemy as in the case of Ps 79 or a natural disaster like an earthquake:

79:1 O God, the *nations* have come into your inheritance....

In this case "the nations," probably refers to the Babylonians and the Edomites who sat by and cheered while Jerusalem was being destroyed.

The city-lament psalms genre goes on to detail the aspects of destruction that have taken place. The city and its temple:

79:1 O God, the nations have come into your inheritance;
they have defiled your holy temple; they have laid Jerusalem in ruins.
79:7 For they have devoured Jacob
and laid waste his habitation.

And the inhabitants of the city:

79:2 They have given the bodies of your servants
to the birds of the air for food,
the flesh of your faithful to the wild animals of the earth.
79:3 They have poured out their blood like water
all around Jerusalem,
and there was no one to bury them.
79:11a Let the groans of the prisoners come before you....

Since they believed God had abandoned them, it is to God they plead for their rescue with the belief that God will return and restore them:

79:6 Pour out your anger on the nations
that do not know you,
and on the kingdoms
that do not call on your name.

79:8b let your compassion come speedily to meet us,
for we are brought very low.
79:9 Help us, O God of our salvation,
for the glory of your name;
deliver us, and forgive our sins,
for your name's sake.
79:10b Let the avenging of the outpoured blood of your servants
be known among the nations before our eyes.
79:11 Let the groans of the prisoners come before you;
according to your great power preserve those doomed to die;
79:12 Return sevenfold into the bosom of our neighbors
The taunts with which they taunted you, O Lord!
79:13 Then we your people, the flock of your pasture,
will give thanks to you forever;
from generation to generation we will recount your praise.

Seven-seven Times

In 79:12 the sevenfold return of their neighbors taunts are reminiscent of Lamach's desire in Gen 4:24 to avenge not just seven times but seventy-seven times, which Jesus addresses in Matt 18:21-22 when he tells Peter he should not forgive just seven times, but seventy-seven times. (See Session 9 for how far the Israelites were willing to take their revenge.)

Dorsey (175) identifies Ps 79 as having three-part symmetry:

a5 report of harm done to Judah by the nations (79:1-4)
- the nations have poured out their blood; they have given the bodies of your servants to the birds
- we have become a taunt to our neighbors

b CENTER: prayer for God's help and forgiveness (79:5-9)

a5 cry for vengeance for harm done to Judah by the nations (79:10-13)
- the nations; let the outpoured blood of your servants be known among the nations
- repay sevenfold the taunts of our neighbors

The structure of the city-lament genre is such that one can use it both to express grief and to ask questions about almost any national disaster that occurs. Although written almost 2,500 years ago, hear the beginning words of Psalm 79 as applied to 9/11/01 and the continuing terrorist attacks around the world:

O God, the nations have come into your inheritance;
    they have defiled your holy nation;
    they have laid the world trade towers in ruins.
They have given the bodies of your servants
    to the birds of the air for food,
    the flesh of your faithful to the wild animals of the earth.
They have poured out their blood like water
    all around New York, Baghdad, Beirut, and London,
    and there is little left to bury.
We have become a taunt to our neighbors,
    mocked and derided by those around us.
How long, O Lord? Will you be angry forever?
    Will your jealous wrath burn like fire?
Pour out your anger on the nations
    that do not know you,
and on the kingdoms
    that do not call on your name.

Even though psalms classified as laments are among the most prominent of all the psalms they are rarely used in Christian worship services. Yet it is these very words that help us put words to our grief and help us approach God with our questions, our doubts, our anger. They allow us to share the psalmist's assurance that, no matter what, God is still there. We need to reclaim these psalms and use them for the times of grief that come to every person and every nation.

Reflections

1. Are the questions raised in the psalm ones we have learned to ask when national disaster, either natural or human in origin, strikes? Or, are the questions raised in the psalm ones that are innate in the human heart when the unthinkable happens?
2. How does the Christian perspective shape our desire for vengeance and our need to forgive? How do we balance the tension between the call to forgive and the powerful emotional response such events raise in us? If we forgive in the name of Jesus, do we then hold those who have brought the destruction accountable in some way? What should happen to Osama Ben Laden, Saddam Hussein, or other terrorists?
3. How willing are we to be honest with God about our "negative" emotions/questions?
4. The Psalmist concludes: "Pour out your anger on the nations that do not know you, and on the kingdoms that do not call on your name." But the terrorists who attacked the World Trade Center and Pentagon in 2001, along with many of the suicide bombers today, were fervent believers in the same God, whom they call Allah. How do we reconcile the fact that Christians and Muslim extremists both call on the name of God and believe God is "on their side?"

The Justice of God

Lectionary Loop

Proper 10 and 15, Year C, Psalm 82

Just Judges

In 2005, the court system of the United States allowed a husband to remove the feeding tube of his wife, Terri Shiavo, who was ruled to be in a "persistent vegetative state." This ruling led to Terry's death and embroiled the United States in difficult questions: Should judges be guided by their religious beliefs as well as by the laws of the United States? What should the proper religious position of a judge be? Should that position affect the way a judge rules? Should the laws of the United States be changed to reflect a specific religious viewpoint or standard about life? In Ps 82, God has come to judge those who judge the earth. For God there is a specific standard of what it means to judge justly.

The movement of Ps 82 flows from God taking a seat amidst the council of gods, to God confronting the council itself: God is concerned about their unjust judgments, God reveals the criteria they should be using to judge and the consequences of their failure to follow those criteria, and the end result that God will now judge the earth and all its nations, not just the Israelites.

Divine Council

In v. 1, God comes and sits amidst the divine council. Based on the Hebrew, this council could be a term borrowed from the neighboring Canaanite religion, referring to the pantheon of gods under the Canaanite high god El, showing that it is not El who is the high god; rather it is the Israelite God who is the high God. (There is evidence within the Bible of "borrowing" or "adapting" material from the surrounding religious cultures.) The divine council could also refer to the divine beings or angels that minister on the earth for God (Deut 32:8). Or, it could mean the earthly rulers God had placed in positions of authority on the earth (Deut 1:9-18; Judg 2:16; 2 Chr 19:4-7; Ps 72; Prov 29:14; Rom 13: 1-2). In any case, God had come to sit in judgment of those who are responsible for judging and ruling on earth to see if they have upheld God's standards.

Standards for Judges

In v. 2, God clearly outlines what these standards are: They are not to judge unjustly by showing partiality to the wicked, ignoring the weak, the orphan, the lowly, the needy, and the destitute. Rather, they are to rescue them from the hand of the wicked. That is what they have been called to do as judges of the earth. They are not to help take advantage of the powerless as others have done (Mic 3:9-11; Prov 24:23-24; Luke 18:2; John 7:24), but, rather, they are to help them. The standards God referred to are clearly outlined in the covenantal agreements God had with the Israelites.

If they chose to follow God and God's laws, which included providing for the orphan, the widow, the poor, the needy, God would bless all of Israel. But if they chose to disregard God, to side with the wicked and neglect those in need, God would curse them and the earth. The rulers God judges in Ps 82 have clearly rejected God and God's covenant, and now the consequences will be severe.

Shaken Foundation

Verse 5 reflects that the very foundations of the earth are being shaken because of the actions of these biased judges. "The foundation of the earth" is a phrase found throughout the Old Testament and usually refers to the pillars that are viewed as holding up the plate of the earth in the ancient Israelite view of how the world is structured (1 Sam 2:8; Job 9:6; 38:4-6; Ps 75:3; 104:5; Zech 12:1). It can also have a symbolic meaning that the very foundations of society are being shaken by the actions of these unjust judges.

Study Bible

See "Excursus: Covenant," *NISB*, 113, and "Excursus: The Righteousness of God," *NISB*, 2001

Verse 5b stresses that these judges have no idea that the very "foundations of the earth" are being shaken because the judges are not fulfilling the covenant. Because of that, v. 5a could be read in two ways. 1) It is the weak, orphan, lowly, needy and destitute who are walking around in darkness because the judges are not giving them the knowledge or the understanding to help them against the wicked; hence the very foundations of the earth are shaken. Or, 2) it is the judges who are walking around in darkness, lacking knowledge or understanding of the consequences of their unjust judging, which has shaken the very foundation of the earth.

Monotheism

In v. 6 God goes on to call those in positions of power "god,"; yet, they will all die like mortals. Jesus quotes this verse when he argues he was not blaspheming by calling himself God's son:

> NRSV: If those to whom the word of God came were called "gods"—and the scripture cannot be annulled—can you say that the one whom the Father has sanctified and sent into the world is blaspheming because I said, "I am God's Son?" (John 10:34-35).

Jesus' use of v. 6 still does not conclusively help define who the "gods" are. Are they human rulers who have received the word of God? Are they members of the pantheon of the High God, listening to the divine word at the council in v.1? Are they heavenly beings who minister on earth for God? We do not know, but the psalm assures us they will die like any mortal or fall like any prince who does not obey God.

The psalmist ends by calling on God to rise up and judge the earth. It is an inclusive cry that God is judge of ALL the nations, for only God can justly judge the whole earth and all those in it (Gen 18:25; 1 Chr 16:33; Pss 9:7-8; 58:11; 75:7; 94:2; 96:10, 13; 98:9; Isa 2:4; 3:13; 33:22; Heb 12:23b). McDaniel (175) interprets Ps 82:7-8 as once and for all putting away the question of polytheism, henotheism, and monolatry as all the gods of the nations are doomed to death and only one God (monotheism) is called upon to judge the earth.

Reflections

1. How do you understsand the tension between a judge's religious belief and the laws of the state or nation? What is the role of religious belief in the judicial process (jury duty)?
2. What are the injustices happening in our society that would draw the judgment of God on our nation? What injustices should we be doing something about?
3. What criteria do you use to vote for the candidates running for the various positions in your community and in the nation? Do you see it as part of your Christian responsibility to vote? How do he laws of the United States reflect the Judeo-Christian values of life?
4. What is the value of the separation of church and state in the laws of the United States? For the church? For the State?
5. How accountable are those in power to the promises they made to win the position and to the needs of the community?
6. How can we halp the powerless in our structures of society? As an individual? As a church?

Psalm 82 is a prophetic oracle in which God has come to judge those who judge the earth. There is not enough evidence found within Ps 82 to place it historically. The title tells us Ps 82 is a psalm of Asaph (Session 6) and is found in book three, which contains 17 psalms ascribed to or for Aspah or the sons of Korah. It does not use the name Yahweh at all but rather uses the name *Elohim* for God.

Psalm 82 contains an inclusio based on the concept of the power of God. God is seen in v. 1 as coming to sit in the midst of the council to pronounce judgment on the rulers of the earth and, in v. 8, the end of the psalm, it is God who will now judge the earth and all its nations.

In the New Testament it is Jesus who will come to judge the earth (John 5:27; 9:39; Acts 10:42; 17:31; 2 Tim 4:1; Jas 4:12; 1 Pet 4:5), and the parable of the sheep and the goats in Matt 25:31-46 highlights the fact that all of us have a responsibility, whether we consider ourselves in positions of power or not, to reach out a hand and help the powerless in our society for that is the law of love, the essence of the very foundations of the earth.

God's Dwelling Place

You only have to read the book of Psalms once through to have it affect your life. Inevitably one psalm or even one verse of a psalm will grab you in a way you were not expecting, as it begins to speak to your life. Psalm 84 is one of those psalms for me. Johannes Brahms put all of Ps 84 in his German Requiem (Opus 45). As soon as the music for the fourth movement begins to swell, and the chorus enters, you can almost imagine how truly beautiful God's dwelling place must be.

Sam Shoemaker, one of the co-founders of Alcoholics Anonymous, based his poem, *I Stand by the Door*, on Ps 84:10b with his desire to help people enter the doorway to God:

> I had rather be a door-keeper ...'
> So I stand by the door.

One of the fascinating and frustrating things about the Hebrew language is its ability to use one word to mean more than one thing. Many words in the Hebrew language have layers of meanings. This can also happen in the English language, which is why it is so important to understand the context of a text. As the classic example goes, there is a huge difference whether you are in front of a firing squad or in a burning building when you yell the word, "Fire!" The Old Testament writers often used the multiple meanings of words to their advantage. They would play with a word using it in such a way that, even knowing the context of a text, it is hard to decipher with certainty the meaning of the word. Or maybe the writer purposely wrote

Lectionary Loop

Second Sunday after Christmas, Year A, B, C, Psalm 84
The Feast of the Presentation of our Lord, Year A, B, C, Psalm 84
Proper 25, 84, Year C
Proper 16, Year B

it that way so that both meanings are equally viable, so that it means both things at the same time.

Layers of Meaning: Lovely/Beloved

The opening verse of Ps 84 contains such a word. The Hebrew word *yadid* that gets translated as "lovely" in the NRSV can also mean "beloved." Beloved is normally used when we talk about a person, but it can also be used in this case to mean the beloved place where Yahweh dwells. It is a very human trait for us to become so comfortable in a home in which we live or grow up in that it becomes beloved to us. The psalmist could well have written the word to mean both things: How lovely and beloved are the places where Yahweh dwells. The Hebrew word, which the NRSV translates as "dwelling place," is actually a plural form in the Hebrew, probably used for emphasis.The Hebrew word behind the NRSV's English translation "hosts" (*tsava'*) can be interpreted to mean "the armies of Yahweh," or "Yahweh, the Almighty." Hence, Yahweh, the Almighty, the head of all the powers of heaven and earth, lives in beautiful and beloved dwelling places.

In v. 2, the psalmist reveals that his soul, heart, and flesh all long to be with God. These words comprise the totality of a human being: the physical body (*basar*, the flesh), the place of decisions (*lev*, the heart), and the very life being (*nefesh*, the soul). Every part of the psalmist longs to be in the courts of Yahweh.

For the psalmist, the courts of Yahweh were at the temple. The very first tabernacle included inner and outer courts. By the time Herod's temple was erected, it contained four courts: the court of the Gentiles, the women's court, the court of Israel, and the priests' court. It was at the temple that the psalmist felt closest to Yahweh.

In vv. 3-4, not only does the psalmist feel at home in the temple courts but also the birds, the sparrow and the swallow feel at home there. It is almost as if the psalmist envies their ability to live in the temple courts, constantly singing praise to God.

Pilgrimage to Zion

In v. 5, happy are those who not only live in the temple, but who find their strength in Yahweh and are on their pilgrimage to Zion.

Reflections

1. Take some time to listen to Brahm's German Requiem and experience how the composer used and envisioned Ps 84.
2. Compare and contrast Psalm 84 with the poem, "I Stand by the Door" by Sam Shoemaker. (www.faithatwork.com/history/shoemaker/shoemaker–I_Stand.html)
3. When you think of the dwelling place of God, where and what do you think it is? What do you think heaven is like and why?
4. Trace the terms "heaven" and "Kingdom of God" throughout the Bible. Based on your research, how would you now define each of these terms?

Study Bible

See the "Excursus: Heart," *NISB*, 829.

In v. 6, the Valley of Baca can mean "the Valley of Weeping" or "the Valley of Balsam Trees." It is hard to know if the psalmist was referring to a valley (the Valley of Weeping), a place that is usually hard to traverse, but is now easily traveled through because of the early rains; or to a valley that is shaded by trees (the Valley of Balsam Trees), full of water, additionally blessed with the early rains. Either reality would constitute a blessing.

In v. 7, moving from "strength to strength" has been interpreted to mean either the gathering of the throngs of pilgrims as they draw closer to Jerusalem, or how a set number of pilgrims moves safely from rampart to rampart as they strategically approach their God of gods in Zion.

In vv. 8-9 the psalmist raises his voice in prayer to Yahweh, the God of his ancestor Jacob, asking God to bless the pilgrims' shield, the anointed of God, the king of Israel.

In vv. 10-12 the psalmist made the comparison that it is better to be the doorkeeper at the house of the Lord than to spend one day in the luxurious tents of the wicked. Happy/Blessed are the people who put their trust in Yahweh for it is God who guides (sun), protects (shield) and provides all that is needed for those who walk correctly in the paths of Yahweh.

Psalm Classification

Psalm 84 has been classified as both an "Individual Psalm of Confidence" where the psalmist shows trust and confidence in God no matter what else is happening as well as a "Psalm of Zion" written as a hymn of praise to God's sovereignty in Zion and used as pilgrims approached the city of Zion.

For Christians, this Psalm takes on a whole new meaning. When Jesus is asked to give a sign for why he drove the money changers out of the temple, he answered, "Destroy this temple, and in three days I will raise it up" (John 2:19). John goes on to explain that Jesus is talking about the temple of his body. It is through the temple of the risen Christ that the Christian is given the gift of eternal life in the beautiful and beloved dwelling place of God.

How Lovely Is Your Dwelling

Ps. 84 *Jean Janzen, 1991*

Jean Wiebe Janzen is a published poet who also teaches poetry writing at Fresno Pacific College and Eastern Mennonite College. She began writing hymns at the invitation of the Mennonite Church for their Hymnal: A Worship Book *(1992) where this text appears with the setting by Heinrich Schütz.*

Tune: ES IST EIN' ROS'
altered to 7.6.7.6.7.7.6.
Catholische Geistliche Kirchengesäng, *Cologne, 1599*

Revenge!

Lectionary Loop
Proper 22, Year C, Psalm 137

No "Sanitizing"

One of the things often noted about a number of the biblical stories is that the storytellers do not "sanitize" the lives of the biblical characters. They tell the stories of the biblical characters, warts and all. For example, we see David's love of God as well as his adultery with Bathsheba and the consequent murder of her husband Uriah (2 Sam 11). We read about Elijah's ability to stand up to 450 prophets of Baal (1 Kgs 18:1-40) and his inability to stand up to Queen Jezebel when she threatens his life (1 Kgs 19:1-3a). We follow Moses as he first asks God to send someone else to go free the Israelite slaves in Egypt (Exod 4:13) and then spends the next forty years leading them out of Egypt to the borders of the Promised land (Deut 34). Psalm 137 also does not "sanitize" the experiences of the exiles in Babylon. We read in these verses their grief, their humiliation, their anger, and their desire for revenge.

Communal Lament over Zion

Psalm 137 is considered a communal lament. It begins by sharing the grief the exiles felt as they sat by the rivers of Babylon remembering their homeland of Zion. The term "Zion" had come to represent Jerusalem, its temple and its people. It is one thing to go away to camp or to school and be home sick. It is a totally different experience to be dragged off as captives of war not knowing what your fate will be or if you will see your homeland again. The exiles sat and shared their memories of home, of what had been and what might never be again. As they reminisced, they wept.

As the exiles were grieving, their Babylonian captors began to make fun of them and mocked them to sing one of the songs of Zion. The term "Zion" also had theological connotations, as Zion was regarded as the seat of the Lord's enthronement as King over Israel and the cosmos (*NISB*, 961). One can imagine the painful irony of what it would be like to sing one of the psalms about how great and mighty Yahweh was while being held captive by the Babylonians. Where was this mighty Yahweh who led the Hebrew people through the wilderness now? Was it not the god of the Babylonians, Marduke, who was really the most powerful god of all, king of the cosmos?

Study Bible

See the "Excursus: Zion in Prophetic Literature and in the Psalms," *NISB*, 960-61.

Vows

The Israelites refused to sing and symbolically hung their harps on the trees growing nearby. They took a vow to put Jerusalem as their highest priority, and, if they did not, then their right hand would wither and their tongues would cling to the roofs of their mouths. We have a number of examples throughout the Old Testament of vows being taken that entail retribution if the action was not carried out. For example: Reuben promised his father Jacob that if he did not bring his brother Benjamin home safely, his father could kill his two sons (Gen 42:37); King Saul cursed anyone who ate food before they had avenged his enemies (1 Sam 14:24), a vow that almost cost him his son Jonathan's life. We also see an example of this in the New Testament when a group of forty men vowed not to eat or drink until they had killed Paul (Acts 23:12-13). The Israelites vowed to set the restoration of Jerusalem above their highest joy. This was now their goal in life.

Revenge

The biblical text records that when the Babylonians destroyed Jerusalem, the Edomites stood by and watched them carry off the wealth of Jerusalem and then gloated over the Israelites' distress (Obadiah). In the language of our day, the Edomites were "cousins" to the Israelites. The Bible refers to them as brothers. They were the descendants of Esau, the brother of Jacob, their father being Isaac. Instead of standing up and helping their Israelite relatives, they sat back and cheered while Jerusalem fell. The exiles wanted revenge. Not only did Israel want Yahweh to remember what the Edomites had done, but they also put a blessing upon anyone who avenged the Babylonians for what they had done to them. The text reads, "O daughter Babylon." The title, "Daughter Babylon," refers to the city and all its inhabitants. The next line can be read either as "you devastator" or "you who are devastated." It is not clear whether the psalmist intended to name Babylon as the devastator of Zion who needed to be dealt with or as the devastator who was about to be devastated. Although it sounds very harsh to our ears today, the Israelites put a blessing on anyone who took revenge on the Babylonians: Happy would be any one who took the Babylonian babies and dashed their heads upon the rocks. As disturbing as it seems to us, dashing children to the ground was a common practice for the victors of war (2 Kgs 8:12; Isa 13:16; Hos 10:14; 13:16; Nah 3:10).

Psalm Outline

Dorsey (178) outlines Ps 137 with a four part symmetry:

a present sorrow of exiled Jews in *Babylon* (137:1-4)

b vow to *remember Jerusalem* (137:5-6)

b' may Yahweh *remember* the evil Edom did against *Jerusalem* (137:7)

a' future blessedness of those who bring evil upon *Babylon* (137:8-9)

I find it interesting that the lectionary includes all of Ps 137. Although the biblical text tries not to "sanitize" the human behavior of the biblical characters, the lectionary tends to leave out some of the scriptures that reveal the extremes of human behavior. We need to hear and read the biblical text in its entirety to understand and acknowledge how God calls us to behave and not to behave. The Bible clearly teaches that vengeance is God's. But human beings need to be able to offer up true emotions in prayer and give them to God and allow God to begin the healing process.

Reflections

1. Why do we try to "sanitize" the lives of our heroes and have a need to make people larger than life who are flawed like we are?
2. What are appropriate ways for us to express our emotions so that they can be honestly felt and healthily dealt with?
3. Have you ever acted out of anger when someone has hurt you? How did you feel afterwards? How would Jesus have wanted you to act (WWJD)? In retrospect, how do you think you should have handled the situation?
4. Jesus teaches that we are to take up our cross and follow him. The cross was an instrument of torture and death. How do you view a faith that honestly admits suffering is a part of what it means to follow Jesus as Lord and Savior?

Study Bible

See the "Excursus: Enemies and Imprecations," *NISB*, 857.

If we cannot be honest with God in prayer as this psalmist was, then who can we be honest with? How healthy is it for us not to acknowledge the emotions we are feeling, or to give them to someone who can help us to face them honestly and deal with them? There are times all of us wish that someone who has hurt us would get theirs. Why not give that desire to God allowing God to deal with our hurt and the cause of that hurt? "Sanitizing" emotions and actions helps no one. If anything, it often allows the behavior, the sin, to continue unabated. In today's society every terrorist attack is a reminder of what happens when a religious zealot's prayer is lived out in human terms.

The Law of Love

Chrisitans may want to read Psalm 137 in light of the New Testament. Jesus teaches that we are not to have a "get even" mentality: "an eye for an eye and a tooth for a tooth" (Exod 21:23-25; Lev 24:19-20; Matt 5:38); rather, we are to love our enemies, do good to those who hate us, bless those who curse us, and pray for those who persecute us (Matt 5:44; Luke 6:27-31). We are to live the "golden rule": do to others as we would have them do to us. When someone mistreats us, we are not to seek revenge, but, through the power of the Holy Spirit, we are to reply in love. We are not to be overcome with evil but, rather, overcome evil with good and trust that God will take care of the rest. In other words, leave the vengeance to God (Rom 12:17-21). It is easier said than done in the midst of persecution, but that is the high calling Jesus asks his disciples to follow.

By the Babylonian Rivers

Ps. 137:1-4
Ewald Bash, 1964

LATVIAN MELODY 8.7.8.7.
Latvian Melody
Arr. by Ewald Bash, 1964
Harm. by Paul Abels, 1966

I Will Praise God

> **Lectionary Loop**
> **Proper 5, 21, Year C, Psalm 146**
> **Proper 18, 26, 27, Year B, Psalm 146**

Hallel Psalms

Psalm 146 is the first of what is known as the Hallel Psalms (Pss 146–150). Each of these Psalms begins and ends with the words, *Hallelu-jah*, literally *Hallelu*, "praise," and *Yah*, a shortened form of the name Yahweh. Each of the Hallel Psalms explores different reasons and ways to praise God reaching the climax and final benediction of Ps 150, which teaches us *where* to praise God (v. 1), *why* to praise God (v. 2), *how* to praise God (vv. 3-5) and finally *who* should praise God (v. 6) finishing once again with the words *Hallelu-jah*! (In the Hebrew Bible, there are 150 psalms. In the Greek translation of the Hebrew, called the Septuagint, there are 151 psalms.)

Psalm 146 opens up with the words *Hallelu-jah*, and then the psalmist begins these Hallel psalms by first claiming that he, himself will praise God and why. In vv. 1-2, the psalmist writes that his soul will sing praise to God his whole life long.

In vv. 3-4, the psalmist warns his readers not to put their trust in any other human being for they too will die and their plans with them. Psalm 146:3 brings home the difference in translations that we first looked at in Session 2 where we looked at Ps 8:4 and the difference in the English translations of the Hebrew *ben adam*.

Son of Man

The NRSV translates it as "mortal," understanding it as the generic rendering of all human beings, while the NIV translates it as "son of man."

NRSV 8:4 what are human beings that you are mindful of them,
mortals that you care for them?
NIV 8:4 what is man that you are mindful of him,
the son of man that you care for him?

In Ps 146:3, even though the Hebrew word is still the same, *ben adam*, the NIV chose to change its English translation:

NRSV 146:3 Do not put your trust in princes,
in *mortals*, in whom there is no help.
NIV 146:3 Do not put your trust in princes,
in *mortal men* who cannot save.

If the NIV remained true to its first English translation of *ben adam* it should read:

146:3 Do not put your trust in princes,
in the *son of man* who cannot save.

From the Christian perspective, it makes for an interesting theological dilemma if you strictly interpret the term "son of man" as being a foreshadowing of the historic person Jesus of Nazareth. One needs to be aware of the various English translations of the Hebrew biblical text and the theology that guides those choices. *Ben adam* may have simply been used by the psalmist in v. 3 as a play on the similar sounding Hebrew word for earth used in v. 4, *adamah*.

Reasons to Praise God

In v. 5, the psalmist turns the readers'/hearers' attention to the only being who deserves praise, the God of Jacob, for happy/blessed are those whose help is in the Lord their God.

In vv. 6-9, the psalmist begins to enumerate why the God of Jacob is to be praised: God is the creator of heaven and earth, gives justice to the oppressed, feeds the hungry, sets the prisoner free, opens the eyes of the blind, lifts up those who are bowed down, loves those who do right, watches over strangers, orphans, and

Reflections

1. Write a psalm of praise to God including who should praise God, where God should be praised, why God should be praised, and how God should be praised. Now write a personal psalm of praise including why, where, and how you are praising God.
2. Take time to explore different English translations of Psalm 146, including the reason given for each particular translation of the biblical text, the guidelines given for how the biblical text was translated into English and the reading level (i.e. 3rd grade reading level, 7th grade reading level, etc.) chosen. Why is it important to know the reasons behind the English translation of the biblical text? Do you agree with the statement, "Every translation is itself an interpretation?"

widows, and makes the wicked to be bowed down in ruin. These verses bring to mind the similar words of Isa 61, which Jesus later reads in the synagogue in Nazareth and then tells those assembled that this scripture was fulfilled in their hearing (Luke 4:18-19). They are also the words he gives the disciples of John the Baptist to assure them of his identity (Luke 7:18-23).

In v. 10, the psalmist ends Ps 146 with words of victory: the God of Zion will reign forever, for all generations. Hallelujah! Praise the Lord!

Resources

A. A. Anderson, *New Century Bible The Book of Psalms* Volume 1 (Paulton, Somerset, England: Purnell and Sons Ltd., 1972).

____. *New Century Bible The Book of Psalms Volume 2* (Paulton, Somerset, England: Purnell and Sons Ltd., 1972).

Jouette Bassler, "Phillippians" in *NISB*, 2099-2106.

Walter Brueggemann, *The Message of the Psalms: A Theological Commentary* (Minneapolis: Augsburg, 1984).

Peter C. Craigie, *Word Biblical Commentary Volume 19: Psalms 1-50*, Eds. Bruce M. Metzger, John D. W. Watts, James W. Watts. (Nashville: Thomas Nelson Publishers), 1983.

Toni Craven, "Psalms" in *NISB* (Nashville: Abingdon Press, 2003), 753-892.

Mitchell Dahood, *Psalms 1:1-50*. Anchor Bible 16 (Garden Cty, N.Y.: Doubleday, 1966).

David A. Dorsey, *The Literary Structure of the Old Testament: A Commentary on Genesis-Malachi* (Grand Rapids, Michigan: Baker Academic, 1999).

David Albert Farmer, "Unselfish Prayer" in *The Pastor's Bible Study, Volume One* (Nashville: Abingdon Press, 2005), 1:159-184.

Gordon D. Fee, *The New International Commentary on the New Testament: The First Epistle to the Corinthians* (Grand Rapids, Michigan: William B. Eerdmans Publishing Company, 1987).

S.E. Gillingham, *The Oxford Bible Series: The Poems and Psalms of the*

(continued on page 204)

(continued from page 203)

Hebrew Bible. Eds. P. R. Ackroyd and G. N. Stanton (Oxford University Press, 1994).

Donald Jay Grout, *A History of Western Music Revised Edition.* (New York: W. W. Norton & Company Inc., 1973).

Walter J. Harrelson, "Introduction: Psalms" in *The New Interpreter's Study Bible With the Apocrypha* (Nashville: Abingdon Press, 2003), 749-752.

Derek Kidner, Psalms 1-72: A Commentary, Tynedale Old Testament Commentaries, Vol 14a, ed. D. J. Wiseman (Leicester, England/ Downers Grove, Illinois: Inter-Varsity Press, 1973).

____. *Psalms 73-150: A Commentary* (*Tynedale Old Testament Commentaries*, Vol 14b, ed. D. J. Wiseman (Leicester, England/Downers Grove, Illinois: Inter-Varsity Press, 1973).

James Limburg, "The Book of Psalms" in *The Anchor Bible Dictionary,* ed. David Noel Freedman (New York: Doubleday, 1992), 5:522-536.

Tremper Longman III, *How to Read the Psalms* (Leicester, England/ Downers Grove, Illinois: Inter-Varsity Press, 1988).

Thomas F. McDaniel, "The Ten Commandments" in *The Pastor's Bible Study, Volume Two* (Nashville: Abingdon Press, 2005), 157-221.

Renew! Songs & Hymns for Blended Worship (Carol Steam, IL: Hope Publishing Company, 1995), 103.

Marvin E. Tate, *Word Biblical Commentary Vol. 20: Psalms 51-100*, eds. David A Hubbard, Glenn W. Barker John D. W. Watts. (Nelson Reference and Electronic, 1990).

(continued on page 205)

(continued from page 204)

Samuel Terrien, *Critical Eerdmans Commentary: The Psalms: Stophic and Structue and Theological Commentary* (Grand Rapids Michigan/ Cambridge U.K.: William B. Eermans Publishing Company, 2003).

The Hymnal of the United Church of Christ (New York: United Church Press, 1979, 257).

The New Century Hymnal (Cleveland, Ohio: The Pilgrim Press, 1995), 558 and 600.

The United Methodist Hymnal: Book of United Methodist Worship (Nashville: The United Methodist Publishing House, 1989), 60.

www.cyberhymnal.org

www.faithatwork.com/history/Shoemaker_I_Stand.html

KINGDOM OF GOD

A STUDY BY

ANNE CRUMPLER

Anne Crumpler, a freelance writer and editor, works as a contract editor for The Upper Room Daily Devotional Guide *and* Devo 'Zine.

THE KINGDOM OF GOD

Outline

I. Introduction

II. Session 1—Kingdom and Covenant: Genesis 12:1-3 and 17:1-8, Deuteronomy 26:5-9, Exodus 20:1-7
   A. The Covenant with Abraham: God, People, Land
   B. Exodus, the Covenant at Sinai, the Promised Land

III. Session 2—Kingship: Genesis 1:1–2:3, 1 Samuel 8:1-22, 2 Samuel 7:1-29
   A. God: the King of Creation
   B. God: the King of Human History
   C. God and Kings

IV. Session 3—Prophets, Exile, Images of Kingdom of God: Amos 4:7-13, 5:22-24, 9:13-15, Isaiah 42:14-16, 43:5-7, 49:8-13, and 51:11, Isaiah 25:6-10a, Micah 4:1-8, Zechariah 8:1-8
   A. Amos: In the Context of Covenant and Kingdom
   B. Exile
   C. Post-Exile
   D. Images of God's Kingdom

V. Session 4—Christ and Kingdom: Luke 4:18-19, Matthew 5:1-12, Luke 6:20-26, Matthew 20:1-16, Mark 4:30-32
   A. Proclaiming God's Kingdom
   B. Parables
   C. God's Kingdom Come Alive
   D. Eating and Drinking

VI. Session 5—Life, Death, Resurrection: Mark 14–15, Luke 4:16-30
   A. Crucifixion: Who and Why?
   B. Resurrection

VII. Session 6—Living for God's Kingdom: Matthew 6:25-33, Romans 14:17-19, 2 Corinthians 5:16-21
   A. In Between Christ and Kingdom
   B. Seek First God's Kingdom

Introduction

The Kingdom of God

The kingdom of God is what God wants for the world and for human society. It is the fulfillment of God's purposes. The Bible describes the kingdom of God as a new social order grounded in justice, mercy, righteousness, generosity, peace, and equality—not to mention neighbor love, good health, glad rejoicing, and, yes, rousing parties.

The kingdom of God is the core of his teachings and the guiding light of his ministry. His parables begin, "The kingdom of God is like. . . ." His sermons ask us to live for God's kingdom. To know Jesus—both what he says and who he is—we need to understand the kingdom of God.

The early church believed that the kingdom of God was just around the corner. The coming of Jesus, the Messiah, signaled change. Any day now, he would return and establish God's new order.

God's kingdom didn't come. After a generation or two had passed, the church began to think through different ways of understanding Jesus and the kingdom of God. Perhaps God was waiting to usher in a new order until the whole world repented and believed. Maybe the kingdom was a future event and communities of faith were the forerunners of the new order. (Read 1 Pet 3, which exemplifies the struggle for understanding God's not-yet-come kingdom.)

Church people today have little understanding of the kingdom of God. Asked for definitions, some say that the kingdom is heaven, a cloudy place with angels and gold-paved streets, where we go when we die. Others define the kingdom as a change of heart, a spiritual renewal of each individual in faith. Still others say that the kingdom is the church, the community formed in the word and spirit of Christ. Few talk about the new social order promised in the teachings of Hebrew scripture and the preaching of Jesus. Almost no one says that the kingdom of God requires us to make moral decisions or to live in the world in new and innovative ways. Ask people about the kingdom of God. They stare blank and shrug their shoulders.

What's happened? Why have people forgotten the kingdom of God, the new promised social order?

At least twice in the twentieth century, the church revived its hopes for social change. The first was in the social gospel movement at the turn of the century, which applied biblical teaching to social progress, notably problems associated with industrialization, and encouraged people to get involved for change. The social gospel assumed that human beings were basically good and that people could live in accord with God's purposes. The social gospel ended with World War, and hopes for human righteousness died in the fires of Auschwitz.

More recently, in the 1960s, the civil rights movement and the peace movement were grounded in the conviction that God's kingdom will come on earth. Dr. Martin Luther King, Jr., envisioned God's kingdom, a dream of equality and peace, and spoke words of scripture: "Let justice roll down like waters and righteousness like an ever-flowing stream" (Amos 5:24). When the 1960s ended, King had been assassinated and college students shot down for protesting the war in Vietnam. People were disillusioned. Perhaps they thought nothing could change—God's kingdom is just a pipe dream, a utopia of failed hopes. People have given up on the kingdom of God, disillusioned by the failure of social change. Maybe we're afraid to believe in God's new order. Proclaiming God's kingdom means standing up for change and gets us in trouble. Society silences words that threaten the status quo.

Americans suffer from nostalgia. We look backward to the glory days of the past—to the 1950s, when rules for living were well-established and children filled our

Teaching Tips

Write on a large sheet of paper the definition of the kingdom of God and display it for all the lessons. At the beginning or the end of each lesson, invite people to write new insights, questions, words of scripture, and so on that help them to understand the meaning of God's kingdom. At the beginning of each lesson, invite the group to read responsively Psalm 96.

Sunday schools. Looking forward is difficult. We have no vision of what our nation could be. Perhaps today's turmoil—terror, close-to-home crime, corruption in government, rising racial tempers, widening economic gaps between the rich and poor, and the oppression of corporate culture—keeps us busy just getting by. We have no imagination, much less energy, for envisioning the future. In the church, we learn the stories of biblical heroes and heroines, and we talk about the mighty acts of God, past tense. We look backward. We struggle to enter a biblical world. Maybe hope for God's future falls flat in the turmoil of today's seemingly hopeless social-economic-political situation.

Popular religion in America today is oriented to the individual. Jesus is in our hearts. We are each saved. Social consciousness has given way to personal piety and spiritual growth. What happened to the kingdom of God?

The lessons in this chapter will suggest ways to recover a biblical understanding of the kingdom of God, to envision God's purposes fulfilled, to suggest ways of dealing with God's kingdom not-yet-come, and to look at what the kingdom of God requires of us in the world today.

Reflections

1. What words describe our society?
2. What words describe the kingdom of God?
3. How would your faith change if you believed in salvation as social, political, and economic?
4. Why is believing in the kingdom of God difficult for us?

Sources

David Buttrick, *Preaching the New and the Now* (Westminster John Knox Press, 1998).

John Fuellenback, *The Kingdom of God: The Message of Jesus Today* (Orbis Books, 1995).

Rudolf Schnackenburg, *God's Rule and Kingdom* (Herder and Herder, 1963).

Michael Welker, "The Reign of God," in *Theology Today*, January, 1993 (Volume XLIX, Number 4).

Session 1 — Genesis 12:1-3 and 17:1-8, Deuteronomy 26:5-9, Exodus 20:1-7

Kingdom and Covenant

When Jesus came preaching the kingdom of God, he didn't need to define his terms. His audience—the disciples, the crowds, the Pharisees—brought with them an understanding of the kingdom of God. They looked for a new social order that would fulfill the promises of God. They expected God to establish a new society founded on justice, righteousness, and peace.

The kingdom of God sums up the relationship between God and God's people. So we look at the origins of God's people. In the events that defined them and the covenants that established their relationship with God are ideas that begin to form the concept of God's new social order.

The Covenant with Abraham: God, People, Land

Read Gen 12:1-3 and 17:1-8. The covenant with Abraham includes three components of the kingdom of God: God, people, and land. The kingdom of God is first of all a relationship between a sovereign God and God's people. God makes covenant not only with Abraham, but also with his children and grandchildren. The covenant stretches out from Abraham to include all humanity for all time. For all the generations of Abraham's family, for a multitude of nations, God "will be their God."

In Gen 12:2-3, Abraham will be the ancestor of "a great nation," which will be a blessing to "all the families of the earth." In one image of God's new order, Jerusalem, the city of God, becomes the hub of God's kingdom on earth. God's word goes out from the city and gathers all the nations into God's new society. The nations learn God's ways, and they are blessed. In both the covenant and the image of God's kingdom, God's blessings emanate from a center, like highways circling a city, gathering in more and more people until all humanity is blessed.

In Gen 17:4, God promises to make the descendents of Abraham "a multitude of nations." They will live in the land of Canaan, where Abraham is "now an alien." The kingdom of God is not a spiritual communion. It is landed, a down-to-earth society of God's people. God's kingdom stretches out from the Promised Land to include all the earth, where no one is a stranger. In God's new social order, everyone is embraced in the love of God and neighbor.

Abraham's wife, Sarah, was barren, yet gave birth to Isaac, according to God's promise. The prophet Isaiah later describes God's new social order as a city. On a crowded street, a woman looks around baffled. "I was barren," she says. "Where did all these children come from?" (See Isa 49:19-21.) The Promised Land, Canaan, was rocky soil and dry, hot wind—a barren land—and it was occupied. In God's new order, fountains bubble up in the desert, and dry soil blooms with flowers (Isa 41:18-19). Like God's covenant with Abraham, God's kingdom is to be proclaimed to a barren world, to offer fulfillment, promise, and hope for the future.

Exodus, the Covenant at Sinai, the Promised Land

Read Deut 26:5-9, a creed that states the history of the Hebrew people from their beginnings until they are established as God's people in the Promised Land. This is the story of salvation.

The children of Israel went into Egypt, where they were foreigners. They prospered according to God's promise and became a great nation. The Egyptians, frightened by their numbers, made them slaves, forcing them to work, like chain gangs, building cities. Oppression gave way to genocide (Exod 1:15-22). God heard the cries of God's people and saw their affliction and brought them out of Egypt "with a terrifying display of power." The people who first spoke the creed would have remembered the stories of

Moses, the plagues, the angel of death passing over their homes, flight in the darkness, the wide-open sea that closed over the armies of Pharaoh. The Lord guided God's people across the wilderness to a new land, "flowing with milk and honey": the Promised Land. In the story of Israel's salvation—the Exodus, the wilderness, the Promised Land—are roots of the kingdom of God.

God is victorious over the king of Egypt and his armies. Scripture often describes God's victory prior to the establishment of God's kingdom. God is victorious over God's enemies and the enemies of God's people. When God's people are exiled, God prepares for war, leading the nations of the world to battle, and, once victorious, restores Israel's fortunes. God is victorious over sin, punishing the wicked; but then God pours out justice and righteousness on earth. God is victorious over death and raises up a new life of neighbor-love and peace.

God is present with God's people. God hears their cries and sees their affliction. God leads the people out of Egypt and through the wilderness. God provides for them, guides them, and forms them into God's people. In the new order, God is with God's people. God dwells in the holy city and walks through the streets healing the sick, wiping away tears, teaching people to love one another. God provides a harvest and clean water—enough to fill the hands and bellies of every child—and everyone is satisfied.

God leads the people out of Egypt, where they were oppressed and brings them to a new land "flowing with milk and honey." Salvation reverses the fortunes of God's people and establishes a new community. The kingdom of God is a reversal of life as it is now. Wrongs are righted; the oppressed go free; those who have lived in darkness see light, greed gives way to generosity, the rich are tumbled out of seats of power, people live together in God's justice, righteousness, and mercy. In the kingdom of God, people settle down, and everyone has enough.

Read the Ten Commandments in Exod 20:1-7. The Ten Commandments are rules for individuals, but God's

Resources

Refer back to the studies by Tom McDaniel in *The Pastor's Bible Study*, Volume 2 and to the commentary on these verses in the *NISB*.

law is also for the community of God's people. At Sinai, on the way from Egypt to the Promised Land, God's new society is formed. The kingdom of God is a social order—a society, grounded in God's purposes. Read the Ten Commandments as laws governing a society. For example: Honoring mother and father may be a guarantee of healthcare. Sabbath laws may translate into clear-sighted labor laws. "You shall not murder" may eliminate war and capital punishment as well as crime gone rampant. Consider also that "You shall not" may be reversed to give us a sense of God's purpose fulfilled in God's kingdom. "You shall not covet" means that greed should give way to generosity, and "You shall not bear false witness" imagines a judicial system that tells the truth in love.

The kingdom of God, a vision of the future, has its roots in the covenants of Israel. The kingdom describes the relationship between God and God's people and the society created by the fulfillment of God's purposes. The first mention of God as king is in the Song of Moses, a joyous celebration of victory and freedom and God's graciousness in providing a home for God's people. Read Exod 15:17-18:

> You brought them in and planted them
> on the mountain of your own possession,
> the place, O Lord, that you made your abode,
> the sanctuary, O Lord,
> that your hands have established.
> The Lord will reign forever and ever.

Teaching Tips

Diagrams are sometimes helpful. Invite people to diagram the covenant with Abraham in Gen 12:1-3 and then in Gen 17:1-8. How are the diagrams similar? different? What does the structure of the covenant say about the kingdom of God?

Suggest that the class tell the story of the Hebrew people in Egypt, the Exodus, the trek through the wilderness—including Sinai—and their establishment in the Promised Land. Ask someone to draw the story on a large sheet of paper. At what points and in what ways is the kingdom of God similar to the Israelites' salvation from Egypt?

Reflections

Invite the group to consider the Ten Commandments as laws of the land. What would a society be like if it were governed by God's law?

Invite people to write one sentence descriptions of God's kingdom, based on what they have learned from the covenants. As a closing prayer, ask volunteers to read the sentences they have written. Encourage the group to respond to each sentence with the words: "The Lord will reign forever and ever."

Session 2 Genesis 1:1–2:3, 1 Samuel 8:1-22, 2 Samuel 7:1-29

Kingship

God: the King of Creation

"In the beginning, God created the heavens and the earth." The first sentence in the Bible announces the rule of God over the universe, over the heavens and earth. God creates an ordered universe from the swirling seas of chaos. God separates night from day and sets the suns in the sky to run its daily course, marking the days and seasons. God gathers up the seas and plants the dry land. God fills the waters with fish and the air with birds and populates the earth with animals. God makes human beings something like God, provides for them, and gives them dominion over all the earth.

The story of creation provides images of God's kingdom, which later writers call God's new creation. Projected into the future, creation is pools of water in the desert and trees planted by rivers with roots deep in the soil. It is all of creation at peace—the wolf with the lamb, the calf with the lion (Isa 11:6-9). It is human beings living free, secure, and unafraid in harmony with one another and with all the universe.

First of all, God is creator, ruler of the whole universe. God is king not only of a human society, but also of land, water, the unfathomable reaches of space, the farthest stars, and the tiniest cells. God rules all of creation. The kingdom of God is perhaps a wider dominion that we thought at first—not just God, people and land, but a whole wide world ordered by God's purposes. The rule of God is universal.

God is not enthroned in heaven, a creator God who sits back and watches creation play out. Rather God is active. Creation is not only "in the beginning" but continuing action. God creates each day new. God sustains creation, bringing seed to harvest, watering the plains, ordering the relationships among God's creatures.

So, second, God is past, present, and future. God created the world; God will establish a new creation in the future; and God is creating, bring God's purposes to fulfillment.

What about dominion? The story of creation establishes a relationship among God, people, and the rest of creation. People are created in God's image and given dominion. Gerhard von Rad, in his commentary on Genesis (pages 57–58) notes that in many nations images of the ruler are created to remind people who is in charge—think of the statue of Saddam Hussein in Iraq or likenesses of Stalin in Russia. In the same way human beings are created in God's image. When we see other people, we should think of God and be reminded: Ultimately God is in charge. Dominion belongs to God, the king of creation. People are to represent God, point to God's rule, and live for God's purposes.

Study Bible

See Theodore Hiebert's excursus on "Domininon or Dependence," in the *NISB*, 8.

Sources

Gerhard von Rad, *Genesis* (Louisville: Westminster John Knox Press, Revised edition, 1973).

Terrence Fretheim, "Genesis," in *New Interpreter's Bible*, vol. 1, 340-47.

God: the King of Human History

The God of the universe is also the God of Israel and our God. God the Creator also rules human history. The hymn sings,

Praise ye the Lord,
the Almighty, the King of creation!
O my soul, praise Him,
for He is thy health and salvation!

God is both king of creation and the ruler of human history. In the beginning, God chooses the people of God, frees them, leads them across the wilderness to a new land. In the course of history, God elects human beings ("You are my people; I am your God") and leads them across ages and generations to a new social order grounded in God's purposes of health, love, justice, peace—the words of salvation. God is the God of all space, creation, and history.

God and Kings

God brought the Hebrew people out of Egypt and across the wilderness. They settled down in the land of Canaan. Their rulers were tribal chiefs and then judges and prophets chosen by God. After many years, the people requested a king and God granted their request.

Israel became a monarchy in a storm of controversy. Read 1 Sam 8:1-22. The people wanted a king for two reasons. 1) Samuel set up his sons as judges; and they were corrupt, taking bribes and perverting justice. 2) With a king, Israel would be like other nations. They wanted a war hero to go before them into battle—with flags flying high in blue skies. Samuel warned the people that a king would draft their sons and put their daughters to work in service to the king; he would take their land and tax their crops. The people would be slaves in their own land as they were slaves in Egypt.

God is king. To ask for a human king was to reject God as ruler. It was to choose war over peace, a gulf between rich and poor rather than a fair distribution of wealth, forced labor instead of work: foreheads sweaty in the hot sun and feet dug deep in the soil for a harvest of good. The comparison of life under the rule of a king and life under God's rule is like the comparison between Egypt and the Promised Land. It is also a comparison between our lives now and life in God's kingdom: war and peace, corruption and justice, tightfisted greed and mercy overflowing in generosity, darkness and light. To be like other nations is to reject God's social order. Yet God gave in to the Israelites' request. They would have a king.

Kings should be representatives of God. Like human beings, who have dominion over the earth, kings have dominion over God's people. When we see the king, we should know that ultimately God is in charge. So in the scripture is a list of good kings and bad kings, judged by whether or not they ruled according to God's purposes and served God. Did they build up weapons of war or live in peace? Did the national budget reflect God's concern for the poor, the sick, the orphans? The people understood that kings were appointed by God and were supposed to serve under God.

Study Bible

See Carol Grizzard's notes on 1 Sam 8:1-22, 403-404.

Source

See Bruce Birch's comments in 1 and 2 Sam, *New Interpreter's Bible*, vol. 2, 1026-31.

Reflections

If the kings of Israel were corrupted by power, why did God promise David that his house, his line, would be established forever? Read the Covenant with David in 2 Sam 7:5-17 and David's response in vv. 18-29.

The kings of Israel, like rulers today, were caught up in politics and power. Their policies sent Israel to war and plunged the nation into debt. Even David, Israel's shining star, was no bargain.

"You established your people Israel for yourself to be your people forever.... The Lord of Hosts is God over Israel," David said. God's promise is a promise for a future in which God will dwell among God's people and be their God. God's promise to David is that God's kingdom will come.

Isa 11:1-5 expresses Israel's hope for a king who will rule in the spirit of God, with wisdom, understanding, righteousness, equity, faithfulness. God's covenant with David, over time, became hope for a king who would establish God's kingdom and rule over God's new creation. The covenant is a promise that God's kingdom will come and that a king will rule according to God's purposes so that when we see him, we will know that God is in charge.

God made covenant with David and David's descendents, who had little to commend them. God's promise of a new social order is to be proclaimed in times when corrupt kings and mealy-mouthed politicians run the world. Someday God will establish God's kingdom; and justice, righteousness, and peace will reign in all the earth.

Study Bible

See Carol Grizzard's notes on 2 Sam 7:5-29, 450-51.

See Bruce Birch's commentary on 2 Sam 7:5-29 in the *New Interpreter's Bible*, vol. 2, 1256-63.

Reflections

What does the story of creation say about the relationship between God and creation? between people and the rest of creation?

How do you imagine the new creation?

In what ways do you see God involved in creation, guiding it toward fulfillment in a new creation?

Sometimes God's kingdom is described in negatives—for example: no more corruption, no more dying. Consider 1 Sam 7-8 and today's social-political-economic situation. Make a list of negatives that describe God's kingdom. Then turn the negatives around and write a list of positives, describing God's new social order—for example: "no more corruption" reversed might be "honesty in government."

Discuss:

How do you see God guiding human society toward the kingdom of God?

What do the stories of Samuel and David say about people who govern?

Read Psalm 96:1-13 as a song of praise. Or write a psalm praising God, the king of creation and the king of human history. If your group likes to sing, invite them to sing together "Praise Ye the Lord."

Session 3

Amos 4:7-13, 5:22-24, 9:13-15, Isaiah 42:14-16, 43:5-7, 49:8-13, and 51:11, Isaiah 25:6-10a, Micah 4:1-8, Zechariah 8:1-8

Prophets, Exile, Images of the Kingdom of God

The prophets are central to understanding the kingdom of God. Prophets speak God's word to particular people in particular situations; but their words span generations, calling God's people back to the covenant and forward to God's kingdom. They speak promise, judgment, salvation, hope—— depending on the situation. But they are bound by God's relationship with God's people and caught up in the vision of a new social order, God's promised kingdom.

The people of God have not been known for faithful devotion. Soon after their creation, Adam and Eve chose self-fulfillment over obedience and ate from the tree of the knowledge of good and evil (Gen 3:1-7). Before Moses walked down the slopes of Mount Sinai, the Hebrew people had fashioned a golden idol to worship (Exod 32:1-9). Settled in the Promised Land, the Israelites became a nation, with a government, a court system, a military, commerce, religious and educational institutions, and socio-economic divisions: rich and poor. The nation looked nothing like the society God had planned. The nation was corrupt, the courts unjust, businesses dishonest. The rich got richer, the poor scrambled for daily bread.

Amos: In the Context of Covenant and Kingdom

Read Amos 4:7-13, 5:22-24, 9:13-15. The prophet speaks words of judgment, but judgment is grounded in the covenant: "I am your God; you will be my people." The purpose of punishment is to bring the people back into relationship with God. Judgment in Amos 4 is punctuated by God's despair: "Yet you did not return to me." God is faithful; judgment is tempered by covenant love.

Amos does not call people to turn their hearts to the Lord in prayer. He calls a society to establish justice, righteousness, social and economic parity. Being faithful to the covenant is living for God's kingdom, when justice and righteousness will once-and-for-all fill the human community—like waters rolling through the desert.

Judgment is followed by restoration. God gathers in God's people and gives them land: a harvest of wheat and wine, cities built up and settled. In Amos, we discover again the three components of God's kingdom: a sovereign God, God's people who live together in righteous harmony, and a promised land. Amos envisions a society of God's people, bound together by God's purposes; he calls the people to obedience, to live as God's intends.

Exile

Soon after the reign of King Solomon, Israel split into two kingdoms, North and South. Tiny nations susceptible to military attack, both finally collapsed. In 721 BCE, the northern kingdom fell to the Assyrians. Twenty-seven thousand Israelites were exiled, their land given over to other people conquered by the Assyrians. Second Kings 17:18 says that the Lord, angry with Israel's faithlessness, "removed them out of his sight," leaving only the tribe of Judah, the southern kingdom. In 587, Judah fell to Babylon. The people of God were taken into exile. Second Kgs 24:14 notes that "all the officials, all the warriors, ten thousand captives, all the artisans and the smiths" were deported, and "no one remained, except the poorest people of the land."

Exiled, the people lost their land. They were no longer a people, bound together by structures of culture. The Temple, which centered their religious life, was destroyed. The exiles began to doubt the sovereignty of God. If Israel's God was sovereign, why was Israel overtaken by other nations? Was God weak, a second-rate God unable to protect the people? Or had God simply abandoned them? Lost in a strange land, the exiles' faith faltered.

Study Bible

See John Barton's notes on Amos 4:7-13 in the *NISB,* 1285-86; 5:22-24, 1287; and 9:13-15, 1291.

Resources

See Donald E. Gowan's reflections on these passages in Amos in the *New Interpreter's Bible*, vol. 7, 380–81, 394–95, and 430–31.

God heard the cries of God's people, freed them from captivity, and led them home. Read promises of return and restoration in Isaiah 42:14-16, 43:5-7, 49:8-13, and 51:11. Isaiah describes a new Exodus. God, the king of creation and history, will arrange for the people's liberation. God will guide them along a great highway through the wilderness, sustain them with fresh water that springs up in the desert, and establish them once again in the Promised Land.

Isaiah expanded the concept of God's kingdom. When the people of God had no land, the prophet promised that God would return them to Jerusalem. But Isaiah was clear: God is the God of all nations. God's rule extends to every corner of the earth. Even though the people lived in a strange land, God was not confined by national boundaries. God heard their cries and redeemed them. Cyrus, the Persian king, did not know God's name, but God gave him the victory over Babylon. God's people came from all directions to stand in God's presence and to walk the highway to the Promised Land. God redeemed Israel so that all the earth would know that God was king.

Study Bible

See Susan Ackerman's notes on Isaiah 42:14-16 in the *NISB*, 1013; 49:8-13, 1025, and 51:11, 1028-29.

Post-Exile

The exiles did return to Jerusalem, but Jerusalem was not the golden city they remembered. It was broken-down buildings, cracked pavement, empty lots grown high with grass, the eerie empty sounds of a city abandoned. Disillusioned, they set about rebuilding the Temple.

Post-exile, Israel's faith changed. First of all, the promises for God's kingdom were pushed into the future. Someday, God would establish a new Jerusalem where people would live secure, healthy, and content in God's presence. Someday, God would bless the people with peace, justice, full-bellies, and the simple joys of a community bound together in God's love. Second, the people of God hunkered down to live their lives. Like twenty-first century believers, the Israelites were busy just getting by. Wisdom became a virtue. Wisdom was not only common-sense intelligence, but also the ability to see God at work in the human community day by day. Wisdom was discerning God's purposes in and for creation.

The changes affected the prophets' understanding of the kingdom of God—and ours. The kingdom of God is a future hope. Someday God will establish a new social order defined by justice, righteousness, peace, generosity, neighbor love. And God is bringing about the kingdom in the ordinary daily lives of human beings. Does the kingdom of God come in glory at the end of time? Yes. But it also comes quietly as God's purposes of justice and righteousness are played out in human history.

Images of God's Kingdom

Perhaps most important are the images the prophets created of God's promised social order. We can describe God's kingdom with words like *justice, righteousness, mutuality, equality, generosity, peace*. The prophets drew pictures. They described a way of living that is God's intention for all of humanity. Read, for example, Isaiah 25:6-10a, which describes God's reign as an international feast. Or read Micah 4:1-8. The nations come to the mountain of God to learn. God arbitrates among them and supervises as they melt down weapons of war to make tractors and plows. God assembles the outcasts of society, "the lame…and those who have been driven away" and makes of them a strong nation, and God rules over them. Read the promises in Zechariah 8:1-8. The prophet draws a picture of a city park, where older adults bench-sit and children play. The prophets have given us pictures of God's kingdom where all people live together in peace.

The prophets stand between covenant and kingdom, God's promises given to Abraham, Moses, David and a vision of the future, in which all God's promises are fulfilled and a new order of life is established on earth. They speak to God's people, in all the situations of their lives, calling them back to God and into the future where all people will know God's righteousness and all nations will live in God's peace.

What images help you see the kingdom of God? Provide paint or crayons and large sheets of paper. Invite people to create images of God's kingdom on earth.

Study Bible

See notes on Isaiah 25:6-10a, *NISB*, 989; Micah 4:1-8, 1308; and Zechariah 8:1-8, 1343-44.

Isaiahs

Discuss

Prophets called people to be faithful to the covenant ("I am your God; you will be my people") and to a vision of God's kingdom. They spoke to particular people in particular circumstances. What would prophets say to us? What would they say to our nation?

Where do you see God at work to bring about God's kingdom on earth? During the exile and the post-exilic period, the kingdom of God became a future hope for the salvation of all people. Display a map of the world. Imagine people from every corner of the earth gathered into God's kingdom.

Prayer: God, bring all the nations together in your kingdom. Gather in people from the east, west, north, and south (name the nations). Teach them your ways—righteousness, justice, peace—and make them your own.

Session 4: Luke 4:18-19, Matthew 5:1-12, Luke 6:20-26, Matthew 20:1-16, Mark 4:30-32

Christ and Kingdom

The Bible understands Jesus as Messiah, the one chosen by God to establish God's kingdom. Think of the scripture verses we read during Advent and Christmas: the stories of Mary, Joseph, Elizabeth, Zechariah (Luke 1 and 2); the song of the angels; the promises in Isaiah 9:2-7; the theological images at the beginning of John (1:1-18). What does the scripture say about the birth of Jesus? Mary praises God because the coming of the Messiah signals a change in the social order: The hungry will be fed; the lowly will be lifted up. The angels sing of peace and good will for all people. The Gospel of John pictures the birth of Christ as a new beginning, the new creation. At Christmas, we read about the birth of Jesus Christ and about God's promises for a new social order.

Jesus' ministry centered on this one idea: The kingdom of God has come near to us. Jesus preached God's kingdom, and his way of life captured the meaning of God's new social order. Jesus made the kingdom of God come alive.

Proclaiming God's Kingdom

Read Luke 4:18-21. The purpose of Jesus' ministry is summed up in the words of Isaiah: "to bring good news to the poor . . . to proclaim release to the captives and recovery of sight to the blind." Jesus is commissioned to announce the kingdom of God, in which the oppressed go free, and poverty, sickness, and death are no more. Jesus is to usher in a new order of life: good will, generosity, peace, and lots of joy.

Beatitudes do not confer blessing; they celebrate

Resources

See R. Alan Culpepper's overview of the Lukan nativity story in *The New Interpreter's Bible*, vol. 9, 42-75.

Study Bible

See Joel Green's study notes on Luke 4:18-21, *NISB*, 1860–61.

Resources

Read R. Alan Culpepper's comments in *The New Interpreter's Bible*, vol. 9, 104-106.

Teaching Tip

Read Matthew 5:1-12 and Luke 6:20-26. Jesus' teaches about the kingdom of God. The ideas expressed in the Beatitudes are not new, but stand on a foundation of covenant law and prophetic vision. They are promises for a new order of life in God's presence.

Study Bible

See Warren Carter's and Joel Green's study notes on the Beatitudes, *NISB*, 1754 and 1864.

good fortune. Charles H. Talbert in his book, Reading Luke (page 70), suggests that they be paraphrased, "Congratulations to ________________because of ____________." Congratulations to the poor, the hungry, those who weep, and the persecuted! Matthew adds the meek, the merciful, the pure in heart, those who hunger for righteousness, and the peacemakers. "Congratulations," says Jesus, "because yours is the kingdom of God."

The kingdom of God reverses the conditions of the world. The hungry are well fed. The powerless are powerful. Those who weep rejoice. Those who are kind set a precedent for neighbor love. Righteousness, pure devotion to God, defines the social order; and peacemakers occupy all the seats at the table. Jesus came preaching. The Beatitudes describe God's new social order.

Parables

Jesus teaches in parables, many of which begin, "The kingdom of God is like..." Parables are interactive stories designed to disrupt and then to redirect thinking. The parables of Jesus shake us up so that we can see past conventional ways of thinking and living and begin to envision God's new order.

An example: Read Matt 20:1-16. In our society, work is a value. We work hard to pay the rent; and we're unsure of people who don't: those who are unemployed, collecting disability, or living on food stamps, yes, but also the wealthy who live on their inheritance or investments. Work is part of our social ethic. Think of contemporary proverbs: *Equal pay for equal work. No work; no pay.*

Jesus tells a story about a landowner and the laborers who work in his vineyard. The laborers are temporary hires. They stand around in the marketplace waiting for jobs. Some work all day in the heat of the summer sun. Some start at nine, others at three. At five o'clock, the landowner stops in the marketplace and asks the workers, "What are you doing, standing around all day? Why aren't you working?" It's the question we ask of people who are poor, homeless, drifting. Why don't you work for a living? The

Resources

Charles H. Talbert, *Reading Luke* (New York: Crossroad, 1982).

Study Bible

See Warren Carter's study notes on Matt 20:1-16, *NISB*, 1782.

landowner hires them, and they work a few hours in the cool of the day.

When the paychecks are distributed, all the laborers are paid a full day's wage. "Unfair!", the laborers who worked all day complain. Of course they do. Laborers should be paid for the work they do—equal pay for equal work.

The parable confuses us. The landowner in the story represents God, and the landowner doesn't play by the rules. Is God unfair? The parable forces us to change our thinking.

The landowner clues us in on the meaning of the parable: "Am I not allowed to do what I choose with what belongs to me? Or are you envious because I am generous?" In God's new social-economic order, God makes the rules. God distributes wealth—and blessings—as God sees fit. In the kingdom of God, the economy is based not on equal pay for equal work but on God's lavish generosity. God gives and gives and gives, so that, in the kingdom of God, everyone has enough. Jesus' teaching makes us think in new ways so that we can begin to envision God's new order of life.

God's Kingdom Come Alive

Other aspects of Jesus' ministry point to God's kingdom. Crowds of people followed Jesus. In every town, people who were sick, lame, blind, and confused came to him hoping to be healed. Jesus' miracles were signs of God's kingdom, where "hearts are brave again and arms are strong" ("For All the Saints," United Methodist Hymnal, 711), where people are healthy and no one dies. Gathered into the new creation, the lame walk, the blind see, those who walk in darkness see the light.

Eating and Drinking

In scripture, when Jesus breaks bread, we should keep our eyes open. Eating and drinking are usually references to or descriptions of the kingdom of God.

Jesus fed the hungry. Remember the story of the feeding of the five thousand (Mark 6:30-44) in which Jesus fed crowds of people with two loaves of bread and a couple of fish? In the kingdom of God, the hungry will

Teaching Tip

A haiku is a poem of three lines. The first is five, the second seven, and the third five syllables. Ask people to work together to write a haiku about Jesus' birth and God's promises for a new social order—for example:

Jesus Christ is born
peace on earth, good will, sheer joy
angel promises

be full. Public policy will ensure that resources are divvied up so that everyone has enough. The story also brings to mind images of God's kingdom in, for instance, Isa 25:6. In the new order, all people gather together to eat and drink and celebrate.

Who are the people we eat with? They are family, friends, business associates, the after-church lunch bunch. Eating together is a way to solidify relationships and sometimes a way to impress, to grab a little power. Jesus ate and drank with outcasts and sinners—nothing impressive there! Jesus did not condescend to eat with poor people, but enjoyed their company; they became family and friends. The deeper meaning: The kingdom of God draws outcasts and sinners into the joy of God's presence.

How do we know God's kingdom has come near to us in Jesus Christ? "Look," says Jesus. "The blind receive their sight, the lame walk, the lepers are cleansed, the deaf hear, the dead are raised, the poor have good news brought to them" (Luke 7:22).

The idea of the kingdom of God developed over time. It was grounded in covenant promises and early hope for a landed society in which God would rule and God's people would live together according to God's purposes. The prophets called people to return to the covenant and to live for God's kingdom—for justice, righteousness, peace. Jesus' ministry centered on the kingdom of God. He proclaimed God's new order. He lived in ways that made God's kingdom come alive. Christ and Kingdom—in him, we see a new social order in which God is king and all the nations of the world come together, in a glad celebration of God's grace.

Reflections

1. Who are the people named in the Beatitudes? How do they fit into our society? How will their lives change in God's new social order?
2. What are words that describe our economic system? How would you design an economic system based on generosity? What would characterize an economic system that is "good news for the poor"?
3. What events in Jesus' ministry are especially important to you? In what ways does Jesus make the kingdom of God come alive?
4. What do other parables say about God's kingdom?
5. Ask people to form two groups to say the Beatitudes responsively.

Life, Death, Resurrection

Today, in Christian circles, people talk a lot about Jesus, who "died for my sins," "took away my sins," "changed my heart." Faith is personal, and salvation is an internal change that sets each of us on a path to heaven. The death and resurrection is all about me and my salvation.

Scripture understands the crucifixion and resurrection as salvation for us, the establishment of a new social order, in which people live together—healed, forgiven, and free—in God's peace.

The early church struggled to understand Jesus' death and resurrection. Some picked up on images from Isa 53:5: God's servant, chosen to establish righteousness and justice, "was despised and rejected.... upon him was the punishment that made us whole, and by his bruises we are healed." Others read Jesus' death and resurrection in light of Ps 118:22-24: "The stone that the builders rejected has become the chief cornerstone. This is the Lord's doing;... This is the day that the Lord has made; let us rejoice." In Acts 2:36, Peter says, "God has made him both Lord and Messiah, this Jesus whom you crucified." In Rom 6:3-11, Paul writes about dying and rising with Christ: "Our old self was crucified with him.... so that, just as Christ was raised from the dead by the glory of the Father, so we too might walk in newness of life." The Gospel of Mark understands the crucifixion and resurrection as a cosmic change: the suffering of the whole creation followed by Christ's coming in glory to gather in God's people and to establish a new order (Mark 13:24-34).

Notice the reversals: death and resurrection, rejection and exaltation, old and new, suffering and glory. The scripture understands the cross as a turning point. Christ's death and resurrection are the end of one age and the beginning of another. Jesus, who was crucified, has been made the Lord of a new social order. The Bible understands Jesus' death and resurrection in the context of God's promised kingdom.

Study Bible

See Mary Ann Tolbert's study notes on Mark 14–15 in the *NISB*, 1837-43.

Crucifixion: Who and Why?

Jesus preached and lived the kingdom of God. He called people to live for God's purposes. Why was he crucified?

Perhaps we should begin by asking, Who crucified Jesus? Officially, the Roman government put Jesus to death. Rome, protecting its hold on an empire, kept order by crucifying insurrectionists. Records show that thousands of people were crucified; Jesus was one of them. Whenever crowds gathered, Rome got nervous; and the crowds that followed Jesus kept growing. When Jesus turned the tables in the Temple and threw out the merchants (Mark 11:15-19), Rome saw an act of civil disobedience. Jesus' talk of a kingdom of God, an international empire ruled by the king of kings, threatened the power of the Roman administration, which was quick to crucify.

The religious establishment—Pharisees, scribes, zealots, the chief priests, and elders of the people—was also involved in Jesus' crucifixion. Religion acted as a mediator between God and people, speaking for God and interceding for people. Religion divided the world—including people—into clean and unclean (Lev 11–15). Religious rituals purified and cleansed, making people acceptable to God. Religion defined right and wrong, good and bad. People who were good, abiding by religious faith and practice, were included in the community of the faithful and welcomed as God's own. First and twenty-first century religion are not too far apart!

Jesus' understanding of God's kingdom called into question ideas about clean and unclean, good and bad, acceptable and unacceptable. The kingdom of God was good news for the poor, the outcast, the sick, the dispirited. Jesus exploded the narrow concept of just reward—the modern version is: "If you're good, you'll go to heaven; if you're bad, you'll go to hell"—because Jesus proclaimed God's new world in which all people are welcome. The establishment of God's new social order brings sinners and outcasts to the table with pillars of the community. It also takes away the need for established religion: By God's grace, God's unconditional love, all people are accepted and included; and all people know God, who wipes away their tears and teaches them God's ways.

Who else was responsible for Jesus' crucifixion? Read Mark14–15. Make a list of all the people who betrayed, denied, condemned, mocked, or ran away from Jesus. There were chief priests, scribes, the elders, Judas, Peter, James and John, "a crowd with swords and clubs," all the disciples, the council, Pilate, the crowds who cried "Crucify him!" the soldiers, people who passed by, those who were crucified with him—have we missed anyone? Mark wants us to know that everyone rejects Jesus; everyone is, one way or another, responsible for his crucifixion.

Read Luke 4:16-30. Why did Jesus' neighbors threaten his life? The passage suggests three reasons: 1) Jesus, who was a carpenter—a construction worker—and a hometown boy, was putting on airs. Class distinctions in Nazareth, like class distinctions in American towns, limit possibilities for what people can do and who they can become. 2) Jesus didn't come to the good people of Nazareth; he came "to seek out and to save the lost" (Luke 19:10). Many of Jesus' parables address the same issue—for example, the parable of the lost sheep (Luke 15:3-7) and the story of the prodigal son (Luke 15:11-32). Jesus bypasses the righteous to search out the sinners and to welcome them into God's presence. 3) The text in Isaiah is a description of God's kingdom. Consider: What is good news for the poor? What does it mean to let the oppressed go free? The kingdom of God threatens our bank accounts, our cushy way of life, our social distinctions. What happens to health care—doctors, nurses, yes and also big insurance companies and pharmaceuticals—when the sick are healed? What happens to the military

Resources

See comments on Mark 14-15 by Pheme Perkins in *The New Interpreter's Bible*, vol. 8, 695-726.

Study Bible

See notes on Mark 3:23 in the *NISB*, 1811, about parables generally. See also notes about the two "major parables" in Mark on pp. 1812–1814. For further discussion of "parables" and the role they play in Jesus' teaching in Mark, see Mitzi Minor, *The Spirituality of Mark* (Louisville: Westminster John Knox Press, 1996) 13-14.

Teaching Tips

Begin with a picture of the crucifixion. Look at Rembrandt's "Golgotha"or "The Three Crosses" or a more contemporary "Crucifixion" by W.C. Mirico. Tape the picture to a large sheet of paper. Invite the group to write down the names of some of the people in the picture and then to add the names of other people involved in the crucifixion. Encourage them to add the names of groups today who try to protect the status quo and then to add their own names. Write at the top of the sheet of paper. Who is responsible for Jesus' death?

when God makes peace? Truth: Jesus preached the kingdom of God and opened wide the gates to the Promised Land. The only way to protect the status quo is to get rid of Jesus.

Crucifixion was understood as God's judgment. Jesus' execution confirmed everyone's suspicions: What Jesus preached was false, and the way he lived was wrong. They thought that crucifixion was condemnation of both Jesus and the kingdom he proclaimed.

Resurrection

The tomb was empty. God's word got out: Jesus Christ is risen! The resurrection is God's "Yes!" to Jesus and confirmation of his teachings. Yes, the kingdom of God has come near. Yes, God's promises of a new social order are absolutely sure. God's new order will disrupt the status quo and reverse the conditions of our lives now. It is good news for the poor, the outcast, the oppressed, the sick. It is also good news for Rome and the religious establishment and just about everyone involved in the crucifixion, because in the new social order, all people are forgiven and reconciled to God and to one another.

Jesus was a living, breathing symbol of the kingdom of God. He proclaimed God's new social order in his teachings, ministry, and way of life. God's kingdom is a threat to people in power—to Rome and to twenty-first century superpowers, to established religions that distinguish between good people and bad, to anyone invested in keeping the social order as is. The crucifixion is our resounding "No!" to change. But the resurrection is God's "Yes!" God will establish a new social order grounded in mercy, neighbor-love, peace. The cross is a turning point: "Everything old has passed away; see, everything has become new!" (2 Cor 5:17).

Reflections

In what ways is the kingdom of God threatening?

In what ways to we deny, betray, condemn Jesus? How do we deny the kingdom of God?

How do you understand the resurrection in the context of God's promised kingdom?

The cross is a turning point: the end of one age, the beginning of a new social order. What changes when God establishes God's kingdom? Invite people to make a list of reversals. Begin with these: death and resurrection, rejection and exaltation, old and new, suffering and glory. Then write together a prayer of petition using the reversals—for example:

God, in Jesus Christ, you make all things new. Those who are rejected now, let them be exalted. Let the lowly be lifted up. Let the hungry be fed and the prisoners go free. Let all who suffer see your glory. Meet war with peace. Clean up corruption and establish your kingdom on earth. Amen.

Celebrate the resurrection by singing "Rejoice the Lord Is King."

Session 6 — Matthew 6:25-33, Romans 14:17-19, 2 Corinthians 5:16-21

Living for God's Kingdom

In Between Christ and Kingdom

What about timing? When will God's kingdom come? These are possibilities:

1) God's kingdom has already come in Jesus Christ.

2) The kingdom has come in Jesus Christ and will be established once and for all when Christ returns.

3) God's kingdom will come in triumph at the end of time. The earth will be destroyed, and the holy city will come on clouds of heavenly glory.

All three ways of understanding the coming of God's kingdom are problematic. First of all, the kingdom of God hasn't come. Pictures of the world before and after Christ show no significant change. In the world we know the hungry starve, the sick die, the oppressed live in squalor, nations shake their fists at one another. To be honest, Jesus didn't establish God's kingdom on earth. It hasn't happened.

Second, to say that the kingdom of God has come in Jesus Christ and will come again at the end of time is to ignore expanses of history. Before and after Jesus, generations of people have prayed, "Your kingdom come on earth," and have waited for the promises of God to be fulfilled. If God is king of creation and of all human history, then God has not taken a vacation between Christ and kingdom. God is still working to bring about a new order of life.

Third, the biblical images of God's coming kingdom are, for the most part, unpretentious. The prophets talked about animals' lying side by side, nations coming together to make peace, merchants giving away good food and fresh water. Jesus said that the kingdom of God would be healing for the sick and good news for the poor. Jesus described the coming of God's kingdom not as triumphant victory, but like a mustard weed that grows haphazardly into a shrub and provides shelter for birds. (See the parable in Mark 4:30-32.) The kingdom of God will come, not in clouds of glory, but quietly, haphazardly in the created world.

All three possibilities are partly true. In Jesus Christ—his life and ministry—the kingdom of God has been brought near to us. We have seen up-close a new order of life. The resurrection confirmed God's promise: God will establish a new social order grounded in justice, righteousness, generosity, neighbor love. Jesus was right, what he said was true—God's kingdom will come. At some point in the future, unexpectedly, like water that springs up unexpectedly in the desert, the Lord will bring justice and righteousness on earth.

We live in between Christ and kingdom, but in a time when God is still king of creation and history and when God is working to bring about a new social order. In a sense, the kingdom has already come; it's a sure promise of God, a done deal. So the kingdom of God is past and future, but it is also present. Now God is fulfilling God's promises, making a new social order come alive.

Seek First God's Kingdom

We live in between. We stand between memory and vision, Christ and kingdom, covenant and God's future. What does God expect of us?

Read Matt 6:25-33. Jesus says that we should not worry about today. Rather, we should "seek first the kingdom of God and his righteousness" and trust God to provide. Jesus is talking about the hand-wringing worry that drives us to work long hours, to sit in traffic every morning, to pile up vacation time we can't use. He's talking about an economy in which the cost of rent exceeds one person's income and older adults sweep floors to pay for medicine. Trying to provide for ourselves and our families, we direct all our efforts to making ends meet. Don't worry about putting food on

Source

See M. Eugene Boring's comments on Matt 6:25-33 in *The New Interpreter's Bible*, vol. 8, 210-211.

In God's kingdom, God provides all that we need. To seek God's kingdom means relying on God and trusting God to provide.

Michael Welker says, "The reign of God is a twofold experience of free self-withdrawal: the self-withdrawal of others in our favor and our self-withdrawal in favor of others."

Source

Michael Welker, "The Reign of God" (Theology Today, Volume XLIX, Number 4, January 1993).

the table or shoes on your children's feet, Jesus says. Let God's kingdom and God's righteousness be the focus of your life, the aim of all your activity.

Our society is built on individuals who are concerned primarily with their own survival and perhaps the survival of their families. They are focused inward, curled up around their own concerns. They ask, "What will I eat? What will I drink? What will I wear?" Welker suggests that living for the kingdom is opening up and turning around, focusing on others instead of ourselves. Imagine what would happen if all of us purposefully made others the pivot of our concern, asking questions such as, What will you eat? What can I give you to wear? Then imagine what would happen if every community and every nation were concerned for the well-being of others rather than themselves. Wealth would be redistributed, bellies would be full, wide-eyed children would wash in clean water. Everyone would have enough.

Read 2 Cor 5:16-21. As we seek God's kingdom, we look to Jesus as our example. We are "ambassadors of reconciliation" because "in Christ, God reconciled us to himself." In Christ, God has created a new world order in which everyone lives in harmony with God and with one another. The kingdom of God is characterized by peace and good will. Our job is to witness to both Christ and kingdom by working for reconciliation. Proclaiming God's new social order means finding ways to bring together rich and poor; black and white; young and old; rednecks and intelligentsia; labor and management; socialists and capitalists; Democrats and Republicans; Israelis and Palestinians, Protestants, Catholics, Jews, Muslims. In a broken world, we stand between Christ and kingdom, proclaiming peace.

Read Rom 14:17-19. "The kingdom of God. . . . is righteousness and peace and joy . . . Let us then pursue what makes for peace and mutual up-building." God is at work in the world bringing all of creation into line with God's purposes. So what do we do? In concrete, down-to-earth ways, we spend our lives devoted to peace, righteousness, and joy. If God's kingdom means peace, we work for peace. We write letters to senators,

Study Bible

See Carolyn Osiek's study notes on 2 Cor. 5:16-21, *NISB*, 2068.

Study Bible

See James R. Edwards' study notes on Rom 14:17-19, *NISB*, 2031.

Reflections

1. In what ways was the kingdom realized in Jesus' life and ministry?
2. What is your vision of God's kingdom, which will come in the future?
3. How would you describe one day living in God's new social order?
4. Where do you see God working in the world to bring about God's kingdom?

Teaching Tips

Invite people to make a list of words that describe God's kingdom—for example: peace, righteousness, joy, love, generosity, good news, social and economic equality, healing, abundance, freedom. Then encourage people to talk about concrete ways of witnessing to God's kingdom.

Invite people to read aloud Mic 6:8. Then say together the Lord's Prayer.

we stand our ground against war, we find ways to love our enemies, we build up relationships between people and among nations. Righteousness is a social order that's right, one that accords with God's purposes. How do we pursue righteousness? What do we do to bring about social and economic equality? How do we encourage leaders to tell the truth and to work toward a society grounded in peace, justice, generosity, good news for the poor, and healing for the sick?

Seeking God's kingdom is active. It means getting involved everywhere that God is working toward a new social order. Our job is to witness to God's presence in the world and God's promises of a new world. We can't bring about God's kingdom, but we can proclaim the good news: In and through our broken world, God will raise up a new order. Seeking God's kingdom is living joyfully, including everyone we know in a glad celebration of God's grace because we're absolutely sure that God's kingdom will come.

CHRISTIAN COMMUNITY: EATING AND DRINKING OUR WAY TO THE KINGDOM

A STUDY BY

J. ANDREW McTYRE AND SARAH S. McTYRE

J. Andrew McTyre is pastor for the Park Central Presbyterian Church in Syracuse, N.Y. Sarah S. McTyre, an ordained Presbyterian Minister, serves as a consultant for Christian Education in central New York.

CHRISTIAN COMMUNITY:
EATING AND DRINKING OUR WAY TO THE KINGDOM

Outline

I. Introduction
   A. Desire for Community
   B. Biblical Images of Eating and Drinking
   C. The Larger Context
   D. Fear and Anxiety in Community Formation

II. Session 1—I'm Hungry!: Psalm 42 and Psalm 48
   A. Hunger Leading to God
   B. Meals and God
   C. Searching for Satisfaction
   D. Countering Despair with the Stories of Faith

III. Session 2—Did You Hear Who Got Invited?: Luke 14:7-24
   A. Social Customs and Anxiety
   B. Jesus' Reversal
   C. Will the Table Transform Us?

IV. Session 3—Hey! Leave Some for Me!: Exodus 16:1-36 and Matthew 6:25-34
   A. Anxiety in a World of Scarcity
   B. God's Abundant Nature
   C. Jesus Models God's Priorities

V. Session 4—Did I Mention I Don't Eat . . . ?: Daniel 1 and Revelation 3:14-22
   A. Wanting to Avoid Controversy
   B. Daniel's Stand with Authority
   C. Hot or Cold vs. Lukewarm
   E. Affluent Indifference

VI. Session 5—How Many Leaves Does This Table Have?: John 21:15-19 and Acts 2:42-47
   A. Table Fellowship Leads to Service
   B. Caution for Disciples
   C. Community of Faith Around the Table

Introduction

The Pastor's Bible Study on Christian Community: Eating and Drinking Our Way to the Kingdom

Desire for Community

We live in a world where people are hungry for meaningful connections and, hungry for significant relationships. Sports teams, music groups, political action committees, and a plethora of other communities spring up in an attempt to meet our hunger. We have all these communities, and we still haven't found what we're looking for. Bono, lead singer for the popular band *U2*, sings those very words, "…but I still haven't found what I'm looking for" in the lyrics to the song that spoke to our collective emptiness and yearning.

Faith communities offer a singular way of making the relational connections we seek. As Christians, we are nourished through sharing stories together in community. As people of the book, we are formed by the nascent stories of our faith in the Bible. If we are to learn about *Christian* faith communities, we are compelled to look at our sacred texts. What does the Bible tell us about the richness of relationships within the Christian community? How might our life together be shaped by the Bible's stories?

Biblical Images of Eating and Drinking

Over and again, biblical texts use images of hunger, food, feeding, banquets, and eating together to teach us about our relationships with God and each other. Many of us learned who we are at the family dinner table. It was there that we heard the stories of where our ancestors came from, how they came to be where they were, and their successes and foibles along the way. As many in communities throughout the southern United States say, the table is where we ask and answer the question: "Who are your people?"

For those in communities of faith, the dinner table is also often where we learned who our people were. It's where the stories of our faith, taught in Sunday Schools and from the pulpits in our churches got discussed, argued over and lived out. We are hungry for authentic Christian community, and we find it most often as we gather at the table.

It should be no surprise that so many Christian faith communities these days refer to the fact that they love to eat together. Whatever the denomination, it is a com- mon refrain to hear someone say, "Well, one thing that (name your particular church) loves to do is eat." One of the most common fundraisers in churches today comes from the publication of cookbooks. Some offer not only recipes, but also texts for feeding the soul.

The Larger Context

Following the thematic structure of table fellowship, this study uses five organizing foci to explore the development of a biblical Christian faith community. In the first lesson, we explore the theme of hunger, specifically a hunger for God and getting in touch with this hunger. We will ask whether God can really be for us and note our anxiety in that yearning. The second lesson looks at our place at our God's table, as well as the place of others at the same table. The third lesson pushes us to open ourselves up to God's reality that there is plenty, even though we live in a world that tells us we will never have enough. The fourth lesson is equally challenging as it invites us to go into the apocalyptic literature and how it served and can continue to serve the church as we set boundaries at the table. Finally, having identified our hunger, found our place, been fed and developed some sense of limits, we are called in the final lesson to go out and feed others, to share what has been given to us with a world that is hungry and still hasn't found what it's looking for.

The texts we have chosen are by no means exhaustive of the theme in scripture. However, we have been intentional in choosing a variety of scriptural literature. The images of food are found in poetry, parable and apocalypse from the early texts of the Torah through the Revelation to John.

Though we reference various scholastic works on "eating and drinking our way to the kingdom," our attempt is not to cover all scholarly points. What we do hope might happen is that the pairing and building of food images might create a space for new insights to emerge around the table.

Fear and Anxiety in Community Formation

As we did a trial run of the study with a group in our church, we discovered that a small group of ten to fourteen was ideal for this study. We also asked those who participated to make a commitment to be with the group for all five sessions. The reasoning behind this was to allow a trusting community to build as we read, studied and ate together. A small group of committed folks works particularly well for this topic, as this allows for a more open exploration of fears and anxieties that can arise in community formation. The level of trust and sharing can grow from session to session. We also discovered that the pairing of meals with texts caused our group to anticipate each lesson, eagerly reading the texts for the following session in an effort to guess what the meal would entail.

The group at Park Central Presbyterian Church who signed on to become test subjects for this project provided us with valuable feedback on reflection questions. One delightful, and in retrospect, desired result was the strengthening of the Christian community within this group of individuals. It was clear by the end of our time together that we were much more than individuals on a pilgrimage. Indeed, we are on a journey together, eating and drinking our way to the Kingdom.

I'm Hungry!

The Hunger that Leads Us to God and Others

In Anne Tyler's novel, *Dinner at the Homesick Restaurant*, Ezra is a youngest child. His father left the family when the children were young, and the hunger for a sustaining family relationship pervades the book. In middle age, Ezra takes over a restaurant bit by bit as he cares for the dying owner. When he is not at the hospital, he dreams:

> Why not a restaurant full of refrigerators, where people came and chose the food they wanted? ...He'd cook what people felt homesick for—tacos like those from vendors' cars in California, which the Mexican was always pining after; and that wonderful vinegary North Carolina barbecue that Todd Duckett had to have brought by his mother several times a year in cardboard cups. He would call it the Homesick Restaurant" (Tyler, 124).

Ezra's plans well up out of his own hunger. He regularly attempts to get his own siblings and mother to sit down around a table and have a satisfying, loving family meal. These meals often come apart and end with someone walking out long before dessert.

Hunger Leading to God

Like Ezra, our dreams are filled with our hunger. Our need for physical food is a daily survival issue, and our need for relationship follows close behind. This need often goes unsatisfied. We are created to be in relationship with God and each other; and in the deep places of our lives, we hunger for a table where we can linger, then rise with both body and soul satisfied.

From the beginning of the Old Testament God is concerned with both kinds of hunger. God promises concrete provision (Cousar, 453) of food and faithful presence in a covenantal relationship. The two are so tied together biblically that our sacred stories would be greatly impoverished without the resulting images.

Meals and God

Gillian Feeley-Harnik writes about the place of meals and its circumstances as one of the primary ways of communicating about relationships between people and between people and God. She notes specifically that,

1. The power of the Lord is manifested in his ability to control food; to feed is to bless, to confer life; to feed bad food or to starve is to judge or punish, to confer death.
2. Acceptance of the power and authority of the Lord is symbolized by acceptance of his food.
3. Rejection of the power and authority of the Lord is symbolized by seeking after food he has forbidden.
4. People "limit" or "tempt" the Lord—that is, question the extent of his power and authority—by questioning his ability to feed them.
5. The Lord's word is equated with food.
6. Eating joins people with the Lord or separates them. (Karris, 71-72)

The poetry of the Psalms provides our texts for exploring this hunger. Psalm 42:1-3 reflects the personal, intimate nature of hunger. The psalmist is longing, thirsting, yearning for God. His tears have been his only nourishment.

Searching for Satisfaction

Our world leaves us believing that we are alone and that we cannot trust anyone else to be interested in our good. We are always tempted to try to satisfy our own

Sources

Anne Tyler, *Dinner at the Homesick Restaurant* (New York: Berkley Books, 1982).

Charles Cousar, editor, *Texts for Preaching: A Lectionary Commentary Based on the NRSV—Year C* (Louisville: Westminster John Knox, 1994).

Robert J. Karris, O.F.M., *Luke: Artist and Theologian, Luke's Passion Account as Literature* (New York: Paulist, 1985).

James D. Newsome, editor, *Texts for Preaching: A Lectionary Commentary Based on the NRSV—Year A* (Louisville: Westminster John Knox, 1995).

Adam C. English, "Feeding Imagery in the Gospel of John: Uniting the Physical and the Spiritual," in *Perspectives in Religious Studies*, vol. 28, no. 3, Fall 2001, 203–214.

Teaching Tip

Serve participants a very simple, small meal. The idea is not to starve, but to feel our hunger in a physical way. A simple broth and bread do well. Invite participants to live with and notice the hunger until it is time for the next meal.

hunger without having to trust beyond ourselves. The biblical story counters this impulse.

We are often fearful and anxious and turn this on God just like the Israelites in the wilderness. "They tested God in their heart by demanding the food they craved" (78:18-20).

Both texts point to memory and storytelling as a way of countering the despair that erupts when we question God's ability to feed us. Psalms 42 and 43 use the refrain, "Hope in God; for I shall again praise him, my help and my God" (42:5, 11, 43:5). This refrain expresses the faith of the larger community. The psalmist in conversation with God and himself relies on a larger story when he is weak and hungry.

Countering Despair with Stories of Faith

Psalm 78 is intended to be a teaching psalm for children (78:1-8). The psalm lays out the history of the people from Moses to David making the clear point that nobody develops a satisfying relationship with God alone. As the psalm bears out, it is hard even as a community. The community must always remember and retell the exodus events in order to avoid amnesia and despair.

Even though the people question God's ability to give them what they need, God's resolve is to provide and to be faithful even and especially in the wilderness. "The wilderness is a place void of resources, where exposure and vulnerability may lead to death. The marvel is that this place empty of resources for life is filled with God's resolve to preserve life" (Newsome, p. 499).

We may be taken aback by the references to anger and punishment in Psalm 78. However, the psalm teaches the reality that God's provision is not to be taken for granted. God is not available to answer our cravings for junk food. God provides within a covenantal relationship that makes demands on our lives. Obedience as well as gratitude is the appropriate response of those who have been satisfied.

As we will see later, we are not only called to trust, but to participate in God's provision. "The poor shall eat and be satisfied" (22:26). How else will the poor be

Reflection

Talk about experiences anyone has had with fasting. How can fasting help us focus on our hunger for God and authentic relationships?

Study Bible

See notes on 42:1–43:5, NISB, 788.

Reflection

Where in modern culture do we turn to for satisfaction of our yearnings?

Study Bible

See the "Excursus: Beauty," 892.

satisfied except if God's people trust enough, are grateful enough to resist calculation and provide food in celebration with all?

We find it interesting that we both first ran across *Dinner at the Homesick Restaurant* in seminary pastoral care courses in which one learns so much about the meager ways we attempt to feed ourselves and others when there is no rooting in God's provision and the community of faith. We might paraphrase Augustine: our hearts are unsatisfied until we find our satisfaction in Thee.

Reflection

Note that Psalm 72 was intentionally aimed at teaching children in the faith community. What stories might we feed to the children of our community in order to nurture their trust in God? What will they use to nourish themselves if they do not hear our stories of faith?

Teaching Tip

Offer a look ahead and point to the New Testament where we find fulfillment in Jesus Christ. "There is a certain excessiveness with which Jesus provides sustenance. He makes forty gallons of wine, offers water that eternally slakes the thirst, and ensures plenty of leftovers at a meal of five thousand. In this sense, Jesus fulfills Psalm 107:9, 'for he satisfies the thirsty and fills the hungry with good things'" (English, *Feeding Imagery...* 206).

Teaching Tip

Reading Psalm 63 is a good liturgical ending. The open mouth signifies the hunger and thirst turned to prayer, praise, trust—complete openness to God, if only for this moment.

Did You Hear Who Got Invited?

Social Customs and Anxiety

Most of us have heard of Emily Post and her famous book, *Etiquette: The Blue Book of Social Usage*. In the chapter titled "Making One's Position in the Community," Post writes,

> "The bride of good family need do nothing on her own initiative. After her marriage, when she settles down in her new home, she assumes by right the intimate visiting list of her husband's family in addition to that of her own. This means that if she cares to give a general party, she can invite any of them she wants to" (Post, 101).

Behind that short, tidy paragraph stands the complex, rule-oriented, angst-ridden world of society. The questions revolve around who gets invited to what occasion, and much of the 893 pages of Post's book in one way or another boil down to the specific question of who will eat with whom.

Although the customs differed, the same anxieties and complexities applied in Jesus' time. Much has been written about the elaborate conventions connected with Greco-Roman meals including how the couches and table were arranged and how guests were seated. In an article about table fellowship in the Gospel of Luke, Dennis Smith explains the similarities between the Greco-Roman settings and biblical settings. He notes that where one sat at the table showed one's relative rank among the other guests (Smith, 617). The Jews of Jesus' time were strongly influenced by these cultural patterns, but Jewish diners faced even greater complexities. They

Lectionary Loop

Thirteenth Sunday after Pentecost, Year C, Luke 14:1, 7-14

Sources

Emily Post, *Etiquette: The Blue Book of Social Usage* (New York: Funk and Wagnalls Company, 1940).

Dennis E. Smith, "Table Fellowship as a Literary Motif in the Gospel of Luke," in *Journal of Biblical Literature,* vol. 106, no. 4, 1987, 613-638.

Jan Michael Joncas, "Tasting the Kingdom of God: The Meal Ministry of Jesus and Its Implications for Contemporary Worship and Life," in *Worship,* vol. 74, no. 4, July 2000, 329–365.

chose to express their religious differences with Gentiles and with each other through food. Not only would they not eat with Gentiles or eat gentile food, but also sometimes the Sadducees, Essenes and Pharisees ate their own distinctive meals (Joncas, 341).

As a result, a meal was much more than nourishment for the body and was freighted with much social and religious meaning. No wonder Luke reports that "when Jesus was going to the house of a leader of the Pharisees to eat a meal on the Sabbath, they were watching him closely" (14:1).

Jesus' Reversal

Luke takes meals that are already saturated with meaning and uses them to point to the realm of God that is already taking shape. Jesus dispels the anxiety over inclusion and honor at a dinner party, but stirs up a greater anxiety in his guests. No longer do they need to worry over their place at the table; they are instead now being asked to upend the table.

From time to time you see someone who is humble receive an honor, and every now and then we enjoy seeing someone who exalts himself become humbled. However, Jesus calls for both of these things to happen at once and everywhere. The world can change completely at our instigation.

Not only are we to discard our anxiety about status, but also we are to replace it with a profound concern for others. In doing this, we can begin to reach out to and welcome those who have no status or place in the world, no place at the table.

Jesus and those he shared meals with were far from unaware about the impact of the dinner table. They knew well how powerful meal gatherings could be in exclusion as well as inclusion. They understood the roles of dominance and submission, debts and obligations, and power and powerlessness that were played out around the table. "...they understood that to change dining habits was, quite literally, to change the world. For at table, everything that creates a world is present: economics, politics, the potential for rivalry and competition, bonds among friends, boundaries against enemies" (Joncas, 356).

Teaching Tips

In preparing the setting for this session, it is important to create an atmosphere of inclusion and honor. Be sure that your table is either round or square so that there is no "head" or "foot." Use place cards for each person to remind participants visually that they each have an important place at the table. Send out attractive invitations before the gathering to help create the feel of a social occasion. Serve a meal that is tried and true "company food" so that the session has the feel of a dinner party. As participants arrive, have a recording of the spiritual, *Plenty Good Room*, playing.

Reflection

Ask participants to describe situations when they felt left out and situations when they felt not only included, but also honored.

Study Bible

See notes on Luke 14:1-6 for interesting commentary on how Luke sets the stage for the dinner in the Pharisee's home, *NISB*, 1882.

Teaching Tip

Play again the recording of the spiritual *"Plenty Good Room"* and ask listeners to talk about how the world reflected in the music is different from our every day world.

Will the Table Transform Us?

Judgment and grace are held in tension in Luke's Gospel. The invitation to the banquet goes out freely, but there are few who are willing for the invitation to transform their lives. The good news is that Jesus indiscriminately welcomes all. All are welcomed, honored and forgiven in his presence. He feeds the hungry to the point of giving his life.

The church is called to the same pattern when we give a luncheon or a dinner (14:12). Not only are we to be willing to open the table in radical equality, but we are also called to be fully present there. "If Christian households do not regularly join in a common sharing of food and drink accompanied by conversation in all its danger and depth, the Lord's Table will hold little appeal" (Joncas, 359). In other words, if we have no significant interaction around the table in the fellowship hall or in our homes, we are not likely to be open to the transforming power of the Lord's Table.

Reflection

Use the poem below, *Banquet Stories—Luke 14 Read at Holy Communion* by Peter Mullins, at the end of the session as a means of inviting personal reflection.

Banquet Stories—Luke 14 read at Holy Communion

I'm disturbed by the ways in which the Gospel
doesn't transform the lives of those around me
but I'm less disturbed by the ways in which it
doesn't transform me.

I frown at those who scowl at noisy children
and draw back from those who won't shake adult hands
but it hardly occurs to me to ask why this
doesn't transform me.

I marvel that they don't choose lower places
or want to be close to others at the feast
but I cope with the way my celebrating
doesn't transform me.

And all the while there is an invitation
from which new fields, oxen and wives distract
but watching those who're distracted in these ways
doesn't transform me.
So I'll not be marked by my humility
nor can I pretend I have wide sympathy—
I'll just hope I'm among those compelled by one
yet to transform me.

Peter Mullins (*Epworth Review*, vol. 26, #4, October 1999).

Hey! Leave Some for Me!

Abundance, not scarcity, best describes the world's food supply. Enough wheat, rice and other grains are produced to provide every human being with 3,500 calories a day. That doesn't even count many other commonly eaten foods—vegetables, beans, nuts, root crops, fruits, grass-fed meats, and fish. Enough food is available to provide at least 4.3 pounds of food per person a day worldwide: two and half pounds of grain, beans and nuts, about a pound of fruits and vegetables, and nearly another pound of meat, milk and eggs— enough to make most people fat! (Lappé, 5).

Lectionary Loop

Eighteenth Sunday after Pentecost, Year A, Exodus 16:2-15
Thanksgiving Day, Year B, Matthew 6:25-33

Sources

Frances Moore Lappé, "Enough to Go Around," in *World Ark,* May/June 2005, 5.

Walter Brueggemann, "The Liturgy of Abundance, the Myth of Scarcity," in *The Christian Century*, March 24, 1999, 30-31.

Teaching Tip

The key to the meal at this study is abundance. Prepare more than enough food for those in the study. Bountiful pasta dishes do well for this gathering. Use the largest bowls you can find to put fruit and bread on the table. Have containers for folks to take home leftovers. Invite them to reflect on God's abundance as they enjoy yet another meal after the meeting.

Anxiety in a World of Scarcity

We live in a world that tells us day by day that there is not enough and that we have to grab what we need in order for life to be secure. The truth is that there is enough and that what we think we need is often just what we want. This leads to a world of anxiety, disease, hollow places and gluttonous hearts.

The story in our Exodus text relates how the people are given daily bread and a daily opportunity to witness God's steadfastness and generosity. The manna is intended to feed them, but also teach them and challenge them on a deeper level of relationship with God. Throughout their journey in the wilderness, they are learning what it means to be God's covenantal partners.

They had never before received bread as a free gift that they couldn't control, predict, plan for, or own. The meaning of this strange narrative is that the gifts of life are indeed given by a generous God. It's a wonder, it's a miracle, it's an embarrassment, it's irrational, but God's abundance transcends the market economy (Brueggemann, 31).

God's Abundant Nature

It would seem that in the wilderness Israel would turn to God, rely on God. The wilderness itself has no resources to offer them. Yet, instead of trusting God, the people of Israel complained and disobeyed. They tried to work God's miracles to their advantage, as if the miracle, presence and generosity of God were not enough! Even when God provided daily sustenance in the form of manna, they could not trust God's provision. Some tried to hoard it overnight, afraid that somehow God's generosity might not really be present. But no matter how much they tried to gather, in God's economy "those who gathered much had nothing over, and those who gathered little had no shortage" (Exod 16:18).

After they were specifically instructed to gather enough for two days on the sixth day of the week, some tried to gather on the Sabbath day. It was difficult to trust in God rather than believing that having enough depended on their ability to get out there and gather every day. "Sabbath means that there's enough bread, that we don't have to hustle every day of our lives. There's no record that Pharaoh ever took a day off. People who think their lives consist of struggling to get more and more can never slow down because they won't ever have enough" (Brueggemann, 31).

The text from Matthew's gospel is directed to the disciples. It provides instruction specifically for those who want to follow Jesus. This is a call for them to set themselves apart from the surrounding culture, to identify themselves specifically as followers of Jesus Christ. The particular passage we are looking at comes within the Sermon on the Mount, a challenging teaching that we too easily follow piecemeal, choosing the parts we can adapt to our own lives without causing too much adjustment, discomfort, or sacrifice. These verses instruct the

Study Bible

See Excursus: Covenant, *NISB*, 113.

Reflection

What in today's world helps us understand the ancient Hebrew people's reluctance and inability to follow God's instructions concerning how to gather the manna?

Study Bible

See notes on Matt 5:1-7:28, *NISB*, 1754 and specifically 1758.

disciples regarding trusting God's abundance, much like the lesson of manna in the wilderness.

Being anxious and worrying indicate "what monopolizes human goals, identity, and efforts" (*NISB*, 1758). It is particularly instructive for the disciples to hear that there is a difference between striving for the goals and identity related to the religious world they lived in and striving for God's kingdom and God's righteousness.

The first of Jesus' temptations is to make bread for himself rather than trusting and relying on God (Matt 4:1-4). The Lord's Prayer, following an emphasis on God's priorities, leads us immediately to ask God to give us each day our daily bread (Matt 6:11). This is a request that God would continue to be generous; that the abundance would continue. The prayer also reminds us that God is generous and that it is a daily challenge to remember that and not fret and hustle in an attempt to be self-sufficient.

Jesus Models God's Priorities

Jesus models priorities in the way he lives. Abundance can begin with a small boy holding only five loaves and two fish. "Jesus bypasses the temptation to brandish his divine powers. He simply blesses and distributes the skimpy victuals. Yet the loaves and fish do more than suffice the hungry gathering, indeed, twelve baskets full of leftovers are collected. The compiling of all the extra food demonstrates a certain quality about Jesus as the divine feeder. His provisions are always excessive" (English, 206). Jesus rejects anxiety and worrying in favor of extravagance.

Every meal can become an opportunity to experience God's promises and take on an extravagant way of living. This does not have to mean an expensive way of living, but instead it is one that approaches God with a true sense that God will provide. There is a small mission church in an impoverished area of Campeche, Mexico. Their building consists of limbs and twine, and the growing congregation proclaims its faith by the name they have claimed for their church and placed over the door: "Jehovah Jireh." Even the youngest child has learned that this means "God will

Reflection

How might observing the Sabbath affect our tendency to worry and be anxious?

provide." You would think that they scarcely have five loaves and two fish among them, but they welcome scores of neighborhood children and their parents, eager to share the good news of the gospel, the amazing abundance of God's care. When you visit this congregation, you do not go away hungry—in any sense of the word.

Abundance and generosity are God's way to live. When bread is broken and shared, there is more than enough for everyone.

Did I Mention I Don't Eat...?

Wanting to Avoid Controversy

Once a community has been established, boundaries become necessary. Sarah served as a minister in a small southern town before we married. It was one of the places we visited after we became engaged and were meeting each other's friends. One of the particularly poignant stories that Andrew remembers from that visit clearly identified the boundaries of the faith community with whom Sarah had served. During the weeks before and after the most notable demonstrations for civil rights in the 1960's, the whole town was in an uproar. It was not clear where or when something was likely to happen.

Most of the large white downtown congregations, including the one where Sarah was serving, were afraid that their churches would be the next scenes of demonstrations, and they took actions to protect their communities. On Sunday mornings, most of those churches closed the doors and posted large men outside on the steps to make sure that nothing disrupted the worship and programs of the church. All of the doors were closed on Sunday except for those at one church. This church unlocked the doors on Sunday morning and threw them open wide. Ushers stood ready with bulletins to hand out to anyone who wanted to come in and worship. Thirty years later, the story continued to be a defining one for that particular congregation.

It may seem startlingly clear to us now that there should have been no other choice. However, the stories of that time highlight the fear and risk inherent in that bold decision.

Source

Craig R. Koester, "The Message to Laodicea and the Problem of Its Local Context: A Study of the Imagery in Rev 3.14-22," in *New Testament Studies*, vol. 49, no. 3, July 2003, 407–424.

Teaching Tip

Plan a meal with items that taste good only hot or cold. For example, you might have hot soup for an entrée and sorbet for dessert. In addition, prepare small bowls of each item and let them come to room temperature. Invite participants to taste the difference.

Andrew asked why they opened the doors and heard various reasons and stories in response. What became clear in listening to this defining story was that the faith community now clearly believed that the living Christ enabled them to unlock those church doors. They were Christ's church and were defining themselves as such by making it clear that their boundaries were ones that welcomed, even when such welcoming was not acceptable to the surrounding religious culture.

Daniel's Stand with Authority

Christian communities often do not truly take shape unless the members are bold enough or desperate enough to create boundaries. The apocalyptic literature of Daniel and Revelation provides intriguing glimpses of God's people under threat and how they engaged the call to distinguish themselves as peculiar communities.

The first six chapters of Daniel depict the Israelites in a time of exile and portray Daniel as a righteous man, a worthy recipient of the visions that are recounted in chapters 7-12. Daniel's first conflict with Babylon, the oppressing power, concerns food. King Nebuchadnezzar assigns a daily portion of the royal rations of food and wine to Daniel and his companions, and they abstain in favor of water and vegetables. By resisting the lure of the king's food, the young men distinguish themselves when it would have been far easier and safer to blend in with the dominant culture. Sometimes it is important to say who we are not.

The issue here is the relationship with the king's table. The food and wine, in and of themselves, are not at issue. It is clear that Daniel has no problem eating the king's vegetables. The issue, specifically, has to do with the relationship with the king as the highest power of the land, the one called "lord" in that day. Perhaps in our time he would be called the commander-in-chief. The story of chapter 1 clearly points to dependence on God as a defining boundary. Daniel and his companions are brought into the king's court to be trained and are renamed by the palace master, but they manage to retain control over what will nourish them. When Daniel and his companions eat vegetables and water as a test for ten days, God is steadfast. At the end of the ten days, the young men appear "better and fatter than all the young men who had been eating the royal rations" (Dan 1:15).

It is interesting to note that there were presumably lots of young men who had no trouble with the royal rations and gave all their loyalty to the king as commander in chief.

Revelation looks at a similar problem from a different angle. Again the people of God are in a threatening situation. This time, the threat comes from the Roman Empire, and the fledging Christian communities are in danger of being consumed.

The imagery in Rev 3:14-22, the last of the seven letters to the churches, has been much debated. Many commentators suggest that cold means either being passive or being against God. In turn, they offer that hot means being either enthusiastic or for God. However, Craig Koester makes a compelling argument that brings new life to this imagery. He maintains that the "metaphor requires that both hot and cold be understood positively in contrast to being lukewarm, the negative trait that characterizes the complacency of the Laodicean Christians. The question is, how can both heat and cold be viewed positively?" (Koester, 409).

Study Bible

Revelation was written in symbolic language in order to evoke, provoke, irritate and disorient, *NISB,* 2212.

Hot or Cold vs. Lukewarm

Koester compellingly argues that the Christians in Laodicea are rebuked because their works are neither hot nor cold, but have instead been found to be tepid, eliciting a revulsion expressed dramatically in the imagery of Christ vomiting them out of his mouth. Tepid drinks are simply not palatable. They offer no contrast to the room temperature and little refreshment for anyone who does not happen to be dying of thirst. The works of the church in Laodicea offered nothing different than the works of the surrounding culture. There was no way to distinguish them from their contiguous world.

Reflections

What might make the church reluctant to distinguish itself from other communities and other powers in our world?

How do you react to the image of Christ vomiting Christians? What are the dangers of a tepid faith?

What does the challenge to the Laodician church have to do with being a disciple today?

Affluent Indifference

With a poignant relevancy to our own time and culture, we see that this lukewarm quality in the church comes out of a self-satisfaction that has emerged from affluence. "The call for works that are cold or hot summons readers to actions that are distinguished from the familiar pattern of wealth breeding complacency, and instead express the relationship with the risen Christ that sets the Christian community apart" (Koester, 415).

How Many Leaves Does This Table Have?

Table Fellowship Leads to Service

During the time we were developing this series of lessons, we visited Heifer International's working educational farm in Massachusetts with a group of youth and adults. Heifer has helped millions of hungry people all over the world through the gift of livestock and the training in their care. Our group gathered for a devotional before we went to the farm, and one elder reported later that the gospel reading about Jesus feeding the five thousand was stunning and simple. Jesus cared about feeding people. This thoughtful man had considered the spiritual aspects of feeding many times, but Jesus' physical feeding of people time and again came home to him in a new way as the gospel was paired with the care of goats that would ensure a family's survival.

When we enter the post-resurrection scene of John 21, Jesus has already given himself completely for the world. He has given his life. Earlier in John's Gospel, Jesus describes himself in this way:

> Jesus said to them, "I am the bread of life. Whoever comes to me will never be hungry, and whoever believes in me will never be thirsty . . . I am the living bread that came down from heaven. Whoever eats of this bread will live forever; and the bread that I will give for the life of the world is my flesh" (John 6:35, 50-51).

Jesus has given his own body as food for the world. Yet in John 6 and John 21, Jesus' ultimate gift is paired with feeding both the crowds and the disciples with

Lectionary Loop

Third Sunday of Easter, Year C,
John 21:1-19
Fourth Sunday of Easter, Year A,
Acts 2:42-47

Sources

John Fuellenbach, *Church: Community for the Kingdom* (Maryknoll: Orbis Books, 2002).

Lorraine V. Murray, "Feeding His Sheep," "*America: The National Catholic Weekly*," vol. 183, no. 2, July 15 2000. http://www.americamagazine.org/gettext.cfm?articleTypeID=9&textID=764&issueID=307.

Teaching Tip

The preparation for the meal for this session should be shared. Those who do not cook can bring bread, drinks or flowers for the table. Sharing dishes emphasizes the call to each of us to feed the sheep. It also nourishes the spirit of generosity around the table.

bread and fish. The bread of life and the bread for the stomach are not separate, but inextricably conjoined in John's Gospel. The concrete images in John over and again have a quality of "more," while, notably, at the same time also having concrete real value. The vivid details John offers in the stories of Jesus interacting with others point not simply to the spiritual nature of Jesus as the living water and the bread of life. Unmistakably, Jesus is also concerned about providing very real H_20 and baked grain. Even after the resurrection, John makes a point of telling us that Jesus "came and took the bread and gave it to them, and did the same with the fish" (John 21:13). Jesus has prepared a satisfying meal for the disciples to eat after a long night of work. Whatever else Jesus has in mind for his disciples, he makes sure that their empty stomachs are filled.

When the disciples finish their breakfast, Jesus then puts the mission of the church into Peter's keeping by asking Peter to feed his sheep. The images of the shepherd and sheep are so abundant in scripture that we easily miss the connection with practical feeding. We often hear Jesus' command to, "Feed my sheep," as a solely spiritual calling that involves the tending of souls. However, Jesus' actions in feeding his disciples remind us that souls come with hungry bodies. The mission of the church is to feed souls and bodies.

Reflection

When you hear, "Feed my sheep," what other biblical stories and passages about sheep and shepherds come to mind? Some examples are Psalm 23, Isa 53, Luke 15:1-7—The Parable of the Lost Sheep; John 1:29—Jesus named as the Lamb of God; John 10:11-18—Jesus naming himself as the good shepherd

Caution for Disciples

Further, lest Peter or we begin to believe that feeding sheep is an easy mission, Jesus gives Peter a prediction about his death in verses 18 and 19. It may seem odd that Jesus would commission Peter and talk about his death in the next breath, but the text is a reminder that feeding sheep is a risky business. Peter will expose his life to danger by living out his love for Jesus. He will ultimately lose control: lose his life for the sake of feeding Jesus' sheep.

Jesus fed hungry people, offered water to the thirsty, and then also gave his body and blood to save the world. In this text, Jesus is handing over this ministry to Peter. With it come joys and sorrows, delights and hardships, spiritual and physical elements. Soul tending and stomach filling ministry go hand in hand for Peter

Reflection

Read John 13:34-47 and John 15:12-14, alongside John 21:18-19 and reflect on what it might mean to feed Jesus' sheep in our context.

and for all those that follow him even until today. Adam English has summarized the calling of this passage with a vivid image. "While this process is sometimes termed apostolic succession, it might be better thought of as one holy, apostolic, unbroken food chain" (English, 213).

The passage from Acts is an encapsulated look at how that holy, apostolic food chain began to grow in the early church. This summary of life in the first Christian communities following Pentecost "offers an ideal to which believers aspire." This short, pithy passage focuses on four characteristics of the believers' community: 1) remaining dedicated to the teaching of the apostles, 2) the sharing of spiritual communion and possessions, 3) prayer and 4) the sharing of food both in meals and in the ritual of the Lord's Supper (*NISB*, 1961).

Community of Faith Around the Table

The breaking of bread is mentioned twice within these six verses. In fact, the text even describes the prevailing attitude of the people around the table; they ate with glad and generous hearts. "Generous" is usually a term reserved for the character of God. In Acts, we are given a developing picture of a community that is taking on God's generous nature by sharing what they have, especially food. The disciples, who were fed by Jesus, are now taking their place in the divine ministry of feeding.

Eating together became both a means of nourishing the fledging community and a way of expanding it. Day by day the numbers increased, and one can imagine the disciples constantly figuring out how to add another leaf to the table. As they ate together, they discerned what it meant to feed and tend Jesus' sheep.

In his book *Church: Community for the Kingdom*, John Fuellenbach asserts,

> "Only the community can provide the atmosphere, the concern, the mutual love, and the experience of Christ risen and alive that will enable the disciple to live true discipleship. Outside of the community we cannot live discipleship" (Fuellenbach, 117).

It has been said that it takes a village to raise a child.

Study Bible

See Acts introduction for helpful information on placing this summary text within the larger scope of the book, *NISB*, 1953–1954.

Teaching Tip

Ask group members to read Lorraine V. Murray's brief *Faith in Focus article, Feeding His Sheep*, in the July 15, 2000, online issue of *America: The National Catholic Weekly*. Use the article as a means of reflecting on how God might give us the support and time we need to feed sheep and add a few leaves to God's table.

Reflection

Is offering food and drink to the hungry and the thirsty an optional or key piece to being the church? Can we divide the physical and spiritual care of sheep and remain true to Christ's calling?

Our study of these scripture passages also makes it clear that it takes a community—specifically a community table—to raise a Christian.

SPIRITUAL GIFTS

A STUDY BY

KEN CARTER

Ken Carter, senior pastor of Providence United Methodist Church in Charlotte, N.C., is the author of The Gifted Pastor *and* A Way of Life in the World.

SPIRITUAL GIFTS

Outline

I. Introduction

II. Session 1—Spiritual Gifts and Community: 1 Corinthians 12
   A. The Language of Gifts
   B. Accepting Our Gifts
   C. Honoring the Gifts of Others

III. Session 2—Connecting Spirituality and Church: 1 Corinthians 14
   A. A Private Prayer Language, or Public Speech?
   B. What is Spirituality?

IV. Session 3—Spiritual Gifts and Transformation: Romans 12
   A. Transformation
   B. Listing the Gifts

V. Session 4—Spiritual Gifts and the Equipping of the Laity: Ephesians 4
   A. The Calling of the Laity
   B. The Purpose of Gifts

Introduction

Spiritual Gifts

There are four classic texts in the New Testament that focus on Spiritual Gifts: 1 Cor 12, 1 Cor 14, Rom 12, and Eph 4. In these Bible Studies, we will reflect on them in that order, in a kind of pastoral commentary. If a pastor is to ground the life of the church in spiritual gifts, he or she will need to become acquainted with these texts and the issues they explore. A study of these gifts will help individuals grasp the way God is calling them to serve, and the study will also help a congregation offer more effective mission in the world.

Paul writes to various congregations in the NT and a number of them are in the midst of conflict (for example, 1 Cor 1:10; and Phil 4:2 ff. In a sense, Paul is seeking to bring order out of chaos, and he looks to the gift of God's creative spirit as the source of this possible new creation (2 Cor 5). Where the spirit of the Lord is, there is a diversity of gifts, and yet these are placed in the One Body (1 Cor 12:12).

Most pastors and many lay leaders understand the divisions that exist in congregations. We are often led to discover resources beyond the church (mediation, conflict resolution), and God can use these resources for the good of the church. It is also true, however, that authentic unity is always a gift of God, a movement of the Holy Spirit.

The apostle Paul was inspired to see the gifts of the Spirit, their presence in the lives of the faithful, and their placement in the One Body as God's way of moving beyond divisions toward mission in the world. As you prepare for these studies, pray for the presence of the Holy Spirit in your teaching and for a receptivity among those who will engage in these biblical passages. Remember the words of Jesus: "I ask that they may be one, as you Father are in me and I am in you…so that the world may believe that you have sent me" (John 17:20-21).

Sources

Ken Carter, *The Gifted Pastor: Finding And Using Your Spiritual Gifts* (Nashville: Abingdon, 2001); see especially chapter two.

Lloyd Edwards, *Discerning Your Spiritual Gifts* (Cambridge: Cowley, 1988). Richard Hays, *First Corinthians. Interpretation: A Bible Commentary For Teaching and Preaching* (Louisville: John Knox, 1999).

Study Bible

See Gen 1:2; Luke 4:18-19; John 14:16; Acts 1:6-8; Acts 2:1-13. The Spirit (wind) of God moves over the waters in creation and activates the prophecy of Isaiah. (See Isa 61:1-2, later quoted by Jesus in Luke 4.) After the resurrection, Jesus breathes on the disciples and grants them the gift of the Holy Spirit (John 20:22). In Acts, Jesus promises the gift of the Spirit, prior to his ascension (Acts 1:8), and on the Day of Pentecost, the gift of the Spirit is given to those gathered in Jerusalem (Acts 2; compare with Gen 11).

Spiritual Gifts and Community

First Cor 12 serves as the beginning of a portion of scripture that concludes at the end of ch. 14 and includes the chapter on love (13). When Paul notes that he does not want the reader to be "uninformed," he is stressing that the primary sign of the Holy Spirit is *love*, not glossalia, or speaking in unknown tongues. Paul then reminds the reader that not all inspired speech is from God (12:2). As F. F. Bruce has noted, "Ecstasy or enthusiasm is not the criterion of spirituality; attention must be paid to the words spoken." (*New Century Bible*). Those who persecuted Christians forced them to say Jesus was *anathema* (cursed), often as an entry into a sect. "Jesus is Lord," (12:3) is the most basic Christian creed. Note the important connection between Jesus Christ and the Holy Spirit. The Holy Spirit leads us to do those things that Jesus did.

In 12:4-6 there is a trinitarian structure: Spirit-Lord-God. The unity of the Spirit is expressed in the diversity of gifts (*charismata*), services (*diakonia*), and activities (*energmata*). Richard Hayes is helpful in noting that Paul "had no explicit doctrine of the Trinity; this doctrine was not articulated formally by theologians until hundreds of years later. The passage shows, however, that he *experienced* God as Trinity; he can describe the activity of God in the community in three synonymous parallel clauses as the working of the Spirit and of the Lord Jesus and of God."

The gifts of God are given for the common good (v. 7), and nine manifestations are listed in vv. 8-10. The gifts are:

Lectionary Loop

Second Sunday after Epiphany, Year C, 1 Cor 12:1-11
Pentecost, Year A, 1 Cor 12:3b-13
Third Sunday after Epiphany, Year C, 1 Cor 12:12-31a

Sources

Richard Hayes, *First Corinthians. Interpretation: A Bible Commentary for Teaching and Preaching* (Louisville: John Knox, 1997), 210

- Wisdom—*an insight borne of maturity*
- Knowledge—*an inner apprehension of the truth*
- Faith—*trust and confidence in the miraculous work of God*
- Healing—*the work of God that brings about salvation and wholeness of body, mind, and spirit*
- Miracles—*the capacity to do mighty works*
- Prophecy—*the practice of building up the community*
- Discernment of spirits—*having a clarity about what is true and what is false*
- Various kinds of tongues—*a private prayer language*
- Interpretation of tongues—*the communal interpretation of someone's private prayer language*

Each gift has its origin in the one Spirit (v. 11), thus, there is unity within diversity. Paul next begins a discussion of gifts through the image of the body of Christ, in vv. 12-26. This image had appeared earlier in the letter. For example,

> "Do you not know that your bodies are members of Christ?" (1 Cor 6:15)
>
> "Because there is one bread, we who are many are one body" (1 Cor 10:17).
>
> "All who eat and drink without discerning the body eat and drink judgment against themselves." (1 Cor 11:29).

These scriptures refer to the interdependence of members within the body of Christ, the church, and serve as a corrective to the privatization of our spiritualities and our temptation to withdraw from community. Because we have been baptized, the distinctions within the church disappear (1 Cor 12:13), and so we drink of the one Spirit, the invitation of Jesus to all who are thirsty (John 7:37-39).

Paul insists, in vv. 14-22, that all parts of the body are important and necessary; in fact, the weaker parts of the body are indispensable (12:22). Paul is appealing for unity—that there be no dissension in the body. This requires an understanding of the interdependence of members of the church, in suffering and rejoicing

(12:26). There follows a listing, in v. 28, of eight spiritual gifts, which do not correspond to the list of nine earlier:

- Apostles—*those who are sent by God*
- Prophets—*those who declare the mind of God in the present*
- Teachers—*those who instruct and guide others in the faith*
- Power— *the capacity to do mighty works*
- Healing—*the work of God that brings about salvation and wholeness of body, mind, and spirit*
- Helping—*extending compassion to the weak, poor and vulnerable*
- Leadership—*those who order the life of the community*
- Tongues—*a private prayer language*

And in vv. 29-30, there is a third listing of gifts, again slightly different. The chapter ends with an affirmation that the greatest spiritual gift is love. This chapter, so often read in celebrations of marriage, is best understood in its context. The spiritual gifts, taken to their extreme and expressed in their most dynamic form, are no match for the gift of love, which "builds up" (1 Cor 8:1).

The Language of Gifts

Indeed, the body does not consist of one member, but of many (1 Cor 12:14)

Paul's letters to the Corinthians were written in the middle of the first century. The primary theme of 1 Cor is the matter of how Christians can live together without splitting into factions. "I hear that some of you are saying that 'I belong to Apollos' or 'I belong to Cephas' or 'I belong to Paul,' " he reports. But then he asks: "Has Christ been divided?" (1:13).

There are problems in the Christian community at Corinth. There is bizarre sex and overwhelming greed (ch. 5). Also, there are lawsuits and scandals (ch. 6) among visible participants in the church. Of course, there are real parallels between modern North America and first century Corinth!

Paul is attempting to make sense out of the gospel in a culture marked by fraud, deceit, and self-centeredness—a culture very much like our own. These Christians had heard the message of Galatians, that they were free in Christ, no longer bound by the constraints of the law, but liberated to follow Jesus. Their interpretation, however, needed a corrective: they understood their relationship to God as a special knowledge and privilege and as a freedom from having to live a life of integrity and faithfulness. The Corinthian Christians understood freedom as freedom *to do as they pleased.* Somewhere, Paul must have felt there had been a breakdown in communication.

Study Bible

Read the notes from Gal 5 on Christian freedom and the role of the law in the life of the Christian.

Reflections

How did Paul choose to respond? By using the language of gifts—gifts that God places within us, gifts that have a purpose and gifts that allow us to serve others, diverse gifts. How can we read this letter from Paul and hear it as if he is speaking to us?

Reflection

See Henri Nouwen, *Life of The Beloved* (New York: Crossroad, 1992) and his meditation on the Christian's life as one that is taken, blessed, broken, and given.

Accepting Our Gifts

We can accept our own gifts and become comfortable with them. This is difficult for many of us. I imagine that each of us would like to be something other than who we are, in some way. In this life's journey we are prone to neglect *who we are* in favor *of what we perceive in another person*. We are inclined to measure ourselves against others; usually we fall short. And so we deny the very gift, the very uniqueness, of who we are.

Jesus Christ frees us from all of that. We are called to accept our own gifts, to rejoice in our own uniqueness. Each of us is created in God's image. Each of us has a gift to share with others, and that gift is not so much what we do as *who we are*. Read 1 Cor 12 closely, especially the section about the body, the hand, the eye, etc. (vv. 14-26). Pay attention to issues of importance, honor, respect, and judgment. Reflect on the way individuals are treated in your own community. Are some visible and others invisible? Have you ever felt invisible? Can you recall an experience when your gift was noticed, or accepted by others?

Honoring The Gifts of Others

We can rejoice in our own gifts. We can also honor the gifts of others. I am convinced that we are initially attracted to people as marriage partners because of their differences, because of their uniqueness, and then we spend all of our time and energies trying to sand those rough edges and to make them more like... like us. This is really a lifetime project. That wonderful personality trait in your husband or wife that brought a smile to your face and a lump in your throat and a faster beat within your heart while you were dating can become an irritant, a thorn in the flesh. And deep down, we are asking, under our breath, *"Why can't you be more like me?"*

We are unique, we are different, and that is precisely God's design for the church: *"God has arranged the members of the body, each one of them, as he chose* "(12:18). The body is strong because each muscle, each joint, each ligament has a different function. Where there is weakness, Paul insists, take note: The members of the body that seem to be weaker are indispensable, for God enters into the world and overcomes the world through a crucified Lord.

Connecting Spirituality and Church

"Pursue love and strive for the spiritual gifts...so that the church may be built up." (v. 1 and v. 5). Somehow a couple of important words have come to mean two different things. "Spirituality" means one thing, and "church" means something else. Spirituality means something good. Church means something bad. It is not evident, or obvious, that people in our time connect the words "spiritual" and "church." These two issues—what it means to be spiritual and what it means to be the church—are at the heart of our scripture. And Paul's struggle with these issues can help us, as a gathered body of believers and as individual Christians. There is an obvious concern: What to do about those folks who speak in tongues at the church in Corinth? Paul offers clear advice, laced with a practical, constructive appeal to his listeners, and it is grounded in the frequency of the word "upbuilding."

Those who prophesy *build up* other people as they speak to them (v. 3).

> No one understands those who speak in tongues,
> but those who prophesy *build up* the church (v. 3).
> Those who speak in a tongue *build up* themselves,
> but those who prophesy *build up* the church (v. 4).
> The one who prophesies is greater than the one who speaks in tongues, unless someone interprets, so that they may *build up* the church (v. 4).

> Strive for the spiritual gifts, in order to *build up* the church (v. 12).

When you come together, each one has a hymn, a lesson, a revelation, a tongue, or an interpretation. Let everything be done to build up the church (v. 26).

By our presence, by our gifts, we *build up* the community. I remember an elderly gentleman who attended a rural church I once served. He had been deaf for many years. Someone asked him, "Why do you still come to 'preaching'?" as they called it. He responded, *"I want people to know which side I'm on!"* We are to be on the side that *builds up* the church!

Sources

The Message (Colorado Springs: Navpress, 2002), 2086.

A Private Prayer Language, or Public Speech?

Paul is teaching us, encouraging us, pleading with us to *build up* the church. We can understand his appeal in another way, by listening to a more recent translation of this passage from *The Message* by Eugene Peterson. In it he translates the Greek word for "tongues" (*glossalalia*) as "prayer language":

The one who prays using a private prayer language certainly gets a lot out of it, but proclaiming God's truth to the church in its common language brings the whole church into growth and strength. I want all of you to develop intimacies with God in prayer, but please don't stop with that. Go on and proclaim his dear truth to others.

The spiritual life is important, Paul says, but it is always life to be shared with others. Our private, personal spiritual lives are essential; but isn't it wonderful when that intimacy with God bubbles to the surface and is a blessing to others? The Holy Spirit comes into our midst in actions that are public: wind, fire, debate, audible speech, confusion, questions.

The word Paul uses to contrast the private prayer language is "prophecy." A prophet does not predict the future. A prophet speaks God's word in the present. A prophetic word is a word that *builds up,* that sets right, that gives insight, that orders, maybe even changes our lives.

Study Bible

Read the excursus on "Creation: Ordering Chaos" (Gen 1:2) and "Speech, Hearing and Silence" (Prov 25).

Always speak a word that builds up the community, Paul insists. The Christian community gathers in order to share gifts with one another. We gather in our strengths and weaknesses. We come together to receive the grace of God.And, yes, we come together in order that we might be fed spiritually: by one another, by the Word, by music, by prayer.

What is Spirituality?

It is fine that we have private, personal experiences with God. But biblical faith is always corporate: the Old Testament is the history of a people, Israel, and much of the New Testament consists of documents circulated among first-century congregations. John Wesley wrote, "I shall endeavor to show that Christianity is essentially a social religion, and that to turn it into a solitary religion is to destroy it." The private prayer language of the heart of which Paul speaks is valued, but a communion with Jesus Christ is being drawn more and more into a dynamic, living relationship with him through his body, the Church.

There is more to the Christian life than personal spirituality. God has designed the Christian life to be lived in community. In his book, *Paul, The Spirit and The People of God*, Gordon Fee poses this scene:

> "A single person is sitting at home in front of the TV; a Christian broadcast is on, a sermon is preached, an invitation is given, and the person responds by "accepting Christ." But the only "church" the person attends is by way of the TV, with no connection to a local body of believers. The question is: Is this person saved? I would answer: Only God knows, but such salvation lies totally outside the New Testament frame of reference."

God's design for the Christian faith is that we live it together. Every time you share with me, every time I encourage you, every time you forgive another person, every time you allow yourself to receive love or grace from someone else, the church is being built up. We cannot do it alone. We need God, and we need each other.

Can a church be spiritual? If we can truly make love the guiding principle of all that we do, if we can seek to know and share our gifts, if we can build up one

Source

Gordon Fee, *Paul, The Spirit and the People of God* (Peabody, Maine: Hendrickson, 1996), 63, 72.

Study Bible

Stephen Gunter, *The Quotable Mr. Wesley* (Atlanta: Candler School of Theology, Emory University, 1999), 56.

another ... then we are a spiritual body, and then we are truly the church of Jesus Christ. Gordon Fee again says it well:

> "To be saved, in Paul's view, means to become a part of the people of God, who by the Spirit are born into God's family and therefore joined to one another as one body.... God is not simply saving diverse individuals and preparing them for heaven; rather he is creating a people for his name, among whom God can dwell and who in their life together will reproduce God's life and character in all its unity and diversity."

Strive for the spiritual gifts, to build up the church, Paul insists. Our task is to hear the call of the scriptures, to connect these two great words, "spirituality" and "church."

Reflection

Why does life in a congregation often seem void of spirit? How is spirituality in the culture often unrelated to the church?

Spiritual Gifts and Transformation

It is helpful again to place this text in its context. In the first seven chapters of Romans, Paul reflects on the reality of human sin in light of God's grace, with full attention to our struggle to be faithful. Rom 8 marks a transition: *there is no condemnation for those who are in Christ Jesus* (Rom 8:1). The Holy Spirit sustains as we enter into our status as children of God (8:16), and we are encouraged in the promise that nothing can separate us from the love of God (8:28-38). Rom 9-11 is a meditation on a question close to the heart of the apostle: what will be Israel's destiny? Rom 12 marks yet another transition: how are we to live as God's chosen people, as God's adopted children, as those who are elected and included in the saving purpose of God?

Transformation

In Rom 12:1 Paul argues that the Christian life is shaped by the structure of God's grace. The sacrifice acceptable to God (our burnt offering) is the whole of our lives. This is our reasonable (logical) service, in light of all that has been given to us. We are then challenged: do not be conformed to this world! As *The Message* translates it:

> "Don't become so well-adjusted to your culture that you fit into it without thinking" (Eugene Peterson).

The transforming work of God in us helps us to discern the will of God—namely, what is good and acceptable and perfect. (Peterson translates this as "*mature, coming to fruition.*")

Lectionary Loop

Fourteenth Sunday after Pentecost, Year A, Proper 16, Romans 12:1-8
Fifteenth Sunday after Pentecost, Year A, Proper 17, Romans 12:9-21

Study Bible

See the excursus on "Sanctification" (Rom 6:1), and read the notes on Rom 8:1 (the introduction of the Spirit) and Rom 12:1-8 (the new life in Christ).

In Rom 12:3-13, Paul focuses on the experience of grace within the Christian community (compare with Phil 2 and Eph 4). Remember: Christians have been adopted into a new "family" (Rom 8). This also rules out the spiritual pride that leads us to think that our gift is superior to the gift of another. In v. 4, Paul again argues for a diversity within the one body (12:4) that leads to our interdependence on one another (12:5). "We have gifts that differ according to the grace given to us," he insists in 12:6. Paul Achtemeier has suggested that "...The difference between Christians is not that some have spiritual gifts and some do not. The difference consists in the fact that not all have received the same gift."

Sources

Paul Achtemeier, *Romans*, Interpretation series; (Louisville: John Knox, 1985), 197.

Listing the Gifts

Another listing of the spiritual gifts is contained in Romans 12:6-8. Again, there is no hierarchy of gifts; each is important. There are seven:

- **Prophecy—*declaring the mind of God in the present***
- **Ministry—*service to God's people in a practical way***
- **Teaching— *instructing and guiding others in the faith*?**
- **Exhortation—*encouraging others toward holiness***
- **Generosity—*sharing out of one's own gifts***
- **Leadership—*ordering the life of the community***
- **Compassion—*doing acts of mercy with cheerfulness***

After listing the gifts, Paul appeals to the importance of love. Eugene Peterson translates 12:9 in this way: "*love from the center of who you are*." Christians are to love one another (12:10). A deepening understanding of spiritual gifts always has love as its foundation.

Some of the literature on spiritual gifts draws too great a distinction between the gifts of the Spirit and the fruits of the Spirit. Love clearly is both a gift of the Spirit (1 Cor 13) and a fruit of the Spirit (Gal 5). The priority of love in each case is obvious. Writing about the fruits of the Spirit, Philip Kenneson notes:

That love heads Paul's list of the Spirit's fruit is hardly accidental. Indeed, many Christian thinkers across the ages have insisted that the fruits of the Spirit listed by Paul are not nine separate fruits, of which love is simply the first. Rather, love—as embodied in Jesus Christ and poured into our hearts by the Holy Spirit (Romans 5.5), most fully reflects the character of God.

Source

Philip Kenneson, *Life on The Vine* (Downer's Grove: InterVarsity Press, 1999), 37.

Gifts are both expressions of what we do and who we are, our identities and our vocations. An appeal to love *"from the center of who you are"* (*The Message*) illustrates how the fruit of the Spirit shape the gifts of the Spirit.

Reflection

What fruit of the Spirit are most present in your own life?

Spiritual Gifts and the Equipping of the Laity

In the letter to the Ephesians, we are introduced the grace of God that saves us apart from our works (2:8-9). We are also confronted with God's ultimate plan and purpose, to "gather up all things in Christ, things in heaven and things on earth" (1:10). Chapter four begins with the words, "I, therefore"; God's grace is the priority; our human response is the result. Theology precedes ethics. Spirituality precedes ministry. Here the letter's first three chapters are connected to the latter three with a word: "therefore." In verse one, we are challenged, in the language of the King James Version, to

> "walk worthy of the vocation wherewith ye were called."

The Message is just as vivid:

> *I want you to get out there and walk—better yet, run on the road God called you to travel.*

The Calling of The Laity

Our calling defines our vocation, our common task as the *laos*, the people of God. We live into our callings in humility, gentleness, patience. While not a translation, the *Living Bible* communicates truth:

Be patient with each other, making allowance for each other's faults because of your love (4:2)

Patience is longsuffering (RSV) and persistence and contributes to the unity of the Spirit within the community (4:3). The writer of Ephesians lists the seven elements of this unity in 4:4-6: one body, one Spirit, one hope, one Lord, one faith, one baptism, one God and Father.

Lectionary Loop

Eighth Sunday after Pentecost, Year B, Ephesians 4:1-16, Proper 13(B)

Ninth Sunday after Pentecost, Year B, Ephesians 4:25–5:2, Proper 14

Study Bible

Read the notes from Eph 4:1-32 (Practical instructions for Christian behavior).

Reflection

How is your congregation most unified? And where are divisions most present?

Within this unity, however, is the insistence that we receive different gifts (4:7). They are:

- **Apostle—*one who is sent by God***
- **Prophet—*one who declares the mind of God in the present***
- **Evangelist—*one with a burden to announce the good news of Christ***
- **Pastor—*one who shepherds God's people toward safety and growth***
- **Teacher—*one who instructs and guides others in the faith***

The Purpose of Gifts

The purpose of these gifts is 1) to "equip the saints" (Christians) for the "work of ministry" (*ergon diaconias),* which could also be translated as "the task of servanthood" and 2) to build up the body of Christ. This text speaks directly to the authentic purpose of gifts of the Spirit, and to the danger of their privatization. The church often errs in its practice of having the clergy perform the work of ministry and the laity function as spectators. The result is that clergy sometimes over-function, and laity become passive. The body of Christ is not as strong, or as healthy, as it could be. The mission is diminished.

In the New Testament, the saints are equipped for the active Christian life. The saints (all Christians) are called to the work of ministry. The church that equips the laity for ministry is strong and healthy, and its mission is expanding. This is indeed the pattern given to us in the New Testament. One by-product of such a pattern is that our external focus (toward others in mission) leads to a decrease in the internal conflicts that often afflict the church. The way beyond internal conflict is a unity that flows from an empowered laity in ministry. The pastoral calling, in this pattern, is no longer conflict resolver but equipper of the saints.

Reflections

How are laity equipped for ministry in your congregation? How might your own pastoral vocation be shaped by a reading of Eph 4?

SOURCES

Sources

The Gospel of Luke

Bondi, Roberta C. *A Place to Pray: Reflections on the Lord's Prayer*. Nashville: Abingdon Press, 1998.

Bonhoeffer, Dietrich. *The Cost of Discipleship. New* York: Macmillan, 1959.

Brown, Raymond Edward. *The Birth of the Messiah*, rev. ed. New York: Doubleday, 1999.

Carroll, John T. and James R. Carroll. *Preaching the Hard Sayings of Jesus*. Peabody, MA: Hendrickson, 1996.

__________. *Response to the End of History: Eschatology and Situation in Luke-Acts*. Atlanta: Society of Biblical Literature, 1989.

Coleridge, Mark. *The Birth of the Lukan Narrative: Narrative as Christology in Luke 1-2,* Sheffield: JSOT Press, 1993.

Conzelmann, Hans. *Theology of St. Luke*. New York: Harper & Row, 1960.

Crosby, Michael. *The Prayer that Jesus Taught*. Maryknoll, NY: Orbis, 2002.

Crump, David. *Jesus the Intercessor: Prayer and Christology in Luke-Acts*. Grand Rapids, MI.: Baker, 1999.

Dunn, James D. G. *Jesus Remembered*. Grand Rapids, MI/ Cambridge, England: Eerdmans, 2003.

Ellis, E. Earle. *Eschatology in Luke*. Facet Books Biblical Series, vol. 30. Philadelphia: Fortress, 1972.

Garrett, Susan, R. The Demise of the Devil: Magic and the Demonic in Luke's Writings. Minneapolis: Fortress, 1989.

Green, Joel. "Let them take up the Cross Daily': the Way of Discipleship," in *Theology of Luke*. Cambridge, MA: Cambridge University Press, 102-120, 1995.

_________. "To Proclaim Good News to the Poor: Mission and Salvation" in his *The Theology of the Gospel of Luke*. Cambridge, MA: Cambridge University Press, 76–100, 1995.

Hornik, Heidi J. and Mikeal C. Parsons. *Illuminating Luke***.** Harrisburg: Trinity Press International, 2003.

Ilan, Tal. *Jewish Women in Greco-Roman Palestine*. Peabody, Mass.: Hendrickson, 1996.

Kraemer, Ross Shepard and Mary Rose D'Angelo, editors. *Women and Christian Origins*. Oxford: Oxford University Press, 1999.

Kroeger, Catherine Clark. "Luke," in *The IVP Women's Bible Commentary*. Downers Grove, IL: InterVarsity, 561–584, 2002.

Lapide, Pinchas. *The Sermon on the Mount: Utopia or Program for Action?* Maryknoll, N.Y.: Orbis, 1986.

Lane, Thomas. *Luke and the Gentile Mission: Gospel Anticipates Acts.* Zurich: Peter Lang, 1996.

Malina, Bruce and Richard Rohrbaugh. *Social-Science Commentary on the Synoptic Gospels*. Philadelphia: Fortress, 1992.

Nouwen, Henri J. M. *The Wounded Healer: Ministry in Contemporary Society*. Garden City, NY: Doubleday, 1972.

Parsons, Mikeal C. *The Departure of Jesus in Luke-Acts: The Ascension Narratives in Context*. Sheffield: Sheffield Academic Press, 1988.

Prior, Michael. *Jesus the Liberator: Nazareth Liberation Theology (Luke 4:16-30).* Sheffield: Sheffield Academic Press, 1995.

Reid, Barbara. *Choosing the Better Part? Women in the Gospel of Luke*. Collegeville, Minneapolis: Liturgical Press, 1996.

Sanders, James A. "What Happened at Nazareth?" in *God Has a Story Too: Sermons in Context*. Philadelphia: Fortress, 1979.

Schaberg, Jane. "Luke," in *The Women's Bible Commentary*. Carol A. Newsom and Sharon H. Ringe, eds. Louisville: Westminster/John Knox, 275–292, 1992.

Seim, Turid Karlsen. *The Double Message: Patterns of Gender in Luke and Acts.* Edinburgh: T&T Clark, 1994.

Stevenson, Kenneth. *The Lord's Prayer: a Text in Tradition*. Minneapolis: Fortress Press, 2004.

Swipe, A. W. *The Ascension of the Messiah in Lukan Christology.* Leiden: Brill, 1997.

Van Voorst, Robert. Luke-Acts in my Reading the New Testament Today. Belmont, CA: Wadsworth, 2005.

Waetjen, Herman C. *Praying the Lord's Prayer: An Ageless Prayer for Today.* Harrisburg, PA.: Trinity Press International, 1999.

Willimon, William H. *Lord, Teach Us: The Lord's Prayer and the Christian Life.* Nashville: Abingdon Press, 1996.

Wright, N. T. *The Lord and His Prayer*. Grand Rapids: Eerdmans, 1997.

Wilson, John C. *The Gentiles and the Gentile Mission in Luke-Acts*. Cambridge, MA: Cambridge University Press, 2005.

The Book of Genesis

Brenner, Athalya, and Luise Schottroff, editors. *A Feminist Companion to Genesis.* Sheffield: Sheffield Academic Press, 24–201, 1993.

Dube, Musa. "The Postcolonial Condition" in *Postcolonial Feminist Interpretation of the Bible*. St. Louis: Chalice Press, 2000.

"Excursus: Israel Among the Nations: The Political Map in Genesis," *NISB*, 21–22.

Felder, Cain Hope. "Race, Racism and Biblical Narratives" in his *Stony the Road We Trod*. Minneapolis: Fortress Press, 1991.

Fewell, Dana Nolan, and David M. Gunn. "Shifting the Blame," in *Gender, Power and Promise: the Subject of the Bible's First Story*. Nashville: Abingdon Press, 1993.

____________________________. "Keeping the Promise," in *Gender, Power, and Promise*. Nashville: Abingdon, 39-55, 1993.

Fox, Everett. *The Five Books of Moses: A New Translation with Introductions, Commentary, and Notes*. New York: Schocken Books, 1995.

Friedman, Richard E. *Commentary on the Torah: With a New English Translation.* San Francisco: HarperSanFrancisco, 2003.

Meyers, Carol. "The Family in Early Israel" in *Families in Ancient Israel*, Leo G. Perdue et al., eds. Louisville: Westminster/John Knox Press, 1997.

Nash, Peter T. *Reading Race, Rereading the Bible*. Minneapolis: Fortress Press. 2003.

Niditch, Susan. "Jacob and Joseph" in *A Prelude to Biblical Folklore: Underdogs and Tricksters*. Chicago: University of Illinois, 2000.

Sarna, Nahum. *The JPS Torah Commentary: Genesis*. Philadelphia: Jewish Publication Society, 1989.

The Complete Parallel Bible. (Includes NRSV, REB, NAB and NJB.) New York: Oxford University Press, 1993.

Teubal, Savina J. "Sarah and Hagar: Matriarchs and Visionaries," in *A Feminist Companion to Genesis*. Athalya Brenner and Luise Schottroff, eds. (Sheffield: Sheffield Academic Press, 235-250, 1993.

Trible, Phyllis. "A Love Story Gone Awry" in *God and The Rhetoric of Sexuality*. Philadelphia: Fortress Press, 72–143, 1978.

___________. "Hagar: The Desolation of Rejection" in *Texts of Terror*. Philadelphia: Fortress Press, 1984.

___________. "Tamar: The Royal Rape of Wisdom" in *Texts of Terror*. Minneapolis: Fortress Press, 1984.

Weems, Renita Weems. *Just A Sister Away*. San Diego: LuraMedia, 1988.

Williams, Delores S. "Hagar's Story: A Route to Black Women's Issues" in *Sisters in the Wilderness: The Challenge of Womanist God-Talk*. Maryknoll: Orbis, 1993.

www.crosswalk.com

Psalms

Anderson, A.A. The *New Century Bible The Book of Psalms,* Volume 1. Paulton, Somerset, England: Purnell and Sons Ltd., 1972.

__________. *New Century Bible The Book of Psalms* Volume 2. Paulton, Somerset, England: Purnell and Sons Ltd., 1972.

Bassler, Jouette. "Phillippians" in *The New Interpreter's Study*. Nashville: Abingdon Press, 2003.

Brueggemann Walter. 1984 *The Message of the Psalms: A Theological Commentary*. Minneapolis: Augsburg, 1984.

Craigie, Peter C. *Word Biblical Commentary Volume 19: Psalms 1-50*. Bruce M. Metzger, John D. W. Watts, and James W. Watts, eds. Nashville: Thomas Nelson Publishers, 1983.

Craven, Toni. "Psalms" in *The New Interpreter's Study Bible*. Nashville: Abingdon Press, 2003.

Dahood, Mitchell. *Psalms 1:1-50*. Anchor Bible 16. Garden Cty, NY: Doubleday, 1966.

Dorsey, David A. *The Literary Structure of the Old Testament: A Commentary on Genesis-Malachi*. Grand Rapids, MI: Baker Academic, 1999.

Farmer, David Albert. "Unselfish Prayer" in *The Pastor's Bible Study, Volume One*. Nashville: Abingdon Press, 2005.

Fee, Gordon D. *The New International Commentary on the New Testament: The First Epistle to the Corinthians*. Grand Rapids, MI: William B. Eerdmans Publishing Company, 1987.

Gillingham, S.E. *The Oxford Bible Series: The Poems and Psalms of the Hebrew Bible*. P. R. Ackroyd and G. N. Stanton, eds. New York: Oxford University Press, 1994.

Grout, Donald Jay. *A History of Western Music Revised Edition*. New York: W. W. Norton & Company Inc., 1973.

Harrelson, Walter J. "Introduction: Psalms" in *The New Interpreter's Study Bible*. Nashville: Abingdon Press, 2003.

Kidner, Derek. *Psalms 1-72: A Commentary,* in Tynedale Old Testament Commentaries, Volume 14a. D. J. Wiseman, ed. Leicester, England/ Downers Grove, Illinois: Inter-Varsity Press, 1973.

__________. *Psalms 73–150: A Commentary*, in *Tynedale Old Testament Commentaries*, Vol 14b. D. J. Wiseman, ed. Leicester, England/ Downers Grove, Illinois: Inter-Varsity Press, 1973.

Limburg, James "The Book of Psalms" in *The Anchor Bible Dictionary.* David Noel Freedman, ed. New York: Doubleday, 1992, 5:522-536.

Longman III, Tremper. *How to Read the Psalms*. Leicester, England/Downers Grove, Illinois: Inter-Varsity Press, 1988.

McDaniel, Thomas F. "The Ten Commandments" in *The Pastor's Bible Study, Volume Two*. Nashville: Abingdon Press, 2005.

Renew! Songs & Hymns for Blended Worship. Carol Steam, IL: Hope Publishing Company, 1995.

Tate, Marvin E. *Word Biblical Commentary Vol. 20: Psalms 51-100*. Eds. David A Hubbard, Glenn W. Barker and John D. W. Watts, eds. Nelson's Electronic Bible Reference Library, Nelson MinistryServices.com, 1990.

Terrien, Samuel *Critical Eerdmans Commentary: The Psalms: Stophic and Structue and Theological Commentary*. Grand Rapids, MI/ Cambridge U.K.: William B. Eermans Publishing Company, 2003.

The Hymnal of the United Church of Christ. New York: United Church Press, 1979, 257.

The New Century Hymnal. Cleveland, Ohio: The Pilgrim Press, 1995, 558 and 600.

The United Methodist Hymnal: Book of United Methodist Worship. Nashville: The United Methodist Publishing House, 1989.

www.cyberhymnal.org

www.faithatwork.com/history/Shoemaker_I_Stand.html

Kingdom of God

Birch, Bruce. 1 and 2 Sam, *New Interpreter's Bible*, vol. 2, 1026–31.

Buttrick, David. *Preaching the New and the Now*. Louisville: Westminster John Knox Press, 1998.

Charles H. Talbert, *Reading Luke*, Macon, GA: Smyth & Helwys Publishing, 2003.

Fretheim, Terrence. "Genesis," in *New Interpreter's Bible*, vol. 1, 340–47.

Fuellenback, John. *The Kingdom of God: The Message of Jesus Today*. Orbis Books, 1995.

Schnackenburg, Rudolf. *God's Rule and Kingdom*. New York: Herder and Herder, 1963.

Welker, Michael. "The Reign of God," in *Theology Today*, January 1993, Volume XLIX, Number 4.

Christian Community: Eating and Drinking Our Way to the Kingdom

Brueggemann, Walter. "The Liturgy of Abundance, the Myth of Scarcity," in *The Christian Century*, March 24, 1999, 30–31.

Cousar, Charles, editor. *Texts for Preaching: A Lectionary Commentary Based on the NRSV—Year C*. Louisville: Westminster John Knox, 1994.

English, Adam C. "Feeding Imagery in the Gospel of John: Uniting the Physical and the Spiritual," in *Perspectives in Religious Studies*, vol. 28, no. 3, Fall 2001, 203-214.

Fuellenbach, John. *Church: Community for the Kingdom.* Maryknoll: Orbis Books, 2002.

Joncas, Jan Michael. "Tasting the Kingdom of God: The Meal Ministry of Jesus and Its Implications for Contemporary Worship and Life," in *Worship,* vol. 74, no. 4, July 2000, 329–365.

Karris, Robert J., *Luke: Artist and Theologian, Luke's Passion Account as Literature.* New York: Paulist, 1985.

Koester, Craig R. "The Message to Laodicea and the Problem of Its Local Context: A Study of the Imagery in Rev 3.14-22" in *New Testament Studies,* vol. 49, no. 3, July 2003, 407–424.

Lappé, Frances Moore. "Enough to Go Around," in *World Ark,* May/June 2005, 5.

Murray, Lorraine V. "Feeding His Sheep," *America: The National Catholic Weekly,* vol. 183, no. 2, July 15 2000,

Newsome, James D. ed. *Texts for Preaching: A Lectionary Commentary Based on the NRS—Year A.* Louisville: Westminster John Knox, 1995.

Post, Emily. *Etiquette: The Blue Book of Social Usage.* New York: Funk and Wagnalls Company, 1940.

Smith, Dennis E. "Table Fellowship as a Literary Motif in the Gospel of Luke," in *Journal of Biblical Literature,* vol. 106, no. 4, 1987, 613-638.

Tyler, Anne. *Dinner at the Homesick Restaurant.* New York: Berkley Books, 1982.

http://www.americamagazine.org/gettext.cfm?articleTypeID=9&textID=764&issueID=307

Spiritual Gifts

Achtemeier, Paul. *Romans: Interpretation Series.* Louisville: John Knox, 1985.

Carter, Ken. *The Gifted Pastor: Finding And Using Your Spiritual Gifts.* Nashville: Abingdon Press, 2001.

Edwards, Lloyd. *Discerning Your Spiritual Gifts.* Cambridge: Cowley, 1988.

Fee, Gordon. *Paul, The Spirit and the People of God.* Peabody, Maine: Hendrickson, 1996.

Gunter, Stephen. *The Quotable Mr. Wesley.* Atlanta: Candler School of Theology, Emory University, 1999.

Hays, Richard. *First Corinthians. Interpretation: A Bible Commentary For Teaching and Preaching.* Louisville: Westminster John Knox, 1997.

Kenneson, Philip. *Life on The Vine.* Downer's Grove: InterVarsity Press, 1999.

The Message. Colorado Springs: Navpress, 2002.

LECTIONARY

Lectionary

Year A

Year B

Year C

SCRIPTURE INDEX

Scripture Index

Christian Community: Eating and Drinking Our Way to the Kingdom

Spiritual Gifts

HOW TO USE THE COMPACT DISK

How to Use the Compact Disk

The compact disk located in the back of *The Pastor's Bible Study: Volume Three* may be used to supplement and enhance the study experience. The disk includes:

- A QuickTime® video introduction to *The Pastor's Bible Study: Volume Three* by general editor David Albert Farmer
- The full text of *The Pastor's Bible Study: Volume Three* in Adobe Reader® (.pdf) format
- PowerPoint® presentations containing outlines for each study within the volume, in both PowerPoint® Presentation (.ppt) and PowerPoint® Show (.pps) format
- Study outlines and reflection questions in rich text file (.rtf) format that may be edited, printed, and given to group participants.

To access any of this material, insert the compact disk into the CD-ROM drive of your computer and browse to the item(s) you wish to select using your PC Windows Explorer, or your Macintosh Browser.

Viewing the QuickTime® Introductory Video

To view the QuickTime® introductory video of *The Pastor's Bible Study: Volume Three*, you must have QuickTime® software installed on your computer. If you wish to install this free software, download it from the web at www.apple.com/quicktime/download/.

> *Note: The QuickTime® program is not included on* The Pastor's Bible Study: Volume Three *disk. Technical support for QuickTime® is available at www.apple.com.*

Once QuickTime® is installed on your computer, browse to the file named **Video** on the disk and double click on it to play it.

Using the Adobe Reader® Book

To use the Adobe Reader® book containing the full text of *The Pastor's Bible Study: Volume Three*, you must have Adobe Reader® software installed on your computer. If you wish to install this free software, download it from the web at www.adobe.com/products/acrobat/.

> *Note: Technical support for installation of the Adobe Reader is available at www.adobe.com.*

Once Adobe Reader® is installed on your computer, browse to the file named **PastorsBibleStudyV3.pdf** on the disk and double click on it to open it. After opening the **PastorsBibleStudyV3.pdf**, you may search any keyword or phrase in *The Pastor's Bible Study: Volume Three*.

Another useful feature of the Adobe Reader® file is the addition of links to other resources on the supplemental disk. These links are at the beginning of each of the six studies. Clicking on a link will open the selected resource on your computer in its default program. Just be sure that *The Pastor's Bible Study: Volume Three* compact disk is in your CD-ROM drive.

Viewing PowerPoint® Presentations

There are twelve PowerPoint® files on the disk, two for each of the six studies. These two PowerPoint® files contain presentations of study outlines. All PowerPoint® files are in a folder named **PowerPoint**. To view the PowerPoint® files that accompany *The Pastor's Bible Study: Volume Three*, you must have Microsoft PowerPoint® software or PowerPoint® Viewer installed on your computer.

.PPT files: The .ppt files are files associated with the full version of Microsoft PowerPoint®. If you have the full version of PowerPoint® software installed on your computer, you may double click on the .ppt files to open them in PowerPoint® and customize your study presentations.

> *Note: The Microsoft PowerPoint® program is not included on* The Pastor's Bible Study: Volume Three *disk. Technical support for PowerPoint® is available at www.microsoft.com.*

.PPS files: The .pps files are "stand alone" files that may be viewed using the PowerPoint® Viewer, which is installed on most computers. If you wish to install this free software, download it from Microsoft at http://www.microsoft.com/downloads/details.aspx?FamilyID=428d5727-43ab-4f24-90b7-a94784af71a4&DisplayLang=en or visit www.microsoft.com and search on the key words "Power Point Viewer".

In most cases, using the .pps files will be the best choice for presenting the outlines to study participants. To begin the presentation:

- Place the disk in your computer's CD-ROM drive.
- Click on the link found on the appropriate study outline in Adobe Reader® to start the presentation. (Or, you may open the .pps file by browsing to it on the disk and double-clicking it.)
- Click anywhere on the slide, or use the page down button, to move through the presentation.

> *Note: If you click past a point in the outline and wish to go back, use the backspace or page up button on your computer's keyboard.*

Using Study Outlines

Study outlines for all six sections are in a folder named **Study_Outlines**. Double-click on an outline to open the rich text format (.rtf) file in your computer's default word processing program. You may then customize your study experience by making changes to the outline. You may also access these files by clicking on the links provided in the Adobe Reader® Book.

> *Note: At the end of each session outline, participant assignments for the upcoming sessions are noted, including Scripture reading assignments and* New Interpreter's Study Bible *references. Providing the outlines to participants will enhance their study experience.*

Using Reflection Questions

Reflection questions for all six studies are in a folder named **Reflection_Questions**. Double click on an outline to open the rich text format (.rtf) file in your computer's default word processing program. You may then customize your study experience by making changes to the reflection questions. You may also access these files by clicking on the links provided in the Adobe Reader® Book.

Contacting Technical Support

To contact one of our Technical Support Representatives, call: **1-615-749-6777, Monday through Friday, 8:00 A.M. to 5:00 P.M.**, Central time.

Notes

Notes

Notes